AT THE POINT OF NEED
Living Human Experience

Essays in Honor of Carroll A. Wise

Edited by
James B. Ashbrook
John E. Hinkle, Jr.

UNIVERSITY
PRESS OF
AMERICA

Lanham • New York • London

British Cataloging in Publication Information Available

"Innocence and Experience: Towards a Theology
of Pastoral Care" © 1988 by Paul Hessert

"Theology and Psychology: Friends or Foes?" © 1988
by Leila M. Foster

"Effective Pastoral Care in the Hospital" © 1988
by John L. Florell

Library of Congress Cataloging-in-Publication Data

At the point of need : living human experience : essays in honor of
Carroll A. Wise / edited by James B. Ashbrook and John E. Hinkle, Jr.
p. cm.
Bibliography: p.
"Bibliography of Carroll A. Wise": p.
1. Pastoral psychology. 2. Pastoral counseling. 3. Wise, Carroll
A. I. Wise, Carroll A. II. Ashbrook, James B., 1925–
III. Hinkle, John E.
BV4012.A88   1988
253.5—dc 19   88–5686 CIP
ISBN 0–8191–6963–3 (alk. paper)
ISBN 0–8191–6964–1 (pbk. : alk. paper)

Table of Contents

v

ACKNOWLEDGEMENTS

We acknowledge with appreciation, the following for permission to reproduce material for which they retain the copyright:

From PASTORAL PSYCHOTHERAPY by Carroll A. Wise, (c) 1983 Jason Aronson Inc., pp.25, 29-30, 34-35, 158, 162, 193, 269, 272, 280, 298, 299, 300. Reprinted by permission of the publisher.

Excerpt from RELIGION IN ILLNESS AND HEALTH by Carroll A. Wise. Copyright 1942 by Harper & Row, Publishers, Inc. Reprinted by permission of Harper & Row, Publishers, Inc.

Excerpt from PASTORAL COUNSELING: ITS THEORY AND PRACTICE by Carroll A. Wise. Copyright 1951 by Harper & Row, Publishers, Inc. Reprinted by permission of Harper & Row, Publishers, Inc.

Excerpt from THE MEANING OF PASTORAL CARE by Carroll A. Wise. Copyright (c) 1966 by Carroll A. Wise. Reprinted by permission of Harper & Row, Publishers, Inc.

Excerpt from PSYCHIATRY AND THE BIBLE by Carroll A. Wise. Copyright (c) 1956 by Harper & Row, Publishers, Inc. Reprinted by permission of Harper & Row, Publishers, Inc.

The Association of Mental Health Clergy for permission to reprint "Response to an Experience of Extreme Stress in the Light of the Ideas of Anton T. Boisen," From AMHC FORUM, Vol. 32, No. 1, September 1979 and The Journal of Pastoral Care, Vol. XXIII, No.4, December 1979, by Carroll A. Wise.

The Journal of Pastoral Care for permission to reprint: "Editorial: The Limitation of the Older Medical Model in Training Pastoral Counselors," Vol.XXII, No.4, December 1968, by James B. Ashbrook, and portions of "The Grandfather of CPE?" Vol. XXXV, No.4, December 1981.

FORWARD

Carroll A. Wise was born in Verona, Pennsylvania, on October 31, 1903. He received his bachelor of arts degree from Ohio Wesleyan University in 1927. His graduate work in theology at Boston University included a bachelor of sacred theology in 1930 and a Th.D. in 1935. His doctoral dissertation was on the subject: "A Study of The Religious Factors in Seven Cases of Mental Disorder." During 1930-31, he was a student in training with Anton Boisen and the Council for Clinical Training at the Worcester State Hospital in Worcester, Massachusetts.

In 1930, he and Addiene Gates were married. Robert Edwin and Patricia Jordon are their two children.

Beginning in 1931, Dr. Wise served as chaplain at the Worcester State Hospital, following Boisen, until 1942. During those years, he served as a counselor for the Worcester YMCA and YWCA on a part time basis from 1936-1940, and as an instructor in Boston University School of Theology on a part time basis from 1932-1940. Between 1942-1944 he functioned as the Director of the Department of Religion and Health of the Toledo, Ohio, Council of Churches. Then, from 1945-1948, he was Minister of Counseling on the staff of the Hennepin Avenue Methodist Church in Minneapolis, Minnesota.

From 1948 until his retirement in 1972, he held a faculty appointment as Professor of Pastoral Psychology and Counseling at Garrett Biblical Institute, which became Garrett-Evangelical Theological Seminary shortly after his retirement with the merging of The Evangelical Theological Seminary in Naperville, Illinois, and Garrett-Biblical Institute in Evanston, Illinois, on the campus of Northwestern University. Through the years of his faculty appointment he also served as a counselor on a part time basis on the staff of the Chicago Methodist Temple.

Active in the founding and development of the American Association of Pastoral Counselors, he served as its third president from 1967-1969. In 1967, the Association honored him, along with Carl R. Rogers, with its Distinguished Contributions Award. In 1981, on behalf of the Association, he presented the same award to his long standing friend and colleague, Carl A. Christensen, M.D.

With retirement from the faculty, Carroll spent a sabbatical year at Lutheran General Hospital, Park Ridge, Illinois, co-supervising the Clinical Pastoral Education residency program. This experience was a return to active CPE Supervision after 27 years. During that same year, he helped organize what had been a pastoral counseling training and service delivery site related to the GETS/NU Ph.D. program into a hospital based outpatient pastoral counseling center. He served as the first Executive Director of the Community Pastoral Counseling and

Consultation Center (now the Pastoral Psychotherapy Institute). After 1973, for more than a decade, he served as consultant, supervisor, teacher, and therapist at the Institute.

Carroll was an ordained clergy member of the Minnesota Conference of The United Methodist Church from 1930 until the time of his death, Tuesday, November 5th, 1985.

Many people have contributed to this volume in his honor. Joan Svenningsen, office administrator in the Department he founded, transferred the edited material to camera-ready copy, a formidable task which required expertise and patience. Professor Walter Cason and Linda Koops, of the GETS secretarial services, assisted with the final work. Mention must be made of the several graduates and colleagues who wanted to contribute chapters but found, for a variety of reasons, that they were unable to do so. Their regret is matched by our regret, for we know something of the quality and substance of the materials on which they were working. Special appreciation goes to David M. Moss, III, for reading the entire manuscript for accuracy and for the energy and ideas that he has put into distribution possibilities.

Carroll deeply impacted a host of lives. He embodied in his own person and work a notable quality of human relationship; a quality at once fundamentally Incarnational, foundationally pastoral, functionally interpersonal, and academically winnowed through the professional disciplines of writing, teaching, counseling, and supervising. This volume is but a small token of the influence that his quality of life had upon others. The book's diversities represent the many directions in which his influence is flowing. Its commonalities reflect an understanding of the quality of life to which he was committed, which he demonstrated, and toward which he pointed. We are all enriched by his vision and benefited by his labors.

James B. Ashbrook/John E. Hinkle, Jr.
Christmastide 1987

PREFACE

It was a lovely spring day in 1984. I was enjoying lunching and reminiscing with Carroll and Adienne. I shifted the conversation to the main agenda - a book recognizing the contribution of Carroll A. Wise.

"I guess the time has come," he answered. "I have always avoided disciples - Wise's guys as they used to quip in the seminary. I wanted no followers and no imitators. I wanted people to be themselves and to think for themselves. But I guess the time has come." With that response he looked across the table to Adienne as though for confirmation. His mind was clear, which was not always the case at that time, and so his conclusion constituted his blessing for this project. Unfortunately, what began as a volume to honor him is now a volume in memory of him and his influence.

We are recognizing the person of Carroll Wise. Yet more than that we are lifting up and affirming the emphases for which he so passionately fought and the concerns for which he so ardently worked. That day we talked of two of these: the clinical and the empirical. From whence came his concern with these?

His answer was immediate: "Working with the staff at Worcester State Hospital." I was unclear whether he was implying that the staff needed "working with" in clinical ways or whether he gained from them the life-long mind-set that human life is to be understood in terms of the dynamic process which is so integral to the clinical method. It was clear that the staff looked to empirical data and not abstract speculation for understanding human need.

We have chosen to introduce the essays recognizing him and more particularly his emphases with two reflections by him. The first experience came very early in his career, though he only shared it publicly at the 50th anniversary banquet of clinical pastoral education. It describes the powerful and poignant chaos of his mentor Anton Boisen turning to him for care. The second experience came very late in his life and represents the impact of his being scalded - almost to death - on his understanding of pain. In each he found himself caught in the swirling undertow of excruciating personal experience. In between these two events he persisted in focusing on the point of personal need. Whereas Boisen pursued "living human documents" to make sense of "the inner world," Wise insisted upon living human experience to ground theological and theoretical formulations.

Before commenting further on Wise's contribution in the areas of the clinical and the empirical it is crucial to identify that which underlay both of these, namely, the pastoral. I had the privilege of serving with him on the first (and the second) special committee to formulate guidelines about the private practice of pastoral counseling for the

American Association of Pastoral Counselors. Prior to that my acquaintance with Carroll was primarily through his writings. However, in the arena of the organization defining itself, I learned the passion and the integrity with which he exemplified pastoral identity. Others may have been confused about whether he was "pastoral" or "psychological." He was not confused. He knew who he was and he insisted that what AAPC as an organization was about was pastoral counseling. Seward Hiltner never recognized the institutionalization of the specialty, but Carroll did. In so doing, however, he never fudged on its pastoral core: the Gospel communicated at the point of personal need.

The Wise tradition involves dealing with the present and the future rather than memorializing the past. The emerging shape of that future has its wellspring in these three convictional emphases: the pastoral, the clinical, and the empirical. Various contributors to the book lift up and elaborate one or more of these. In so doing they are reflecting developments, not mere extensions, of Carroll's contribution. Let me sketch those developments briefly as a testimony to the fact that we are recognizing what Carroll set in motion more than honoring Carroll for himself alone. For that was his intention and that represents his impact on the Department of Pastoral Psychology and Counseling here at Garrett-Evangelical Theological Seminary.

Pastoral Identity has broadened in three quite specific ways. Emma Justes represents the infusion of the pastoral theological tradition of Seward Hiltner and James Lapsley. Edward Wimberly brings the dimension of spiritual values and inner healing. I continue to articulate the parish context as normative for the understanding of the meaning of pastoral. And these three elaborations of pastoral--theological, spirituality, parish base--are concerns found among our graduates and shared by the entire department.

The clinical method has likewise broadened in three quite specific ways. The most crucial is the cross-cultural concerns articulated by John Hinkle and institutionalized in his cultivation of The Asian-American Pastoral Counseling Center. This conviction has been carried in the presence of black graduate students and black faculty. Now it is embodied in Edward Wimberly and institutionalized in his responsibility with The Black Pastoral Counseling Institute of Chicago. A systemic or organizational approach that grows out of the clinical world view comes in the various consultative relationships with pastoral counseling agencies, health care institutions, and church bodies with which the pastoral psychology faculty work.

The empirical orientation also has broadened in three specific forms. This emphasis was the least developed by Carroll himself in terms of implementation but was ever anchoring issues in the arena of consenual validation arrived at by gathering empirical data. Criteria for the psychological assessment of ministerial candidates represents more than a decade of a sustained program of research guided by John Hinkle and Emily Haight and described elsewhere in this volume. My own work with implications of brain research for faith and practice continues the empirical focus in a way that is recognizable even though it would not have been anticipated. Carroll came to the phenomenological as a source of knowledge out of his own excruciating physical and psychic pain. Lallene Rector brings to the Department that orientation and expertise, along with the ethos of the Boston School of Theology's program in the psychology of religion.

I sketch these emergences to underscore Carroll's conviction that the authoritative derives from authentic integrity. He planted and cultivated. Since then the departmental faculty, especially under the leadership of John Hinkle, has implemented and deepened the vision. We continue the work of planting, cultivating, and harvesting, hopefully, sowing seeds of new growth with the same vigor and integrity that he did.

"The time has come" for Carroll A. Wise to be honored for what he released in the world through those with whom he worked. He agreed and we agree. What follows bears his heritage and our generativity.

James B. Ashbrook, Chair
Pastoral Psychology and Counseling
Garrett-Evangelical Theological Seminary

PHOTOGRAPH OF CARROLL A. WISE

PART I

THE MAN AND HIS IMPACT

INSTITUTIONALIZING CONVICTIONS

The following seven chapters identify the quality of Carroll Wise as a person and the impact that had on others and, even more, the meaning that had **for** others.

In accord with Anton Boisen's emphasis on "living human documents" and Wise's emphasis on "the point of need," we offer, first, two pieces by Carroll himself: "A Tough and Tender History," and "My Encounter with Pain." They are linked by their descriptions and analyses of intense personal pain--Boisen's second breakdown, which Wise experienced, and Wise's near death by scalding. Together, the chapters provide a unique glimpse of the power of clinical pastoral education, namely, the way in which Boisen and Wise, as well as virtually everyone in the movement, plumbed the depths of suffering and explored the heights of redemption.

By identifying the healing forces at work in the experience of emotional upheaval, Boisen himself spoke of "breaking an opening in the wall that separated religion and medicine." Because of his contact with Boisen--both in training and in intimate caring for him--Wise learned that a "real pastor" **listens** to people at the point of their need. And such listening enables people to move toward "the fulfillment of the **Imago Dei**" in themselves. Although Boisen's pain arose from internal causes and Wise's came from external causes, both men struggled to find meaning in their pain. Both experienced a regression in which they attended to their inner reality in order to reinvest in others and the world. That process involved giving up their autonomy as they found themselves plunged into a state of dependency. The result, of course, was restored relationships with life.

In recounting these events Wise shares both clinical knowledge and personal wisdom. He shows how guilt for what happens undermines recovery, while responsibility for how one deals with pain facilitates recovery. Most significantly, he finds in his own "regression" a rationale for "living" experience "at the point of need:" namely, an understanding of, and cooperation with, the deep inner, nonrational, processes which are "the roots of religious faith." These processes can be voiced neither by the ideas of psychology nor by the concepts of theology. "One cannot confine the non-rational, dynamic aspects of life or religion in any formula," Carroll writes. We must deal with "experience as experience, not as ideas." It was that conviction which kept him at odds with many conventional theologians and conservative psychotherapists alike.

Tyler Thompson's description confirms Wise's own discussion. As a student of Wise's at Boston, Thompson had the impression that Wise cared little about theology. However, as a colleague over a span of two decades, he came to understand the profound respect Wise had for theology in its contribution to human wellbeing. The theological, he contended, had to be centered in **persons**, and more particularly, in **the dynamics of the personality** if it was to be significant at all. Attention to inner conflicts held more promise than teaching abstract concepts. Clinical experience was central to both the selection and the training of seminarians.

Thompson traces Wise's use of experiential theology through his writings. The themes are there and they are clear: clinical experience belongs at the center of theological education; only living relationships mediate the grace of God; the destructiveness of sin is to be met by the reconciling reality of love; the theological and personal dimensions of pastoral care are related by communicating "the inner meaning of the Gospel to persons at the point of their need." Presence, or personal relationships, is the sine qua non for Carroll. Human presence embodies and mediates the Holy Spirit in both growth and wholeness. Thompson's survey and appreciation leave us with a portrait of Wise as a theologian, a theologian for whom life was deeper than logic. "[D]espite his dissatisfaction with his own tradition," Thompson insists, "there were two respects in which he was strikingly in tune with it: empirical openness in theology and refusal to accept abstraction as truth."

In "**Imago** and introject: A Profile of Carroll Wise," by David M. Moss, the reader will find what it meant--and what it means--to accept truth in the living human document rather than in abstraction. In a unique interweaving of his own experience with that of Carroll Wise, and of his constituting a human bridge between Wise and Heinz Kohut, Moss offers a personal account of suffering in the life of each of them and privileges us with glimpses of the "grace" in each man. Using himself as a paradigm, David shares what it has meant to be "mentored" by both Wise and Kohut, which means to be the recipient of "empathic understanding and thoughtful affirmation," as well as to be the giver of such grace in return.

Moss picks up Carroll's encounter with pain in the accident of his scalding, shares his own brush with death in being broadsided by another automobile travelling at 70 m.p.h., and blends the two in response to Kohut's coronary bypass operation. This intimate human document is primarily a story of caring and sharing. Yet Moss, like his mentors, does not settle for mere story. He, and they, move to generalization, to interpretation, to abstraction. Only now the abstracting is anchored in primary experience and emerges for the sake of other people's engagement in primary experience rather than coming from speculative detachment.

Moss describes the vocation of mentoring as a process of learning from significant others basic trust in oneself and others. It roots in what Freud identified as "memory traces," which are the core of object representations, and intimate identifications, which are expressed by the

4

word "imago." The "imago" becomes an "introject" and, in healthy development, finds its focus in a mentor or mentors. From being the recipient of such a process, the individual "passes on" to others the gifts which have been nurtured in oneself. If Wise serves as an "ideal model" of what mentoring means--and so does Kohut in the description we are given of his relationship with Moss--Moss' discussion provides, not simply an analysis but even more, an experience of what makes image-creating truly grace-ful.

Carroll resisted being idealized or gathering disciples. In truth, he exhibited very human qualities of irritation, anger, stubbornness, and yes, pettiness. Those qualities are shared in John M. Vayhinger's reminiscence of teaching with him in the late-1950s through the mid-1960s. However, Carroll's more positive qualities of care, insight, Christian faith, collaboration, clinical anchoring of theological thought and ministerial practice are also described by John. What we are given is an intimate portrait of two quite different and strong personalities working together: Wise with a psychodynamic orientation to inform his liberal theological views, and Vayhinger with a behavioral psychological orientation to inform his conservative theological views. Together they shaped a converging of clinical concerns and empirical research for the sake of more effective ministers.

While Carroll always held a "respectful attitude toward research," John brought the technical expertise. John's skill with psychological testing matched Carroll's emphasis upon "life processes." The result was one of the most thorough pieces of empirical research on seminarians and ministers which has ever been conducted. For the first time, some of its magnitude and some of its conclusions are in print. Why now and not previously? According to Vayhinger, Carroll simply could not accept the findings that seminary students, and Garrett's students particularly, were more mature, altruistic, and stable than comparable groups in medicine, education, and the sciences. For him, their pathology loomed larger than their health. Even so, the project provided several generations of students with informed feedback about themselves, on the basis of which many sought resources to assist in their personal and professional growth.

John Hinkle, Jr. lifts Wise's more personal pilgrimage into its most proper form, namely, the institutionalizing of clinical convictions and passionate faith, or, as he labels it, "The Legacy." Wise's career carried him from a psychiatric facility into the seminary setting by way of the parish, but the continuous thread was his call to integrate the experiential and the theoretical through teaching. Within the combined structures of Garrett Seminary and Northwestern University Carroll provided a "context" in which psychologists and psychiatrists gave themselves as colleagues in the enterprise to which he himself was committed. Hinkle links Wise's "incarnational-interpersonal-insightful imaginal/associational manner" with his creative crustiness and his empathic realism.

5

Hinkle's essay is both historical and constructive. It chronicles a struggle to remain faithful to a professional practitioner model of training for general and specialized ministries, which combines clinical and scholarly concerns, during the break-up of existing institutional structures. In describing the philosophical--and therefore political--developments, Hinkle articulates a sophisticated program in pastoral counseling/psychotherapy. That program moves far toward meeting the need for the clinical, the empirical, the theoretical, and the dialogical among theological and social science disciplines. From being a recipient of the Wise "legacy"--one which elicits his admiration and appreciation--Hinkle becomes an architect who renews that heritage.

Although working in another institution, Ashbrook has shared the convictions of Wise and Hinkle through the years. At the time Wise orchestrated that initial Ph.D. in pastoral psychology, The Journal of Pastoral Care asked Ashbrook to critique it. His piece on "The Limitation of The Older Medical Model in Training Pastoral Counselors" prophetically links his commitments with those of The Legacy. He outlined a multifaceted approach which included the following distinguishable yet mutually enhancing compontents: (1) "pastoral" models and mentors, (2) delivering direct specialized services, and (3) utilizing psychiatric, behavioral, social science, humanities, and theological resources.

Emerging institutional structures are incarnating Carroll's convictions.

A TOUGH AND TENDER HISTORY[1]

Carroll A. Wise

Anton Boisen had his first psychotic episode in 1920 and was a patient in a state hospital in Boston and later in Westboro, Massachusetts.[2] During this experience Boisen came to believe that he had "[b]roken an opening in the wall that separated religion and medicine." (Boisen, 1960, p.91) This idea occupied his mind for the rest of his life, and he devoted all of his energy to following it up. When the idea of clinical training for ministers first came to him, he saw it as a means to this end.

Boisen was released from the hospital in January 1922. Then followed a period of several years of intensive study in the field of mental illness and religion. Much of this was done in Harvard and in the Boston Psychopathic Hospital under Dr. C. Macfie Campbell, a leading psychiatrist of his day and the author of an excellent book, Delusion and Belief (1926), which subject was a large issue with Boisen. Many more details on this period will be found in the articles by Dr. Powell. (1975, 1976)

In 1924, Boisen was appointed chaplain in the Worcester State Hospital, Worcester, Massachusetts. Here he had the opportunity to carry his studies into the clinical situation, and he made good use of it, doing the research required for some voluminous case studies. His basic theory about mental illness, especially schizophrenia, and religion was already formulated. He was not developing it but amassing clinical data to support it. The years between 1925 and 1930 saw a great deal of creative work while he also spent time raising money for his clinical training program. Among his writings during this period two should be noted particularly. They are "Personality Changes and Upheavals Arising Out Of A Sense of Personal Failure," (Boisen, 1926) and "The Sense of Isolation in Mental Disorder: Its Religious Significance." (Boisen, 1928) The fact that he could be published in prestigious professional journals is witness to the status he was achieving for himself through his scholarly work.

My first contact with Boisen was in 1928 when I took the course he offered in the Boston University School of Theology. Dr. Lewis Hill, psychoanalyst, who later became the associate medical director of the Council for Clinical Training, joined him in teaching the course. He corrected many of the erroneous ideas about psychoanalysis which were floating around that school and gave Boisen excellent support. It was clear then that Boisen's theoretical and clinical ideas were well developed, that he had done much research in his problem of breaking "an opening in the wall that separated religion and medicine."

The summer of 1929 saw me in Worcester as one of his students. The

7

next winter I read papers for him in his Boston University course. I was invited back to Worcester for the summer of 1930 as his assistant, and I had agreed to stay on for one year to take the place of Don Beatty, who had gone on to Pittsburgh to open up the Mayview Hospital. Now the summer of 1930 was a very critical period for Anton Boisen for a number of reasons. That fall he had his second breakdown. You read about some of that in his book Out of The Depths; (Boisen, 1960) and if you have not read it, do.

Shortly after the students had left, he announced to me he was going to Chicago and left me in care of the department. I felt like I felt the first day I was in the hospital when at six o'clock in the afternoon, I found myself the only sane person on the male admission ward. I did not know which way was up. I got through that, though. Yet here again I felt overwhelmed. Now I do not know all that transpired in Chicago; I know some of it, and some is in his book, but about a month later I had a letter asking me to meet him at the train station on a certain night--he was coming back. I did so. He asked to be driven to the hospital, rather than to his room in the city. We arrived at his office, and he asked me to stay with him. Now this is the background for the incident.

Gradually, I witnessed the disintegration of a personality. I had already worked with schizophrenic patients; I knew something of their experience. I had heard Anton talk about the experience of personal upheaval, the profound sense of isolation, alienation, and guilt, the ideas of the end of the world, and a profound sense of mission. Now, I was seeing it in the living document, with all the pain and agony that such a person experiences. I saw below the mechanisms involved in this experience to a deeper sense of the person. He was not talking about upheaval, isolation, and guilt; he was experiencing it right there. I saw him try to bring himself together again only to sink back into despair.

I heard him talk about hell; now I experienced him in hell. The devils he had to deal with were the elemental forces of a human being. I wondered when the constructive, creative forces, of which I had heard him speak, would appear. How would the living God manifest Himself in Anton? Frankly, I was frightened, very frightened. What could I do, what could I say? I remembered him saying once in a seminar, we should not try to do anything for a patient; we should try to understand the patient and the experience of the patient. Well I was trying, but I had my own feelings welling up in me that tended to block my acceptance and understanding. I knew those feelings--I was aware of them.

In such a moment, understanding is not being able to formulate an idea or something in words. [It] is being able to communicate to the other person a sense of acceptance and being able to communicate by manner and bearing. I had heard Anton talking about listening, and now I was learning that listening involved not just my ears, but it meant identifying with him and being able to communicate that I was with him in a deep sense.

What else could bridge his experience of isolation and bring him back to the real world and to himself? Yeah, I was frightened, very frightened, shaken to the depths. After all this man was my teacher, my guide in clinical experience, and in a real sense an ideal, a father figure in a good sense. He had given me the opportunity which I was to discover later saved me for a genuine Christian ministry. Without my years at Worcester--they stretched out to be twelve--I might have continued to be a clergyman, but I would not have been a real pastor to people. I owed him a great deal. Now in his extreme urgency, what could I be to him? The memory of that evening is still very clear in my mind, that [as well as] other talks that followed with him over the succeeding months.

Now why do I bring this crucial incident on this occasion of the fiftieth anniversary of the founding of Clinical Pastoral Education [1975]? In order to say to you, you have indeed a tough and tender history. That the very origins of your history plumbs the depths of human suffering and the heights of human redemption. I do not know all that is happening in clinical training today, I am sort of on the periphery. Whatever it is, it is your responsibility, not mine, [and] I plead with you not to waste your time with the quicky methods of therapy that entice and plague many pastors today. Whatever your clinical setting, you are called upon by your very origins to teach pastors to plumb the depths of human suffering and misery, sin, illness, and bring a redemptive healing ministry to them. By redemptive ministry I mean, in terms of persons, to be to them the kind of pastors who can help them to become their true autonomous and responsible self. To fulfill the potential that they have within them, or if you want it in theological terms, to move toward the fulfillment of the Imago Dei. It is only by helping people experience their depths that we can help them discover their true breadth and their height.

Boisen was psychotic for several weeks before he was committed to the wards of the hospital. Dr. Bryan, the superintendent, wanted to save him from this if possible, but it proved too dangerous, as Boisen was suicidal. He was also very deeply disturbed. I spent hours with him before commitment. I was with him when he took the manuscript of his hymnal, which he was reediting, numbering about 300 pages, and tore it down the middle in one movement. Later I retrieved that manuscript from the wastebasket and saved it for him. After he recovered, he laboriously glued the sheets together and sent it to the publishers. It has always seemed to me that this was a highly symbolic experience, both the tearing and the gluing together.

There was consternation among many of Boisen's friends in the hospital when it was learned that Milton Erickson would be his physician. This assignment was justified on the basis of his position on the staff. [In no way can Erickson be regarded as contributing to Anton's recovery or the founding of clinical pastoral education.]

One of the factors responsible for Boisen's recovery was his heroic effort to bring about a resolution of his conflict. As he said about his first episode and recovery, "The cure has lain in the faithful carrying through of the delusion itself."

Another factor that was responsible was the visit from Dr. Helen Flanders Dunbar of New York. Since I already knew her, I escorted her to the ward to see Boisen. I waited to see her out of the wards after the visit, which lasted at least an hour. Through much of this time, Erickson anxiously paced the ward, wondering what they were talking about. The next day he questioned me at length about their conversation. She had told me nothing, and I could honestly say to him that I knew nothing. However, he was worried. Boisen began to improve from that visit with Dunbar, and soon had recovered sufficiently that he was permitted to come to his office during the day. That visit with Dunbar was a definite factor in his recovery.

Again Boisen resolved the problem of [seeing the window screen as a cross in the sky and hearing voices] in the early twenties during and following that hospitalization. He made a sharp distinction between the mechanism by which voices were experienced and their content. The social value of the content was the important thing, not the mechanism. Indeed, one of the important diagnostic signs for Boisen was whether the voices had a positive social content or not. In his mind this made one difference between a religious experience and a mental disorder. In this he followed several scholars such as George A. Cooley and Charles H. Meade, the psychologist William James, and the psychologist of religion, George A. Coe.

In summary, Boisen's ideas and goals were well formulated before 1930. The program at the Elgin State Hospital after 1932 was essentially the same as he had at Worcester up through 1930. After coming to Evanston in 1948, I visited Boisen at Elgin as often as possible. He finally forgave me for changing the Worcester program from a research to a pastoral emphasis. He said he had come to realize that this is what the pastor needed. In my last visit with him he said he had a mission for me. Addressing me as his son, he said that my mission was to "tell the world that the Holy Spirit is the Mother." That was spoken out of his depths. Taken literally, those words have little meaning. But understood symbolically, they may be seen to have deep meaning.

NOTES

1The editors of this volume have combined remarks Dr. Wise made at the fiftieth anniversary celebration of the Association of Clinical

Pastoral Education in Minneapolis in 1975 with parts of an article he wrote in <u>The Journal of Pastoral Care</u> (1981) refuting the claim that Milton Erickson was the grandfather of CPE.

[2]This article utilizes material mostly from Anton Boisen, <u>Out of the Depths</u>. The reader is referred to the excellent Boisen Bibliography found in the papers of Robert Charles Powell (1975, 1976).

MY ENCOUNTER WITH PAIN:
RESPONSE TO AN EXPERIENCE OF EXTREME STRESS
IN THE LIGHT OF THE IDEAS OF ANTON T. BOISEN[1]

Carroll A. Wise, Th.D.

Response to an experience of extreme stress was the subject selected by your committee from among several suggested possibilities. Then I discovered that I would be speaking at this banquet in honor of Anton T. Boisen. This raised a very interesting question in my mind. Do the ideas of Anton Boisen, developed out of the experience of schizophrenia, throw any light on other kinds of stress experiences? Because of the nature of his illness Dr. Boisen's ideas were narrowed to that kind of experience. The question I am proposing now is whether some of his ideas have application and meaning to other forms of stress experiences, or indeed to our understanding of some fundamental processes in human nature itself, in both its health and spiritual aspects?

This paper gives me the opportunity to bring together two very significant personal experiences--one as a student, friend and colleague of Anton Boisen, [which I have described in the preceding chapters on CPE's "Tough and Tender History,"] and the other an experience of severe injury by burning just two years ago. It will be by no means exhaustive, but I hope it will open some new avenues of thought.

[My] other experience, which occurred on February 19, 1977, was that of being severely burned with hot water. The diagnosis in the emergency room of a hospital was "3rd degree burns over 30% of the body." The burn experience was accompanied by congestive heart failure which almost resulted in death. I shall not go into all of the details of this experience. I am more interested in certain psychological responses and the relation of the experience to Anton Boisen's ideas about the borderline between religion and medicine or spirituality and health. In a real, but different sense, I was on that borderline.

At first sight, these experiences seem radically different, and in many ways they are. But there are some similarities. These similarities do not appear on the surface. They may become evident as one probes deeper. The roots of Boisen's difficulties lay deep within his psyche, and grew out of intense conflicts in his early years, resulting in a personality structure which made satisfying personal relationships very difficult if not impossible in his adult years. His problems in adult life grew out of deep internal pathology that made it impossible for him to achieve healthy goals as an adult. In the conflict-free portions of his being he was very creative, and therefore had to wrestle with his painful experience in order to find meaning in it. He was a sick, but creative person.

13

My experience, on the other hand, grew out of external causes, the malfunctioning of the hot-water system in my home. In less than a minute I was transformed from a person with a fairly good sense of well-being to an injured, helpless one. This sudden change brought deep psychological responses and conditions. It shook my being to its very foundations. The major difference was that my ego remained intact for the most part. It was my bodily ego, or that part of my ego which rests on organic and physiological foundations, which was severely disturbed, which of course threatened my entire being. For some time I faced the possibility of death, and there were several episodes when the doctors thought they were losing me. But I survived!

One of the concepts through which Anton Boisen understood his experience, and that of others in similar conditions, is that of regression. Today this is a rather common concept, and I am sure all of you are familiar with it. Not so in the early to middle twenties when Anton was going through his first episodes and seeking light on their meaning. The concept of regression can be understood only in the light of a genetic and developmental view of the mind. Severe personality upheavals may be viewed as a breaking-up of later mental structure, and the emergence of infantile, intrauterine and primitive modes of thought. The purpose of such regression is to make possible a reintegration of "masses of life experience which had failed to be structuralized into a functional unity." (Boisen, 1926) Indeed, Boisen held that those patients in whom the struggle was most intense and regression the deepest were most likely to recover from schizophrenia.

My regression took a different form. When I was first placed in bed in the intensive care unit a nurse said to me, "You are to do nothing for yourself except press that button. We will then come and do whatever you need." Thus in a few words I was made to realize my state of complete helplessness. Strangely enough my mind was very clear and active. My thought processes were very sharp and intense, so that I can remember them today as clearly as when they occurred. Was I really so badly hurt? The doctors must be wrong. When will I be able to go home? How did the accident occur? What caused it? Why am I so weak? Why can't I do more for myself? Why must I be so dependent? What will it be like--being cared for as an infant? To use a concept popular today, you will see these thoughts as narcissistic, (Freud, 1914) and that is the way they have to be. Suddenly my energy, what there was left, was drawn away from the external world and centered on myself in a very infantile way. Nothing mattered but me. I was aware of what Anton called the "narrowing of attention," but could do nothing about it. Nor did I want to. What I am saying to you is that seriously ill people, whether with mental or physical symptoms, have to become absorbed with themselves. In your ministry to them you must take this into account, if you have not already learned to do so. Recovery is in part a reversal of this process, and the reinvestment of

14

interest and energy in the external world.

Regression was not without conflict. I did not want to accept the helpless dependency nor being cared for like an infant. My weakness told me I could not do much else. My understanding told me that to fight the regression or rebel against my condition might be to tip the scales toward death rather than recovery. A friend of mine, a psychiatrist, who dropped in occasionally for a brief visit, confirmed my ideas about this. To paraphrase the New Testament, if anyone would compel you to go one mile, go with him two in a willing and gracious spirit. Or again, unless you become as a little child you cannot enter the kingdom. Boisen would have interpreted his regression, and certainly I interpreted mine, as "regression in the service of the ego," that is, in order to resolve a serious problem. He would not have interpreted it as pathological regression for the purpose of evasion, rebellion or escape from conflict. He was aware of the difference between instinctual regression, where infantile erotic drives take over and control the ego, and ego regression where dependency, trust, and autonomy become the issues. To me, the most autonomous act of which I was capable at that time was to accept the physical condition into which I had been thrust and make my peace with it. This was a necessary condition to overcoming it.

We move on now to another of Anton's major ideas, the sense of isolation. (Boisen, 1928) The sense of isolation, he held, was the root evil in the sense of guilt. In guilt he felt cut off from all that he loved and idealized, he felt he had failed his family and those who trusted him, and he had failed himself, his own standards, super-ego and ego-ideal. Thus he felt split off from fellowship with others and also he felt a split within himself. Without an internal or external source of strength the experience of upheaval was inevitable. Indeed, this concept was so important to him that he devoted a paper to it, and it found expression in many of his writings.

By the same token, restoration, or cure, or the removal of the sense of isolation rested on the ability of the individual to accept the standards of the group and in this way resolve the problem of conscience, or the split within himself. Greatly influenced by the social psychologists of his day, the idea of socialization appealed strongly to him. From our perspective today it should be noted that restoration into the fellowship of the group depended on the acceptance by the patient of the standards of the group, on the ability to fulfill the expectations of the group. He resisted strongly the idea that the standards of the group should ever be questioned, especially the standards for sexual expression. Sex was so vitally related to the continuation of the group, and of the family, that the group had the right to determine standards. The acceptance of such standards was an integral part of socialization or cure. But he had an hiatus here, for he had intense guilt over the fact that he had never married and produced a son to keep the family name going. How could he correct this failure?

15

The sense of isolation due to feelings of guilt did not figure in my own experience. My problem in this regard was to deal with those persons, of whom there were not a few, who wanted to hold me responsible for the accident and thus make me feel guilty about it. None of these people were even near the scene of the accident. How could they know so many details of its happening? I spent much time in the first few days of my hospitalization trying to fathom the causes. This issue intruded into my thoughts in an obsessional fashion for several days. I could not figure out how I had caused the accident, and I began to resent people who tried to put a guilt trip on me. It was clearly their problem, the externalization of their own guilt, not mine. The intrusive nature of the thoughts about the cause of the accident gradually lessened and after several days completely disappeared. This happened in part because it was gradually becoming clear to me that regardless of the cause of the accident, my job now was that of getting well and going home. It was also accompanied by an experience of a religious nature of which I shall speak in a few minutes.

The only experience I had at all like Boisen's sense of isolation was the experience of aloneness and loneliness. I was in a private room, in reverse isolation, with some limitation on visitors, with everyone including doctors wearing gowns, rubber gloves, and face masks. Somehow it is hard to feel warm and close to someone whose identity is partially and artificially disguised. So the experience of loneliness was very deep. It was offset by visits several times a day by my wife, especially during mealtime in the period when I could not feed myself.

The loneliness was also offset by the daily change of dressings on my burns, an activity which took as long as two hours at first. This was always done by the surgeon assisted by a nurse. During these treatments there was time for conversation. The surgeon was a middle-aged orthodox Jewish man who had deep empathy and understanding, and we found much to talk about. While he was in the room, the loneliness was gone. When he left I was ready for sleep as the change of dressings was usually painful and exhausting.

I have spoken of these experiences to emphasize what you already know but may tend to forget, that caring people are emotionally and spiritually necessary for a patient's recovery. The loneliness which I experienced is quite different than the sense of isolation which Anton experienced and wrote about. The ability to spend some time alone without anxiety is an indication of maturity. People like Anton feel isolated even when with others.

I woke the second morning with my mind rather clear and active on the thoughts I have already given you. I called the nurse, and after taking care of routines, she came close to the bedside and in a quiet voice and manner informed me that my heart had almost completely failed the night before. They thought they were losing me. My family

16

had been there until after midnight when they were told to go home as I was improved and would probably make it through the night. My mind immediately started working on this. I had been unconscious throughout, and so had no awareness of this experience. I was now aware that I had no fear of death. I wondered. People are supposed to have a fear of death. Was I denying something? I thought not, what was there to deny? Within myself I felt something different, mild, vague but strengthening. By inner effort I could not bring this feeling any clearer into focus at that time.

As I pondered my situation during the next few days, including the imminent possibility of death, I noticed that all of my theological training and religious practices had receded into the background and had all but vanished. Prayer in its conventional form seemed quite unreal to me. I was occupied with a deep level of meditation and reflection which contained little of rational processes, but which had much of feeling and experiencing. I wondered about my lack of anxiety about possible death, but had no answer.

Toward the end of the first week I gradually became aware of something which had been emerging all week, and which seemed to throw light on all of these issues. It was a clear and profound inner assurance that I would get well. It was more than a wish or desire. It was a sense of an inner healing force, a power that was part of me, yet definitely transcended me. There was no sense of omnipotence, but of adequacy to the task at hand. There was no dramatic or unusual manifestations, but a deep inner sense of a reality that carried the certainty that I would recover. I wondered about this, but did not doubt it. It came with a pervasive sense of reality, of peace and strength. It would take time, but I would get well. This was an answer to the powerlessness I felt within myself, but not a reaction to that powerlessness. A reaction would have had anxious, compulsive elements in it.

My lack of interest in conventional religious ideas and practices now became clear. They seemed unimportant, and extraneous. The inner certainty that I was in touch with a profound aspect of myself, and yet with a reality transcending myself which had power to heal, was so real that it did not need to be formulated in theological ideas nor put into a religious ritual. In some way the entire experience was prayer, but not in the conventional sense. It was as real as the electronic monitor on the wall which recorded every heart-beat. While this was a very private experience, I also felt that this Power was not unique to me but was available to everyone, and that it was rooted in the nature of the Universe and in the nature of human beings.

I felt no need to fit this experience into a theological system. Indeed, I seemed to sense that trying to "theologize" the experience would have destroyed it. It would have meant structuring it into rational symbols, rather than appreciating the dynamic power of the experience.

17

Psychologizing would have done the same thing, only perhaps added the element of reductionism. There was no need to project this into a system. It was real, and my sense of certainty did not need that kind of support.

Now, to summarize for the sake of clarity and at the risk of repeating. I was aware of a profound inner presence that seemed part of me, and yet to transcend me in the sense of having an existence and autonomy beyond myself. It had a vital relationship to the task of healing. Second, I felt no need for rational verbalization or formulation of the experience. It was real and existed beyond all formulations and independent of them. It was to be accepted gratefully, to be appreciated and cooperated with.

Third, there was a sense that the healing process was beyond my power and that of the doctors. But I was aware that my conscious self did have a part in it. I was not to be a passive object but an active person in the process. My task was to understand and cooperate with what was going on inside of me, especially whatever promised to promote the healing of my wounds. My task was to maintain a relaxed mood, to accept whatever pain was to be involved and to seek relief from pain only when necessary so as to avoid interference with my new inner strength.

Fourth, there was a very firm conviction that the Power which I was inwardly experiencing was more than adequate to the healing task, given proper external conditions. Many of these conditions were the responsibility of the hospital. I was not about to test this new inner conviction. I was not about to jump off the pinnacle of the temple in a demand that my conviction be proven. It was rather there to be accepted.

Fifth, I inwardly felt that this new awareness did not guarantee a smooth process of recovery. There were and would continue to be many ups and downs in this process: impatience at the slowness, boredom at the sameness of each day, some conflict with hospital routines and conditions. But I never doubted the direction I was moving. Only I wanted to get there more quickly. This new and clear sense of communication with my own internal processes seemed to give me an undergirding strength to meet the daily irritations of being a patient, and at times it gave me strength to protest loudly and angrily at conditions.

As I thought about this experience, it became evident that my inner processes were identical with those which are present in all healing, although often on an unconscious level. They are especially present in all genuine psychotherapy, whether by ordained or non-ordained persons. Their effectiveness lies in the attitudes and spirit of both the patient and the therapist. In genuine psychotherapy, the healing of the spirit depends on the understanding and cooperation with the same inner forces with which I was dealing. Any genuine pastoral care or pastoral therapy needs to be practiced with an awareness of this reality in human life. The pastor should remember that it is impossible for him [or her] to produce this experience in [oneself] or in others. There are no "three steps" to its achievement. I suspect that the fact that my defensive ego was almost completely dissolved, leaving me on the bed-rock of personhood, had much to do with it. An issue is whether the interpretation of such an experience is grounded in some pre-conceived theory of personality, or whether the experience is allowed to contribute insights to an understanding of personality.

Not only did I understand that the same forces were present in all healing, so-called physical or mental, but it seemed clear to me that they represented non-rational elements in the human mind and that they could not be fully comprehended nor expressed in rational symbols, either theological or scientific. I was aware of a dilemma here. I felt a need to communicate the experience to others, but such communication is done chiefly through verbal symbols. Yet rational and intellectual symbols seemed quite inadequate to convey the meaning involved. Psychological symbols seemed particularly inadequate since they had no way of expressing the realities of which I was aware. Indeed, the scientific approach seemed rather to deny than affirm realities of this sort. Theological symbols, on the other hand, tended to become descriptive and to lose the dynamic quality of the experience, especially when they are arranged in rational form. Whatever else this experience was or was not, it was not produced by rational means. The more it was rationalized the more it would be separated from its deep, dynamic roots and from my sense of close contact with it.

As I thought about these things, I remembered that professional theologians have been bringing pressure on pastoral therapists and chaplains to "theologize" their work. Some pastors have accepted this pressure and have offered very stilted and lifeless formulations. This should have been expected, as it is grounded in a rejection of the dynamic aspects of religious experience. One cannot confine the non-rational, dynamic aspects of life or religion in any formula. Such formulations can never produce the experience. Energy always flows from the creative levels of the person toward the symbol, never in the reverse. At this point in my thinking and searching I began to feel the falseness in the demand to "theologize" our work. To put it in symbols of a living, insightful nature, yes; to put it in rational symbols of theology, no. Clearly, the letter kills, but the spirit gives life. Rather than this approach, those of us in the pastoral care field should invite the theologians to come in with us and deal with experience as experience, not as ideas. This was the plea of Anton Boisen, to learn to read "the living human document," but it is a plea which has not been greatly heard. The plea to "theologize" our work seems to me to be a counter-reaction to Boisen.

Did this experience change me? This was one of the interpretations of Anton Boisen--that the upheaval experienced by certain patients has for its purpose the resolution of conflict and the reconstructing of the personality. It should be said in support of his interpretation that between the first breakdown and that of 1930, and also after the third breakdown, he entered into periods of great creativity, writing articles and books, and working prodigiously for the development of his movement. While it did not make him a completely different person, his psychotic experience did free him to enlarge on his contribution to theological education.

The experience through which I passed brought to me a new orientation to life. This is difficult to explain, and it is something I feel inside and use in my daily living, but it is subtle and unobtrusive. There is a new meaning and gratefulness in being alive. Many things which seemed important before do not matter now. There is a new openness within myself and with others, which has been commented on by some of my friends. There is a new depth of feeling for others, a greater empathy. When an ambulance goes by, I feel a pain for whoever might be in it. To me this is a sign of strength. I have broken through the hardness which characterizes so much of our society. I have a new sense of awareness and closeness with other persons. There is also a deeper sense of vulnerability and precariousness of life--so often it hangs by a fine thread. Life is rewarding when it can be lived with ever-present awareness of the possibility of death, but not the fear of death. The fear of death is overcome by facing it from inner strength.

The changes in me were not the result of any conscious effort. They seemed to emerge within me as my physical strength returned. I believe they are the result of being shaken to the foundations and emerging again, and of living within the consciousness of the possibility of death over a considerable period of time. I believe they speak of powers of renewal which are the profound heritage of each person, and that they make growth, healing, and creativity possible. They are the deep roots of religious experience, regardless of the form which it takes. Through this experience I learned from within myself what Anton Boisen often emphasized, that in life crises or periods of stress the key to the solution is in the person and the experience, and not outside; in inner forces which are either at peace or war within the person, or those which make it possible for the person to be in peace or conflict with others; in the attitudes, responses, and goals of the individual [self]. Beyond this, and far greater than this, there is a power beyond all living things which makes for wholeness and healing, which may perform its will without any awareness by the person, or which may be consciously apprehended and appreciated, and may, in this manner, bring a sense of peace and strength of spirit which is itself healing.

Now a word about those who came into the room to minister to me regardless of the capacity in which the helper came. In the various people who came I sensed quickly three distinct attitudes. One group were those who reacted with fear or guilt to my experience and who began talking immediately in an unrealistic, sentimental manner, sugar-coating or denying anything that I said about my experience. A second group also responded with fear and guilt, but were more aggressive and controlling, knowing exactly what I should do and not at all backward in giving answers. Persons in each of these groups over-identified with my experience and condition, and suffered with me, but had different ways of easing their pain.

The third group, which consisted of only a few, could see my condition and hear about my experience, but they did not have to react to it. They felt my suffering and could identify with my experience without fear or guilt. It was my experience, not theirs. They could hold this within themselves, listening attentively and with understanding, and when they spoke it was in a positive and helpful manner. In my very weak condition they did not try to take the autonomy of my ego or spirit from me. I was not called upon either to submit to their emotional control or to help them with their problem. Even in my extreme physical condition they allowed me to be as much of a person as I could be. This brought out new strength in me.

Shortly after my discharge from the hospital I wrote the following about pastoral care of the ill: "While the doctors and others are gathering data about the physical aspects of the patient, the pastor needs to be the person who brings to the patient a deep sense of reassurance as to the underlying source and sustenance of life, to offer a sense of strength which does not require any or many words, to make available to the patient the opportunity to speak of the deeper issues of his experience. This is not the place for probing, or interviewing, or analyzing, or 'getting at feelings,' or reflecting feelings. It is the place for a deep empathic understanding of what is going on in the self of the patient as the result of what has happened to [one's] body. It is a time and place for deep spiritual sensitivity, not learned theology or psychology. Indeed, such learned approaches should be held in abeyance so that a word may be spoken out of understanding which supports the patient in his [or her] dilemma. Whatever the word spoken by the pastor, it should communicate a sense of the acceptance of the rootedness of life in a reality beyond the physical in which the patient can find rest, some abatement of the inner struggle, a sense of the presence of a spiritual power which removes isolation and aloneness, and a sense of whatever happens the essential core of him or her is now and will continue to be valued, reliably, even beyond death. Unless these realities, or some of them, can be communicated as a human experience any theological language will be empty. If they are really communicated, the form or language will not matter much. The living God is not dependent on the language of a given school or sect, or scholar, in a specific time and place. Symbolic language will convey much more meaning than theological abstractions. A person who would function in this way needs a profound understanding and

21

discipline of [one's] own spirit, and [one] must be deeply empathic. [One] should have no fear of reaching over the abyss of separation and aloneness to the patient. If [one] cannot do this, [one] has no business being there."

Early in this paper I raised the question as to whether some of the ideas of Anton Boisen have an application and meaning for a much wider group of human infirmities than the schizophrenic experience, or to our understanding of some fundamental processes and realities in human nature itself, in both health and illness. Throughout the paper I have been answering this in the positive sense. It seems to me it is time to put Anton Boisen and his ideas in the larger framework of universal human experience, and discover that when he was telling us about his experience, he was also telling us something about the nature of ourselves and the centrality of the roots of religious faith in human beings. Perhaps it is time we placed much more emphasis on understanding "living human documents," and minstering to persons in the light of that understanding.

NOTES

[1] This article was first given at the Anton T. Boisen Banquet of the Association of Mental Health Chaplains held on May 15, 1979 in Chicago. In its first printed form it appeared in the AMHC Forum Vol 32. No 1, September 1979, and then in The Journal of Pastoral Care, December 1979, Vol.XXXIII, No.4:220-229. It is reprinted with permission.

The scope of material in a paper of this length is necessarily limited. The student will want to consult the Boisen Bibliography in Robert C. Powell's, Anton T. Boisen's "Breaking an Opening in the Wall Between Religion and Medicine." (Association of Mental Health Clergy, Inc., 1975) and the following books by Anton T. Boisen; The Exploration of the Inner World (Chicago, IL, Willett, Clark and Co. 1936) and Out of the Depths, (New York, Harper and Brothers, 1960).

IMAGO AND INTROJECT:
A PROFILE OF CARROLL WISE

David M. Moss, III

My father had a deep love for classical literature and collected fine books all of his life. During many of my childhood years he read to me nearly every week night. At a very early age he taught me how to discern the value of a book and avoid the seduction of "best seller" lists. He started my library with gifts given when I least expected them. He was my first mentor--a trusted counselor or guide. More accurately, he was the mentor of my youth. Carroll Wise was my mentor into adulthood.

Like my father, Carroll was mentor to me in many ways. A mentor is sometimes described as a "tutor" or "coach." Simultaneously, Carroll was both and more. Chronologically, he was my teacher, clinical supervisor, and colleague. For nearly a year we even shared the same office. Later, for a brief but important period, he was my pastoral psychotherapist.

Carroll also encouraged me to publish and urged me to cultivate close relationships with other mentors. One of these people was Heinz Kohut, a man I consider to be Carroll's historical counterpart in the psychoanalytic community. It would not be an understatement to say that Wise was to Boisen, what Kohut was to Freud. Later I will share how I was able to serve as a connecting bridge between them.

In the profile which follows, I will concentrate on features of Carroll's personality, particularly his traits or abilities as an imago and introject--two terms that form the warp and woof of his style of ministry. In addition, I will sketch my perception of him as a mentor and my own experience of him as a pastor.

Imago

The term imago is used by both psychoanalysis and theology but in different ways. Freud referred to early object representations as imagos. Perhaps his clearest comment about their significance in psychic life is the following:

> The nature and quality of the human child's relations to people of his own and the opposite sex have already been laid down in the first six years of his life. He may afterwards develop and transform them in certain directions but he can no longer get rid of them. The people to whom he is in this way fixed are his parents and his brothers and sisters. All those whom he gets to know later become substitute figures for these first objects of his feelings. (We should perhaps add to his parents any other people,

23

such as nurses, who cared for him in his infancy.) These substitute figures can be classified from his point of view according as they are derived from what we call the "imagos" of his father, his mother, his brothers and sisters, and so on. His later acquaintances are thus obligated to take over a kind of emotional heritage; they encounter sympathies and antipathies to the production of which they themselves have contributed little. All of his later choices of friendships and love follow upon the basis of the memory-traces left behind by these first prototypes . . . the imagos--no longer remembered. (Freud, 1914a, p.243).

In other words, Freud considered imagos to be "memory traces" established in our formative years. He believed that they are at the core of all significant object choices from that time on. "Psychoanalytic writers have never taken seriously the notion of the inheritance of object representations." (Rizzuto, 1979) However, Freud's belief that an object representation is a distinct fixed memory trace has consistently characterized most clinical and theoretical studies.

For some of us it seems unfortunate that most of these psychoanalytic studies fail to recognize the rich soil of theology, the locale from which the imago concept actually sprung. More specifically, the concept and doctrine of imago Dei seek to describe a fundamental memory trace: the distinct and peculiar relationship between God and humanity. This distinctiveness or state of unique existence has a biblical touchstone in the creation accounts of Genesis, particularly the passage: "God said, 'Let us make [humanity] in our image, after our likeness'. . . So God created [humanity] in [God's] own image, in the image of God created he . . . male and female" (Gen.1: 26 & 27).

The expression imago Dei is intended to describe the quality of an intimate relationship like that of the father-son bond depicted in Genesis: Adam's son is said to be "in his likeness and image" (Gen. 5:3) That is to say, the biblical expressions of "image" and "likeness" (which mean essentially the same thing) were selected to denote: (1) the absolute difference between God and humanity; and (2) the exclusive place of humanity in God's scheme for reality. As such, Adam (meaning humanity) was originally created in the imago Dei to be:". . .God's vice-regent on earth but most of all to reflect in our nature the nature of God, just as the child is in the image of the [parent]." (Vriezen, 1962)

The New Testament carries this notion further. Jesus of Nazareth is defined as the image of God in simplicity. As the actual Son of God he "portrays the Father and as the incarnate God he makes God visible." (Rahner and Vorgrimter, 1965) Jesus' mode of existence, his moral direction, and the basic ethics of his personality reveal God's will for humanity's growth.

24

Systematic theologian John Macquarrie summarizes the existential meaning of humanity's creation in God's image:

> The full meaning of the claim that [humanity] is made in the image of God can be better conveyed in the contemporary language of "existence." What distinguishes [humanity] from other creatures is that [it] "exists," and to exist is to have an openness, which is perhaps the best clue to the mysterious affinity of God and [humanity]. Just as God opens himself into the creation and pours out being, and therefore has "letting-be" as his essence, so [humanity] is most truly [itself] and realizes [its] essence in the openness of an existence in which [it] too can let be, in responsibility, in creativity, and in love. (Macquarrie, 1966, p.212)

Carroll and I debated Dr. Macquarrie's language more than once, but we always came back to a common agreement: memory traces which lead to an openness of existence--healthy, creative relationships--or life-styles which manifest the Golden Rule, are, in essence, the basic goals of psychoanalytic psychotherapy and the Christian community. It may be true that theology concentrates on a Reality beyond the focal points of psychoanalysis, but Carroll would be quick to remind us that it is a serious mistake for either discipline to ignore the other. The goals of both are "to bind together again" (religio).

Introject

Just as "image" and "likeness" are used synonymously in the doctrine of imago Dei, psychoanalysis originally employed the terms "introjection" and "identification" without any fundamental distinction. Recently, however, the terms have been differentiated. (Schafer, 1968) Currently, the words "introjection" or "introject" and "identification" are used in different ways, one of which is quite suited for our discussion. That definition of introjection is:

> The child's taking into [itself] as a psychic phenomenon the object's (usually parent's) demands as if they were [its] own, so that [the child] reacts in the same way whether or not the object is present. The child does not copy the object as he [or she] would if [the child] identified with it. The regulating, forbidding and rewarding aspects of the superego are formed by the introjection of parental directions, admonitions and rewards. (Moore and Fine, 1968, p.58).

Like many people who studied with Carroll, I had just entered psychoanalytic psychotherapy. I was a graduate student in a new discipline or style of ministry that was not (and, to some extent, is still not) fully understood or appreciated by my ecclesiastical authorities. Under such conditions or circumstances introjection is a natural possibility. Carroll carefully and thoughtfully understood this. From time to time he spoke of it from the perspective of "regression in

the service of the ego." (Hartmann, 1958)   More than once we talked
about this vulnerability with Jesus' words: ". . . whoever does not
accept the kingdom of God like a child will never enter it." (Mk.10:15)
Yet in this condition I never felt Carroll took advantage of me, even
when I tried to provoke him to do so. As a mentor he was patient but
firm. Consequently, he changed my life at the bottom line. He taught
me about the basic trust of myself and others--a gift that I can only
repay by passing it on.

Mentor

Given this last comment I think it is of value to say several things
about myself. At the time I applied to the Garrett-Northwestern Ph.D.
program my career plans had become somewhat directionless. I had a
fine academic record which included four degrees: one in the Fine
Arts; another in Comparative Religion and Philosophy; and two in
Theology.   I was the Assistant Rector of the largest Episcopal Church
in Chicago and regarded by my denomination as a young priest with
innovative ideas.   Nevertheless, I felt a vague sense of uneasiness and
periodically experienced a feeling of angst. Without being aware of it,
I needed a mentor, perhaps even more than I needed a psychoanalyst,
to guide me through the unresolved grief over my father's recent and
untimely death.

I began to inquire about local doctoral programs as a solution to what
I thought might be a need for intellectual challenge.   Then, if by
second nature, I started to ask questions about the professors in these
various universities.   Soon, by a process of elimination, the field of
eligibles narrowed to The University of Chicago and Northwestern.
After nearly a year of evaluating these programs and teachers--in much
the way my father taught me to survey books for my library--I decided
that no other professor in the Diocese of Chicago had a finer
reputation as a mentor than Carroll.

I made this decision in three ways.   First, I talked to people who
were Carroll's students.   Second, I read his published works.   Then, I
studied the dissertations of those who had graduated from the
Department of Pastoral Psychology and Counseling.   I remember
thinking: "These students have paid 'big dues,' but they must have
been encouraged by a sense of purpose."   They were.   Carroll's
appreciation for scholarship was a motivating force behind these
doctoral papers.   References to this were evident in the dissertations
themselves.   Also evident was the fact that Carroll recognized his
limits when it came to formal research.   In such instances, he made
good use of his collegial network to help his students learn
experimental techniques that he was unaccustomed to using.

With these factors in mind I applied to Carroll's program, and was
accepted for the following year with two recommendations: that I
enter psychotherapy; and that I take a couple of courses in statistics.

This angered me, and I tried to see him, but he was on sabbatical. So I took his advice. I began my analytic journey, and confronted a bewildering set of formulas and figures which often mystify me to this day.

The next year my course work with Carroll began. In fact, I met him for the first time in the Fall of 1970, with no idea about his height. None of his students and none of the faculty I had spoken with had ever mentioned his physical size. I must have been expecting "the Great and Powerful Oz" and discovered the shortest giant I have ever met.

Because of the years that followed, I consider Carroll to be my "cherished mentor." (Moss, 1986a) In another tribute I have said: "I find justice to Carroll's life and ministry beyond my intellectual capacities and descriptive vocabulary." (Moss, 1986b) However, there are ways of explaining his place in my life, and the lives of many others, without being vague.

An elementary point is that Carroll engaged in those activities that characteristically define a mentor. He was "a veteran professional who [took] an active interest in the career development of . . . younger professional[s]." (Wright and Wright, 1987) He did the three things mentors typically do.

(1) they encourage the dreams and support the career aspirations of their proteges;

(2) they provide opportunities for their proteges to observe and participate in their work; and

(3) they help their proteges become aware of the unwritten rules and politics involved in the profession. (Bova and Phillips, 1982)

About a decade ago the Harvard Business Review published an article which shows that having a mentor directly correlates with several professional factors: increased job satisfaction; faster promotion and higher salary; firmer career plans; and a greater probability that the protege will also become a mentor. (Roche, 1979) More recent research has confirmed this. (e.g. Missirian, 1982) It is no coincidence that most of Carroll's students reflect such strong professional mobility.

The encouragement of published research is another characteristic of a mentor. (Crane, 1965; Kram, 1980) Carroll did this in several ways but chiefly by example. He shared many of his early drafts with his students and listened to their ideas. Several of us edited his lengthier works. Likewise, he helped a number of us to get "wet with ink" and risk our ideas in print. For instance, he edited three of my earliest papers and reviewed nearly a dozen more. Such direct assistance is a hallmark of the authentic mentor.

Current studies have documented the value of professional networking in career development. (Kram and Isabella, 1985) Mentors help to establish such networks by urging proteges to join professional organizations which increase their visibility and introduce them to other colleagues and opportunities. Mentors also increase the visibility of proteges by including them in intellectual discussions with peers and treating them as equals within a professional organization. (Edlind and Haensly, 1985) Carroll provided such opportunities in countless ways-- at Garrett, Lutheran General Hospital, AAPC, ACPE, local churches, etc., etc.

Perhaps the most important publication on this subject is <u>Mentoring at Work: Developmental Relationships in Organizational Life</u> by Kathy Kram. (1985) This book is the product of a Yale Ph.D. dissertation and, as one might expect, its research is tight, sound, and current. A strong point made by Dr. Kram is that an important benefit of mentoring is the effect the relationship has on the protege's self-image. A mentor provides an acceptance and confirmation of a protege's abilities which can increase the latter's self-confidence. A mentor's respect for the protege's ideas, positions, and opinions is critical to creative tasks because they can be approached, discussed, and conducted without a fear of rejection or ridicule. Dr. Kram could have used Carroll Wise as a model for her research.

Carroll gained much from what he gave, however, For mentors benefit by "passing on" their knowledge, talents, values, and attitudes. A mentor accepts the responsibilities of <u>imago</u> and introject as part of what Erikson calls "generativity." (1963) A mentor willing extends oneself through the next generation of professionals. One writer sums up the benefits of such giving in terms of a male relationship:

> The mentor is doing something for himself. He is making productive use of his own knowledge and skills. . . He is learning in ways not otherwise thought possible. He is maintaining his connection with the forces of youthful energy in the world and in himself. He needs the recipient of mentoring as much as the recipient needs him. (Levinson, et al., 1978, p.253)

Enough has been said for an interpretation to be made: the ideal mentor is a type of <u>imago</u>. He or she seeks to establish and/or renew memory traces in the protege's psyche via empathic understanding and thoughtful affirmation. This intimate relationship naturally spawns a "likeness" between the two while deeply respecting their distinct individualities. Proteges are not clones, and Carroll "rejected discipleship to him by vigorously fostering that which resided uniquely in the psyche of each individual with whom he came in contact." (Ashbrook, 1985)

As I have said, Carroll was my cherished mentor. That means three things: (1) I have followed some of his suggestions resolutely; (2) I continue to cultivate memories about his style of ministry; and (3) I maintain a deep affection for his presence in my life today. In these ways alone he has been, and will remain, a unique figure in my own development as a pastoral psychotherapist and as a mentor to others.

With these points in mind, I want to make another observation about a mentor. I have omitted this characteristic until now because I want to illustrate it in some detail. A mentor is not someone who ceases to be for the protege once the latter has cleared a particular career hurdle or completed the oral defense of a dissertation. Proteges will often return to their mentors for advice and counsel--not because of unresolved dependency needs, but out of genuine respect for collegiality. (Kram, 1983) Mentors, by the same token, may enlist the assistance of their proteges in appropriate situations or projects. (Kram, 1986) I experienced such reciprocity with Carroll many times, but one series of incidents stand out for me. I believe it illustrates how deeply Carroll was committed to the teaching ministry and the multifaceted nature of his mentoring. It also illustrates his basic nature as a pastor.

Pastor

The scenario begins in the summer of 1975 when I left Lutheran General Hospital to take a staff position at The Center for Religion and Psychotherapy of Chicago. I was excited about returning to what I considered to be the heart of the city and doing post-doctoral work at The Chicago Institute for Psychoanalysis. I was particularly interested in working with Heinz Kohut and one of his colleagues, Harry Trossman, who had agreed to be my clinical supervisor. Carroll encouraged me to pursue these plans even though he sensed my sadness about leaving the fine pastoral counseling agency that he had designed. I had been part of that agency for five years and most of that time had been wonderful. Additionally, to leave a structured source of financial security for a group private practice is always a risky venture, to say the least. (Houck and Moss, 1977)

Nevertheless, my practice at The Center for Religion and Psychotherapy blossomed in a manner I had not expected. Many of my former parishioners, particularly attorneys, began to refer to me with surprising frequency. I also found my studies at The Institute for Psychoanalysis to be very exciting. I had met another mentor, Heinz Kohut. Along with Carroll, Therese Benedek strongly suggested that I interview him for a project that was slowly taking shape, an anthology entitled Dialogues in Depth-Psychology and Religion (in process).

Heinz agreed to an interview for publication. He gave me a stack of unpublished manuscripts and several speeches, as well as a personalized copy of his recent book, The Analysis of the Self. (1971) In the front, he inscribed one of his favorite quotations from Eugene O'Neill's play

29

The Great God Brown: "Man is born broken. He lives his life by mending. The grace of God is glue." (O'Neill, 1925; see also, Moss, 1976a, and Scharfenberg, 1980) Naturally, I called Carroll and told him about this. I remember his remark: "Dave, this man is one of the best theoreticians in his field. Listen to him carefully. I think he will guide you well."

After studying Heinz's writings, I interviewed him about narcissism and self-psychology. We also agreed that if we both liked the final product, it could be published again in German. Heinz encouraged me to present part of the interview for a paper in one of my classes at the Institute.

The next day my life was drastically interrupted. On my way to the Loop offices of the Center for Religion and Psychotherapy a policeman driving at more than 70 m.p.h. hit my car broadside. I nearly died. I have recorded the details of this experience in an issue of Pastoral Psychology. (Moss, 1979; 1984). However, I have never discussed how Carroll helped me to recover emotionally from the effects of this tragedy.

During the month I was hospitalized, Carroll called me and wrote a short letter suggesting that I try to avoid fighting regression and self-absorption. He also invited me to visit him in his new home when I could. I gladly accepted his invitation. It gave me something to look forward to, a sense of future.

Two months later I made my first visit to Carroll's home. I had to take a taxi because my left arm was still in a cast and my right hand was not flexible enough to grip a steering wheel. The scars on my face burned from the cold wind. I was still ejecting slivers of windshield glass from my neck and chest. I had lost nearly twenty pounds. In short, I looked terrible and I felt worse. I was severely depressed in a way I had never felt before.

For about six weeks I saw Carroll every Wednesday afternoon for visits of two or three hours. We talked about many things, especially faith. He gave me a paper on Nietzsche that he had written for Anton Boisen. I found this very interesting, partly because of history but also because my first master's thesis was on the Death-of-God movement in the 1960s. (Moss, 1969) More importantly, I was undergoing a faith crisis and did not know it. Carroll did. He skillfully guided me into religious issues that I had never discussed with anyone--except in some intellectual or dogmatic way.

We also looked through countless photographs that he had taken--he was an artist when it came to black and white landscapes. To my surprise, he showed me a series of photos from which he had selected the sunrise portrait that hung in our office at Lutheran General. Once I commented that I had seen only one picture of a human being, an old

Indian woman, among his photographs. "Yes," he said, "I think it's intrusive to take such pictures. The reason why I took that one is simple. She asked me to."

One afternoon we looked through the newspaper and talked about the values which seemed to obsess so many people. Carroll sensed that I was getting bored and suggested that we watch television. "I know just the show for you. It's one of my favorites," he said. Actually, the show was a soap opera about a love affair in a general hospital. I began to wonder if Carroll actually watched this garbage on a regular basis. I remember thinking: "My God, maybe he's losing his cognitive skills!" Then something in that silly dialogue touched me to the point of tears and he asked me why I was crying. I told him how grateful I was for his care; his friendship meant so much to me; and more than that I loved him, even though his choice of television programs worried me. He put his hand on my shoulder and said softly, "Dave, this is nothing. Wait 'til you see the next one." Startled, I looked up at him. He was grinning from ear to ear. We both laughed for a long time. I think it was the first time I had laughed since my accident.

On my last visit I asked Carroll if I could interview him about the early pastoral psychology movement. He agreed but urged me to follow up by interviewing Seward Hiltner. (Moss, 1978) He also urged me to polish up my interview with Heinz so that it could be published. Our interview went well, and when we said good-bye, he gave me a framed copy of his "sunrise portrait." "This is something for you to enjoy," he said. Smiling he added, "I don't think it's ready for publication." I thanked him and suggested, "Maybe it is ready." To his pleasant surprise I arranged for its publication in Pilgrimage shortly thereafter. (Wise, 1979)

Physically, I felt better. My visits with Carroll had definitely lifted my spirits. My practice had resumed, and I continued my studies at the Institute. Then, on Christmas eve, I stopped by Heinz's office to leave a gift for him with his receptionist. It was a kodalith photograph of two drawings superimposed on one another: a heart on the profile of a brain; surrounded by one of Heinz's classic descriptions of "empathy." (Moss, el al., 1977) His office door was open, and I heard him say, "Tell him to come in, of course."

It was the first time I had seen Heinz since my accident. While I looked a lot better, I was still sensitive about the five inch scar on my cheek. I gave him the wrapped photograph. He immediately put it on his desk, took me over to a window, and straightforwardly asked, "How are you?" "I'm a lot better, thanks," I replied. As we talked, he got a little smile on his face. "Now you'll have to change your middle name." "What?" I said. He went on, "If you change MacBeth to 'von' you can pass off that scar as a saber slash." We laughed and he quickly said, "You're in good shape and you've had some very good care." I told him about my long "talks" with Carroll. When we parted he said, "Merry Christmas, David--and the same to Dr. Wise."

My interviews with Carroll and Heinz were published the next year. (Moss, 1976a, 1976b) Heinz informed me that a European publication wanted to contract for a German translation. (Moss, 1977) I was excited and shared this with Carroll, who suggested that I present a paper about my accident at the next AAPC convention. His rationale was simple: "I think you've learned some things that could help others. Pass it on!"

The very next week another tragedy occurred. Carroll was burned severely by hot water due to a plumbing malfunction. "The diagnosis in the emergency room was '3rd degree burns over 30% of the body.' The burn experience was accompanied by congestive heart failure which almost resulted in death." (Wise, 1979) Carroll's friends and colleagues were horrified. Most of us did not know what to do, and some of us knew there was nothing we could do except pray. Naturally, we contacted Addiene, his devoted wife, but otherwise we were powerless. Then I remembered what Carroll had written me when I was hospitalized--"do not fight regression or self-absorption." I sensed that he was in an extremely self-focused process directed toward healing, and I was sure that he was going to live.

Two months passed, and his progress was good. I visited him a couple of times, but we did not talk much. I think he appreciated the silence with someone he knew had also been through "a valley dark as death." (Ps. 23:4)

At the next AAPC convention I presented a paper on my accident and its psychological effects. I mentioned my appreciation for Carroll's help and, along with other contributors to this book, sent him the following telegram: "Like many AAPC members at this Convention, we miss you and pray for your continued recovery."

When I spoke to Carroll again, he thanked me for the telegram. As a result, I got the idea to write him on a regular basis, at least twice a week. They were just short letters, but each one contained three things: (1) a prayerful comment for his recovery; (2) news about what was going on that he would not have read about in the newspapers; and (3) a joke. The first two came easily, but the third required some research. I must have bought every current joke book and maybe there was one suitable piece of humor for every twenty pages. Nevertheless, I knew Carroll's sense of humor to be an aspect of his character that liked to be tickled even at the strangest times. I thought if he did not feel like reading my letters, he could always set them aside because he would quickly catch on to my style. (Years later he told me that I was right; he had had a few laughs and a lot of smiles.)

Relational Influence

In the months that followed, Carroll slowly grew stronger, but he never recovered fully from the scalding incident--except in an emotional way which he related to Anton Boisen's recovery from his last psychotic breakdown. (Wise, 1979) We talked about this more than once. Then one afternoon at his home I read him a draft of my paper on the automobile accident. We discussed it, and I made a lot of notes about his suggestions. I told him how painful it was to write but that I appreciated his encouraging me to make sense out of a seemingly meaningless tragedy. I asked him if he planned to write about his scalding. He said he thought he was going to, and so we agreed not to talk about the subject until after he had completed his paper.

Before I left, Carroll wanted to know if I had made any more literary plans with Heinz. I told him about the German publication of our interview and that we were planning a paper on narcissism and biblical fundamentalism. I intended to introduce him to Ron Lee and Homer Ashby since I thought their work with the MMPI might be useful for such a project. Carroll urged me to follow through. He was also pleased that I had been invited to a small ceremony for Heinz's presentation of the Austrian Cross of Honor for Science and Art later that year.

A couple of months passed before I saw Carroll again. One night he called to ask if I would help him edit some chapters in his new book, Pastoral Psychotherapy: Theory and Practice. (1983) I gladly accepted and, later in the week, he came to my home to leave several chapters. At that time he also gave me an early draft of a paper he had been working on regarding his scalding.

Carroll's Christmas letter of that year clearly reflected the quality of his recovery. The following excerpt nicely expresses his abiding faith: "As the Christmas season returns to us again we have reasons to be grateful. Christmas speaks of the gift of life, of a Life which came into the world. It also speaks of the life in which we all participate, which is in all of us, and which is sometimes threatened. When the threat comes we call upon healing powers in mind, body and spirit-- powers that are again part of the gift--to re-establish wholeness and peace . . . The gift of Life is with us constantly, but at Christmas we celebrate its incarnation in a Child. We can also celebrate the coming of new life into our spirits, and we give thanks. May the gift of healing be yours according to your needs . . ."

In October of the next year the first Annual Conference on the Psychology of the Self met in Chicago. Heinz asked me to meet with one of the participants, Joachim Scharfenberg, a German minster, to see if I could assist in the editing of his paper. (1980) I agreed and shortly thereafter spoke with Carroll about Dr. Scharfenberg. Carroll knew of him via his publications and thought it might be an interesting experience. Moreover, he thought it would be historically valuable for me to record any unusual incidents that might not be published. I told him I would, so the next day I purchased a pocket tape recorder.

Carroll was unable to attend that conference, but I gathered handouts for him. It was an impressive meeting with figures from several countries attesting to the significance of self-psychology and the psychotherapy of narcissistic patients. Religion and art were also subjects of concern. Randy Mason, the Director of the Center for Religion and Psychotherapy, delivered one such paper, and Dr. Scharfenberg presented another. (Mason, 1980; Scharfenberg, 1980) Several times I thought about Carroll's "historical alert" but never thought the occasion was apt. Then, in the final minutes of the Convention, Heinz got up to make some apparently spontaneous remarks. I thought about Carroll's advice and turned on the recorder. Suddenly, I understood so much about Heinz and why his professional life had taken the direction it did. He spoke clearly and his gratitude was evident:

I recall a personal incident which seems fitting as I reflect upon these last few days and the company of this evening. When I was a student of grade school level, I had the opportunity to play the role of a doctor in a class play. I became fascinated by this part and began to think about how things fit together, particularly the brain. My father, a musician, was perplexed by my behavior. I asked him questions that, at first, seemed to be the interests of the physician I had portrayed. In reality, these questions reflected my own interests.

I kept asking these kinds of questions. I can still remember his reactions. He became visibly annoyed with me and said, "Why are you interested in such questions? Why can't you be like the other boys?" I remember being very hurt. I had the feeling that there was some kind of gap--some kind of a distance that existed between my father and me--that there was something in me that I was deeply interested in which annoyed him. This was not his mode of living or thinking. He was a person who tried to express himself in art and sounds but he was not an inquisitive thinker. And I was. I was beginning to think inquisitively and continually asked, "Why is this?" and "Why is that?" I bothered him and it bothered me that he was not proud of my interests. Still, I felt that it was good that I asked these questions even though I knew that there was something unsettling about his not understanding me.

Well, it was a long, long hard road from that time on. I idealized him greatly, yet there was a distance between the two of us, and I felt that he did not try to understand what I was after. But then came the time when I was a late adolescent and I got into medical school and wrote several scientific papers and he was very impressed by my work. One day he said to me, "You know, Heinz, you have

34

done things that I could never do. I'm very proud of you." I was extremely pleased by this, as you can imagine. And there's something about this present moment here that reminds me of that moment. For many, many years now, perhaps for longer than I even realize, I have always felt I wanted very much to have a childhood like the other children. And I tried very much to do all the right kinds of things. However, in the long run, I couldn't. I grew up not quite like the other children. I continued to ask all the kinds of questions which annoyed the other "fathers" that I had. So often I felt very uncomfortable and stuck to myself, but I kept thinking my own thoughts, and I have attempted to rationally articulate new thoughts. Today it seems to me--after all these years--my father finally approves of me.

On the way out of the banquet hall I shook hands with Heinz for the last time. He had a gleam in his eye when he said, "You and your recorder are at it again. I'd like to review what I said after you've transcribed it."

A couple month's later Heinz had an unexpected coronary by-pass operation. His son Tom told me about it. I remember feeling the way I did when I heard about Carroll's accident. One afternoon I went to see Carroll to return the drafts of his final chapters for Pastoral Psychotherapy. He knew about Heinz's operation, and asked me if I had been upset by it. I was and told him how deeply I disliked not being able to do something in such situations, especially when they involved people I loved. To my surprise Carroll said quickly, "Well, then, do something!" "What can I do except pray for him?" I replied. Carroll smiled but was quite firm when he stated, "Do what you did for me. Write him."

I had forgotten about the letters I had written to Carroll during his recovery. He had never told me of their importance for him. In fact, I never expected him to do so. It was just something I did naturally. I thought about his advice for a few days. There was something not quite right about my writing Heinz in the way I had written Carroll. Granted they were "alike" in some ways, but my relationship with Carroll was different from any relationship I have ever had with anyone. So I thought about another avenue. One evening as I was looking at a copy of the Heart/Brain photograph I had given Heinz four years before, the answer came to me. The next week I sent him the following telegram.

Dear Heinz:

Since Tom told me about your operation, I have frequently prayed for your mending. Today, in supervision, Harry Trossman told me that your spirits were high. That reinforces my thanksgiving for your recovery, in spite of my deep regret for the pain you must have experienced during the last several weeks. (Reflecting on my accident, I can relate to you quite well, including several dimensions of anxiety, which I am sure you faced.) Since the heart is an ancient symbol of empathy, I preached about your work last Sunday at Seabury-Western Theological Seminary. I also commemorated the Eucharist to your health.

The touchstone for my sermon was not the appointed text, but a passage you reintroduced me to four years ago today: "Man is born broken, he lives by mending. The grace of God is glue." Mend well, my friend, as you have aided the mending of others.

Agape,

David

A little more than a week later I received the following reply:

My dear David:

I was deeply touched by your message and felt sustained by your multifacted participation in the trial to which I was exposed. It all came quite suddenly--I had not been prepared for surgery or anticipated such a possibility.

All this has its good and bad sides. The pain and anxiety I handled well--the struggle that I confronted was to counteract a sense of emotional estrangement, of feeling suddenly deprived of contact with the activities that relate to the center of my being: my work, my thought, my teaching, my healing. From the very first moment when I awoke after the 7 hour operation I joined the struggle to return to my world with every ounce of strength I had. I tried to learn from my experience--watched my feelings as they dehumanizingly concentrated on the functions of my body rather than on the body as the vehicle for meaningful action and thought. And I was soon making headway and finding myself again when I began to think about each of my patients--what the sudden deprivation might mean to them--and even got in touch with them, via phone, dictated messages, and brief handwritten notes.

My recovery went very well. I left the hospital after 10 days and have continued my convalescence at home. Even though I am not allowed to do clinical work yet for at least a month, I am given the freedom to attend concerts (we did last night) and to increase my physical activity. I am listening to a lot of music, doing more reading, and even beginning to play with scientific ideas--those I had been playing with when the "thunderbolt" interrupted me.

Anyway, you can see I am doing all right. You can also understand now why your message meant so much to me and why I am grateful to you for it. Feeling in every word you wrote that my struggle, my work, my thought now reverberates in others, in you and in those to whom you speak, was more healing and health-giving medicine than any narrow comparison with my physical discomforts would have been. Yes, I am "mending."

Warmly yours,

Heinz

I spoke to Heinz on the phone after I received this letter. I also sent him an offset copy of Carroll's article about his accident. He wrote a brief note about how he appreciated it and was sorry that he did not know Carroll personally. He was busy trying to finish his next book, and his papers were being collected into a two volume anthology which was eventually published as The Search for the Self. (Kohut, 1978) I was also inundated. I had begun to commute to Atlanta on a weekly basis to build a pastoral counseling center which I hoped would serve as an expression of my denomination's pastoral ministry.

The last time I heard from Heinz was via a Christmas note in 1980. He responded directly to the message of my card which was an early 19th century sampler done by an ancestor, Elizabeth Moss: "O that I could the blessing prove/My heart's extreme desire/Live happy in my savior's love/And happy in his arms expire." Heinz's card was Giotto's Flight into Egypt and his note read:

David, dear friend -

A warm thank-you for your Christmas message which is some "distance" from Elizabeth Moss' touchingly concrete affirmation.

I am glad that our paths have met. I know that however differently expressed in our "needlework," we are both living in the service of the same ideals.

The very best for Christmas and the New Year.

Warmly yours,

Heinz

When The Organization & Administration of Pastoral Counseling Centers (Carr, Hinkle and Moss, 1981) was released, my commuting from Chicago to Atlanta finally ended in 1982. However, my conversations with Carroll did not. He willingly gave me advice about my organizing a pastoral counseling center that would meet some standards of AAPC. We decided to spend time together at the forthcoming AAPC convention in Toronto [1981], but I did not know Carroll was going to warn me about Heinz's health. He had heard rumors that the analyst had been pushing himself and that the demands on his time seemed relentless.

After he told me that, I left the convention a day early and stopped in Chicago to visit friends. When I asked about Heinz's health, no one seemed alarmed. However, more than once I heard, "He's pushing himself for a reason." Several months latter Heinz died after a series of lectures at the University of California in Berkeley. He was 68 years old.

Carroll, on the other hand, was in the best of health. He had looked great at the Toronto convention. He was especially proud to introduce his longstanding friend and colleague, Carl Christensen, as the recipient of AAPC's Distinguished Contributions Award, an honor Carroll had received himself 14 years before. Carroll also sounded strong when later he called me about Heinz's death. He listened emphatically and reminded me that Heinz "got a chance to see his dream get realized. I've heard that he left at least one book-length manuscript and another conference in Self-psychology is being organized right now." (e.g., Kohut, 1984, 1985, 1987; Lichtenberg and Kaplan, 1983) Carroll was current, as well as bright.

There were other occasions when I spoke with Carroll on the telephone, and even though I never saw him again, he made many helpful suggestions about the development of my counseling practice in Atlanta. In 1986, I was able to convey a brief message of my gratitude for these suggestions, as well as his life, at a dinner in his honor. The occasion was the 23rd annual AAPC convention in Downingtown, Pennsylvania. The Pastoral Psychology and Counseling faculty of Garrett-Evangelical Theological Seminary invited several alumni to make statements about Carroll and his legacy. What I said then is, in essence, the conclusion of this chapter.

Conclusion

Carroll's death in November 1985 was more than the loss of an individual. Memorial celebrations in his honor, as well as tributes in diverse publications, address our loss of a symbol of authentic pastoral care. It is as W.E. Auden said of Sigmund Freud:

> To us he is no more a person
> Now but a whole climate of opinion. (Auden, 1945)

In this sense, Carroll's "climate of opinion" reminds us of Freud's definition of immortality: "being loved by many anonymous people." (see Stone 1971, p.1)

When you think about the number of clients that have been in psychotherapy with pastoral counselors who were trained directly by Carroll or learned from his profound writings, such a figure becomes abstract. These psychotherapists reflect a basic fact that his wife,

Addiene, summarized quite well:

> I have been hearing from many of Carroll's students, colleagues, and associates. They all testify of his ability to guide and help them in their search for direction . . . They write: "I would not be where I am today if it was not for him." In one way or another, they have said that they have grown because of him and that this is immortality--"passing it on," to use his expression and yours. (Moss, 1986b)

For many of his students and colleagues, Carroll will always retain the position of cherished mentor. We will continue to hold dear his memory with great value. He was a fine parental and/or fraternal model. His image, his imago, has been a force within us which continues to guide or shape our ministry even in subtle ways. He is an introject in that sense. He has left his fingerprints on the soul, the psyche, of the Pastoral Psychology Movement for the church of today and tomorrow. He patiently realized the sound "architectural advice" of the Sermon on the Mount. (Mt. 7:24-25) Carroll built on solid ground with careful counselors, teachers, and authors, many of whom continue to demonstrate his legacy. He was a mentor who ministered to his students with, as well as about, pastoral care. He encouraged our dreams of helping others to help themselves. He provided opportunities for us to participate in his work, and he taught us some of the unwritten rules that accompany true professionalism.

Perhaps the most important thing Carroll taught us was how to share his gifts, as we have experienced them--to develop and pass on those talents that he nurtured in each of us. To quote John Donne (see Moss, 1986b):

> All [humanity] is of one Author, and in one volume; when one [person] dies, one chapter is not torn out of the book, but translated into a better language; and every chapter must be so translated.

CARROLL WISE AS THEOLOGIAN

Tyler Thompson

In 1938 Carroll Wise was my teacher in a "Seminar in Psychopathology" at Boston University School of Theology. Case studies on various forms of pathology were examined and discussed with care. I remember that the first case was an instance of severe manic depressive illness. The purpose of the course was to give us a partial substitute for the preferred alternative: clinical pastoral training. There was no formal discussion of theology. When the subject came up, it was in terms of passing remarks, usually derogatory--or even snide. I remember that Dr. Wise was especially annoyed with use of the notion of sin because of its tendency to produce guilt feelings in those who have more than enough of the same already. I got the impression that he had little interest in theology.

In 1951, I began a 21 year period as his colleague (in philosophy of religion) on the faculty of Garrett Theological Seminary. I soon discovered that his interest in theology was very strong. Indeed, he was prime mover and chief organizer of a monthly discussion group fostering dialog between psychotherapists and theologians, which continued for years.

Was this perceived change of attitude accurate? If so, how did it come about? It struck me that an examination of his writings with these questions in mind should prove interesting.

His first book (Wise, 1942), published the year that he left New England and two years after the termination of his part-time teaching at Boston University, reveals rather clearly that my 1938 perception was in error. What I had mistaken for lack of interest in theology was rather a strenuous objection to the way theology was taught at his own and other theological schools.

> Students emerging from the average theological school today may be experts in Biblical criticism, in philosophical or theological argument, in certain literary devices for sermonizing, in textbook knowledge of psychology and sociology, and in other matters of more or less value. But they are not trained to deal with the fundamental material of the ministry--the human personality. Their thinking and work becomes book-centered, idea-centered, or program-centered, whereas it should be centered in personality. (Ibid., 263)

He believed that theological education in the main was directed to training clergy to "maintain a tradition rather than help persons in need." (Ibid., 261) Courses in theology could be valuable if directed to people's efforts to work out their own world views and resolve their

41

own inner conflicts. However, theology "taught as a series of cold, abstract ideas, in logical sequence, . . . becomes dull and spiritually deadening." (Ibid., 264) The solution, he felt, was to introduce more clinical experience into the training, for such experience concentrates on the living person rather than theological, psychological, or social theories and "leads to the evaluation of religious ideas and behavior in whatever degree of pathology or health, in the light of their function in personality as a whole." (Ibid., xii)

This suggests that Dr. Wise had been engaged in a struggle with his own faculty over this issue even as he worked to pioneer and foster the clinical pastoral training movement. His unpublished autobiography (N.d.a) confirms this and suggests that the struggle played a part in the termination of his part-time teaching at Boston (on "budgetary grounds?) in 1940. All this lends piquancy to his Founder's Day address on "Pastoral Care for the Broken and Forgotten" at his alma mater, delivered on March 12, 1964. He argued that clinical pastoral training needs to be brought from the periphery to the center of theologcal education if students are to be trained for creative pastoral care.

> This means that teachers of Theology, Bible and other subjects should themselves be highly trained clinically and pastorally, and should, in some way be functioning in a direct pastoral ministry to persons. Part of the split which occurs in the mind of the young student is due to the fact that he [or she] spends three years in a divided atmosphere where [one] finds no whole image as a basis for [one's] identity. Somehow the diverse academic points of view which should be represented on a seminary faculty need to be transcended in an integrated approach to pastoral care. (N.d.)

It is evident that he thought an important change which had taken place in most of the major seminaries in the generation since his own theological training in the late 20's--i.e., the establishment of a department of pastoral psychology and counseling--was not enough. Of course, he did not oppose this change: indeed, he was one of its pioneers. Called to the faculty of Garrett Theological Seminary to establish such a department in 1948, he worked constantly to have clinical experience brought into a more central place in the selection and training of candidates for the ministry. That this was in no sense an anti-theological move is made clear in his second book, Pastoral Counseling: Its Theory and Practice, published during the early years of his tenure at Garrett.

This work (Wise, 1951) is all about the kind of "living relationship" which makes effective counseling possible. Intellectual formulations, as such, are downplayed in relation to basic attitudes, (Ibid., 10) but the book is filled with intentional affirmations about the work of the Holy

Spirit. "The counselor is a mediator of the grace of God through a living relationship." (Ibid., 97) "The capacity of the human mind to see into and understand itself and its motives, once it is placed in a secure and understanding relationship with another, is one of the gifts of the grace of God to [humanity]." (Ibid., 141) The minister "tries to create conditions through which the grace of God can operate to produce healing and growth." (Ibid., 221)

Any doubt as to whether the interest in theology arose early or late is dispelled by Dr. Wise in his third book, Psychiatry and the Bible. He makes clear that it was Professor Rollin H. Walker, during student days at Ohio Wesleyan University, who first opened to him "the profound insights and resources of the Scriptures." (1951, xi. The same point is made in the unpublished autobiography.)

Of special interest in this volume is his treatment of sin. The same objection to misuse of the notion mentioned above is to be found here, but in a much more carefully qualified way. "Sin is an objective condition. Feelings of guilt are subjective, and may be produced in us by conditions which are or are not our responsibility." (Ibid., 11)

> It is . . . rebellion against the laws of God that the Bible calls sin. The concept of sin carries with it an element of responsibility on the part of the individual. Because feelings of guilt are so prominent in religious experience, and because [humanity] feels a need to be punished due to [its] relationships, this element of responsibility is often distorted in the direction of punishments and blame. However, in the Christian sense [humanity's] responsibility is more that of seeking to correct the condition of sin through repentance. Likewise the physician does not blame the patient for being sick, but does expect [the person] to take some responsibility for [one's own] cure. The individual either sinful or sick has some power of choice or decision, and this choice seems to be whether or not [one] will identify [one's] hopes and [one's] goals with destructive forces or with creative elements in [one's] experience. It is in this identification that relationships are established or broken; we feel a part of that with which we have identified and separated from that with which we have not identified. And this has a profound effect on the direction in which we are moving, either in terms of sin and salvation or of illness and health. (1956, 20)

Dr. Wise takes his lead in treating the subject from Jesus who was conscious of the reality of sin in human life and understood its destructiveness, but did not try to explain it. Jesus' emphasis was on redemption. He was "not obsessed by the idea" of sin. "His experience and his teaching was firmly rooted in a deeper Reality, the love and mercy of God." (Ibid., 80) Indeed, it is in the life and work of Christ that the love of God becomes most real in human life. It is here we "see a uniting, reconciling kind of love which reaches beneath human guilt and separation and gives those who can realize its meaning a sense of profound belonging in the universe and to God." (Ibid., 121) It is a reconciliation similar to but deeper and more trustworthy than anything we find on the strictly human level.

I am bound to confess that the treatment of sin in this work differs markedly from what I heard from him in 1938, but the emphasis is what he was already looking for:

> In the Christian faith the kind of relationship which God offers to us in Christ is one of love, of acceptance, of forgiveness, or reconciliation. It is through the realization of this love within ourselves, and through identification with Christ, that we gain freedom to be servants of one another through love. (Ibid., 155)

The fourth book, The Meaning of Pastoral Care (1966), states specifically that it is an attempt to relate the theological and personal dimensions of pastoral care. (Ibid., x) This was surely one of the major objectives of Wise's career, and to show how it was done is the purpose of this essay.

> Pastoral care is the art of communicating the inner meaning of the Gospel to persons at the point of their need. Thus pastoral care is not a theoretical discipline, although it may be undergirded by such disciplines as theology or Biblical interpretation. (Ibid., 8)

This is one of his favorite ways of putting the matter. I suspect all of his students have heard it from him, and it appears elsewhere in his writings. For instance, an unpublished paper on "The Psychological Content of the Curriculum of the Theological School," where he continues, "Whether the minister is preaching, counseling or administering a church or engaging in some other activity, pastoral care should be taking place." (N.d.d)

Later in the same paper he states in blunt terms his notion of the relation of his own field to theology:

> Pastoral psychology must free itself from the domination of any theological point of view which insists on predetermining what we shall see in [human beings]; pastoral psychology must be free to recognize in [humanity] whatever it finds. Pastoral psychology must also have a close relationship and continuing conversation with theology, particularly around the doctrine of [humanity]. (Ibid., 4)

He never in his writings repudiates theology unless it becomes ingrown and feeds on itself (1983, x) or becomes "a defensive substitute for understanding experience, rather than an aid to understanding." (Ibid., 269) Indeed, he insists that "the Christian pastor must have a thorough Biblical theological,and historical training (1966, 9) through which the elaboration of the Gospel will take place. He even makes bold to enter into a couple of specific theological disputes. He sides with Wesley against Calvin (Ibid., 18-20) in interpreting prevenient grace, on grounds that the teaching of the former fits in better with the experience of pastoral care. Furthermore, in treating the doctrine of the Holy Spirit--a favorite topic with him--he repudiates the language of "encounter" or "confrontation" in favor of the language of "presence." (Ibid., 29)

This latter distinction is very important to his understanding of pastoral care.

> The pastor must be the kind of person who can be so trusted that another will invite him [or her] to share the realities of [one's] existence, especially those which are painful, in which [one] has already been hurt. Such trust and openness can come to the pastor, not because he [or she] has any particular brand of theology, but because [the pastor] is a genuinely loving, trustworthy person. He [or she] also must have the wisdom to know what really helps and what does harm in various human situations. (1966, 15)

Dr. Wise is quite explicit in regarding the work of the pastor as an instrument through which the Holy Spirit can work--whether it is preaching, religious education, church administration, calling, counseling, or conducting worship.

> But if these forms are engaged in by the pastor without a relationship of love and concern for persons, then they lead to ineffectiveness and disillusionment for both pastor and people . . . The participation of pastor and people in experiences through which the Gospel of redemption becomes real, must be genuinely motivated, or it is nothing. (1966, 67)

Theology comes into the pastoral picture in this way. It is a method of interpretation, whereas the method of the pastor "is that of personal relationships, using interpretation to give intellectual substance to a reality which has been or is being experienced. And when the theologian becomes pastor, as sometimes [one] does, [one] moves from the level of concepts to the level of personal relations." (1966, 41)

An interesting proposal with regard to theological education brings this volume to a close and effectively embodies its central message. Dr. Wise suggests that the symbol of "scholar" needs to be balanced by the symbol of "saint." He asserts: "By saint we mean a person who is growing in genuine love toward God and [humanity], who is honestly trying to cope with the conditions in [oneself] which are obstacles to such love, and who is able and willing to use professional services to this end." (1966, 134)

The final book on Pastoral Psychotherapy: Theory and Practice (1983) was published several years after Dr. Wise's retirement from the Garrett faculty.   It is an extensive development and more technical treatment of the area covered in the earlier volume on pastoral counseling.   He here drops the term pastoral counseling in favor of pastoral psychotherapy, but pervasive exposition of doctrine of the Holy Spirit continues.   There is also a strong emphasis on the doctrine of creation as it applies to human beings.

> The understanding symbolized by the 'Image of God' has a deep significance for pastoral therapy.   It carries the meaning that God has placed within [humanity] as part of [its] created nature, resources which make for wholeness, health, growth, the resolution of conflict, the transformation of instinctive conflict and energy into creative living.   [Humanity] as a creature has the power to take a hand in the creation of [itself] by utilizing and fulfilling the potentials which God has placed in [humanity]. (1983, 34-35)

He says that God should be thought of as present in any process in which self-revelation or growth toward love and faith are experienced. As a person "becomes more aware of his [or her] inner strengths, [one] understands that [one] is using resources which [one] did not create, that [one] finds them within.   They are part of God's creation in the nature of [humanity]; they are also a means of grace and healing." (Ibid., 162)   The proper task of the pastoral psychotherapist is helping people discover the healing forces which God has put in them.

As part of the culmination of this work, Dr. Wise includes some passages which provide his most sophisticated and precise treatment of the role of theology in pastoral psychotherapy.   It is clear to him that: "the therapists need to know [their] way around in the theological disciplines, to have [their] own theology worked out and continuing to grow, and to be able to relate [their] theology to [their] work." (Ibid., 280)   While therapists, unlike the theologians and philosophers, are not dealing primarily with the ontological meaning of religious symbols, they need to recognize how experienced ideas and behavior deny or distort accepted theological truth.   Ordinarily the conflicts these engender within individuals cannot be resolved by rational processes, but they need to be rationally understood.

> The task of the pastor as a therapist is not to "theologize" with people.   It is in part that of helping a person discover how he or she is using religious symbols to support processes of disease and distress.   It is also assisting a person to find the strength through which those decisions and commitments that lead to change, growth, and a new quality of life may be made.   If there is theological talk, it should grow out of and enhance the immediate context of the conversation, and not be theologizing for its own sake.   Such theologizing will probably mean that the pastor or the person, or both, want to avoid some painful realities in the

relationship. The pastor may discover that others do not agree with him [or her] conceptually, either psychologically or theologically, but may still derive much help from [that] ministry. [One's] knowledge of processes, along with [one's] genuine humanity, should help [one] respond in an empathetic and healing manner. In the New Testament language we are speaking of the quality of redemptive love, of a reconciliation which is deeply internal, as well as with others and with God. (Ibid., 300)

The conclusion is that Carroll Wise was not only a person of strong and growing theological interest, but also a creative theologian. His strong emphasis upon the operation of religious symbols within the crises and growth of lived experience casts an interesting light upon a common contemporary expression: doing theology!

A final note concerning his relation to his own immediate theological heritage. There can be no doubt that Carroll Wise had strong objections to the way in which theology was taught to him, although he did not repudiate it directly. Consequently, it is of interest that one of his characteristic sayings is virtually identical with the best remembered saying of one of his grandfathers in the faith. Borden Parker Bowne, professor of philosophy in Boston University for a generation before 1910, was the most influential teacher of several of Carroll Wise's teachers. Many of Bowne's students reported that he was fond of saying in class: "Life is larger than logic." (As far as I am aware, this appears nowhere in his published writings.)

Carroll Wise has written, "Life is much deeper than logic." (Ibid., 272) The saying was at the heart of one of the main thrusts of his teaching. I suspect his students have heard it often in class. Despite the slight verbal difference, I am convinced that the intention of the two sayings was the same. There is a delicious irony here. I can find no evidence that Wise had Bowne in mind. Yet despite his dissatisfaction with his own tradition, there were two respects in which he was strikingly in tune with it: empirical openness in theology and refusal to accept abstraction as truth. His own contribution arose from the kind of empirical data he emphasized as a result of his association with Anton Boisen and his work as a mental hospital chaplain.

TEACHING WITH C.A.WISE: THE EARLY YEARS, 1958-64

John Monroe Vayhinger

My first contact with Carroll A. Wise was in the summer of 1948 when he was a visiting professor in Union Theological Seminary, and I was in my third year at Columbia University across Broadway in New York City. Since I had had no courses in Pastoral Counseling in my four years in seminary, I was much intrigued with this professor from the Garrett Biblical Institute. So, I signed up for the course, the only course I took at Union. It was a fairly low level seminary course. I gained mostly from it in realizing that theology and psychology get along pretty well together, though the lectures were mostly psychological in nature.

Then, in 1952, when I was a Chief Psychologist in a Mental Health Clinic in South Bend, Indiana, Carroll and Garrett invited me to be a visiting professor in the summer school. Carrying on my patient load in Indiana on Mondays and Fridays, I spent mid-week in Evanston. Both the opportunity to room with Millard Burroughs of Qumran Documents fame and the chance to get acquainted with Carroll were highlights of that summer. Furthermore, I found a warm acceptance by the faculty. By 1957, I had reached the point where I felt I had enough experience in parishes (14 years as pastor, including 2 1/2 years as a Chaplain in the Pacific during WW II) and in psychiatric clinics. I was ready to move on in my calling, namely, teaching counseling in a seminary.

One rainy foggy night I met Dwight Loder, president at Garrett, at the parsonage of Bryant Howard in Fort Wayne. After two hours of friendly discussion well-washed in coffee, I took Dwight to the airport to catch his plane to Chicago. We drove around in the fog for a couple of hours before we found the airport. Fortunately, the plane also was held up by the fog.

I had spent seven years in the Clinic, taught psychology for Indiana University, and served Portage Chapel United Methodist Church as pastor. However, that night resulted in an invitation to teach with Carroll on the Garrett Faculty as Professor of Pastoral Psychology and Counseling, PP&C as it was called. My wife Ruth and I prayed about it, and felt strongly that Garrett was the open door to seminary teaching for us. So we moved to Evanston on 1 September 1958.

To have the opportunity of teaching with Carroll Wise was beyond my fondest hopes. My grandfather had attended Garrett in the last decade of the Nineteenth Century, teaching German and Mathematics at Northwestern to pay his way. Grandmother had been a social worker, and the family tradition told that she had worked with Jane Adams while grandfather was in school. Nineteen fifty-eight, then, found

Ruth, our two children Karen and Jack, with our two dachsunds, Trudy and Tippy, furniture, library and high hopes, moving to Evanston.

Carroll occupied the north third of a divided class room on the Garrett Main Hall first floow. I moved into the south third, with Marilyn Butt, our secretary, in the small middle room. Our windows looked out at Howes Chapel and the green lawns between the Seminary and Sheridan Road. The room's inside door became an open path for students seeking advice, academic direction, or counseling.

I intend to let two things show clearly in this chapter. The first is the pioneering work of Carroll in the field of Pastoral Counseling in bringing the theological traditions of the Church back into the fields of psychology and psychiatry, which theologians had abandoned to physicians after 1900. His writings reflect his broad involvement in both Bible and psychology.

The second is that Carroll was a very human person. Some of his strengths proved difficult to live with at times. Character and determination seemed like stubbornness in close relationships. An illustration came in the first year of a research project.

I had thought that while Carroll, with his ten years of seniority at Garrett, was indeed more experienced in seminary teaching, each department came to consensus on policy and curriculum. I believed all members of any department contributed equally to its plans and procedures. Since I knew that a Lilly Endowment grant was paying my salary and that my major responsibility was the development of what came to be called "A Psychological Study of the Theological Student," I entered my title in the American Psychological Association Biographical Directory as "Director of the Garrett Research." When Carroll discovered this, though I certainly had not hidden it from him, he became angry. I was to understand that he was the Director; my responsibility was to design and carry out the Research. So I took the title out of the Directory, and continued to do the planning and procedures. In the two volume report on the Research, Carroll described our relationship in that project:

> This project was carried out in the Department of Pastoral Psychology and Counseling in Garrett Theological Seminary in Evanston, Illinois. Carroll A. Wise, head of the department, was the initiator and supervisor of the project. John M. Vayhinger was the project director, with responsibility for the research design, the collection of the data and the statistical use of the data. This book was prepared by both of us, and it would be difficult to separate our ideas. (p.ii)

More of the study later.

So, it was apparent, soon after arriving, that Carroll expected to make most of the administrative decisions. "Most," I must say, because he was the senior member of PP&C and because there were many periods when we truly made decisions together. Dictatorial, no, not really, but he was firm, and the "senior member of the department."

Carroll had a good laugh at my expense at the end of the first quarter. When final exam time came, I wrote questions which, in my eyes, covered all of the material in the class on "Research Design and Statistics with Religious Data," for doctoral students from Pastoral Counseling, Christian Education, and Sociology of Religion. I had stretched the students with three text books and fast-paced lectures, with demonstrations. Some finished the examination after 50 minutes, while I found a number of students still writing when I returned after chapel. The question was how to grade those who took fifty minutes and those who wrote for nearly two hours. I learned the distinction between "thorough" and "possible" and can still recall Carroll's laugh when we talked about it.

The funds for my professorship came from a three year grant from Lilly Endowment, of Indianapolis, Carroll and Dwight Loder had applied for money to study the personalities of seminary students, and Lilly had granted $17,000 a year for three years. The design was not completed in three years and Harold Duhling of Lilly saw that we received another year, with an additional grant for computer costs. In 1962, I applied to the National Institute of Mental Health, and they granted us $40,000 more, over two years.

Carroll's interest in psychological/psychiatric research went back to his years as Chaplain at Worcester State Hospital in Massachusetts. Not only did he work with Anton Boisen, but he took part in the Schizophrenia Studies being conducted by such famous persons as Helen Flanders Dunbar, Harry Stack Sullivan, and other leaders in the psychiatric world. His keen interest in research continued through his years as pastoral counselor in churches and as seminary professor.

I found this respectful attitude toward research to be a solid bridge between us. Carroll kept close tabs on all stages of the Research, being most supportive of my designs and methods. Every Monday we would spend two hours going over course plans, students, the research design, advancement of the data collection, computer techniques and results, and interpretation of the print-outs. I designed and interpreted the broad and theologically oriented goals that Carroll had developed in the original plan. In order to administer the broad battery of tests that we had chosen, we needed more skilled help. Morris Taggert became my assistant during his years of doctoral study, many times saving my sanity as the work load increased. At various times, we employed six to ten doctoral students from the clinical psychology department of Northwestern University. They administered tests and worked with me in developing new questionnaires and tests.

51

Carroll was extremely busy during those years, teaching, counseling, writing, speaking, and administering the department. Sometimes during our Monday sessions he would doze, sleeping for maybe twenty minutes. Then, he'd wake, and we'd continue as if on a comma instead of an interpruption. I'm sure he often was bored as I tried to explain the mysteries of statistics, how programs worked on computers, and the growing mountain of data. "Just the conclusions, John," he'd say, "Just the conclusions." Some times he'd say, "No, that doesn't agree with my experience," and I'd go back to the drawing board to find some compromise between what I thought I knew about the data and that which would fit his experience and hunches about seminary students. At Columbia I had learned never to compromise data, which was next to Holy Writ to the scientist. Nevertheless, I soon learned that I would get further with Carroll by minor compromises than if I argued for another point of view.

I do not intend to review Carroll's psycho-theology. His works and his lectures have done that, along with memories of conversations. The positions his students occupy in counseling centers, parishes, and professional organization, as well as seminaries and universities, reflect the effectiveness of his teaching. However, I will use some of his ideas to illustrate the atmosphere in which we taught during those years.

Carroll's concerns with the "life processes" came through often and strongly in faculty meetings, while his colleagues were more concerned with theological concepts. This difference stimulated profound discussions and heated confrontations. I recall some of the more existentially and theologically oriented faculty raising their voices at Carroll, who gave them as good as they argued. The respect most faculty felt toward Carroll usually resulted in colleagues backing down, whereupon Carroll would join in a compromise to which they could agree.

Carroll insisted on the pastor's knowing modern psychodynamics and possibly participating in psychotherapy in order to gain "an understanding of the whole person and [one's] life experiences and particularly [one's] responses to those experiences." (Wise, 1983, p.100) Carroll, unlike many liberal theologians, regularly used traditional terms such as "sin," "evil," "only as one serves the needs of others and the community in obedience to God," "the Cross," "resurrection experience," "new life in the Spirit," "rebirth," and so on. Though he often interpreted these in psychological ways, we could converse through this language and find a common base from which to teach. In the same way that I am an unabashed Evangelical Christian, I recall Carroll saying several times, "I'm an unrepentent Liberal." He referred to believers in a literal Bible as "fun-damn-mentalists."

Carroll and I belonged to several groups formed to discuss the relationships of psychology/psychiatry and theology. I can recall how shocked he was when one of the psychoanalysts, in answer to a query as to his motivation in going into psychiatry, answered, "It pays good money." I am confident Carroll was in ministry from altruistic motives. Those groups were an important part of our professional involvement.

In those days, Garrett had a broadly selected faculty. The Bible department, for instance, had teachers with a moderately conservative theology and others with quite a liberal point of view. I never understood nor asked Carroll why he almost never quoted any of his colleagues in his writings. In searching the indexes of his books and through reading those volumes, I could find only three or four names of colleagues. The names of leading psychiatric authors, however, appear often in the same volumes.

An incident in 1961 illustrates the careful way he selected his authorities. Abingdon Press asked Newman Cryer and myself to edit a Casebook in Pastoral Counseling. We used cases submitted by pastors to Together Magazine which were commented on by leaders in the pastoral counseling field. We selected some 56 cases out of a total of approximately 140 for publication. I wrote a paragraph to introduce each case, and Newman and I added a Preface and Index. Howard Clinebell of Claremont Graduate School of Theology used many of these cases to illustrate his Basic Types of Pastoral Counseling. More than half the seminaries in the Association of Theological Seminaries used this Casebook in their classes in Pastoral Counseling at one time or another. However, when Carroll discovered that Newman and I had agreed to edit this book, he took a negative view of the project, demanding we cancel the contract, indicating the cases were too simple and would be ridiculed by our psychiatric colleagues. We went ahead with the book, but I felt Carroll's displeasure.

Carroll's bold and sometimes defiant lectures on psychological descriptions of religious behavior often aroused student resistance, even attacks. He wrote in Pastoral Psychotherapy, after summarizing the New Testament interpretation of confrontation:

> Speaking the truth in love. . . In supervising advanced students in pastoral psychotherapy it is evident that the ability of the student to permit himself or herself to regress is central to [their] teachability. It is also evident in seminary classes where a student's reception of new ideas is accompanied by hostility at the professor or by exaggerated dependence. (1983, p.193, underlining added)

Yet such fears of hostility by students, or even by faculty colleagues, never deterred him from expressing unpopular or threatening concepts which he felt ought be expressed.

Carroll worked through another confrontation in regard to his height.

Though certainly not tiny, he was shorter than many. Students sometimes unkindly referred to this, as though his ideas and attitudes were also small, especially when his lectures hit home. He would share some of those cruel remarks with me, and I appreciated his trust in our relationship. In private, he would characterize those confrontations with psychiatric terms, listing the ego-defense mechanisms he believed were operating in the students', sometimes faculty's, belittlements, i.e., transference, projection, regression, etc.

Carroll contributed to my growth in teaching. I had ranked, and still do, Carroll with the four or five pioneer leaders in the field of Pastoral Counseling. These were Paul E. Johnson of Boston, Seward Hiltner of Chicago and later Princeton, Wayne E. Oates of Southern Baptist, and Anton A. Boisen of Boston and Elgin State Hospital. My own teachers had exposed me to psychology and theology in a broad and positive way, but I had little in Pastoral Counseling. These special people in my life included: Frank Morris and W.D. Turkington of Asbury; Edwin Lewis, Stanley Romaine Hopper, and Lynn Harold Hough of Drew; B.F. Skinner and Margaret Mead at Columbia; Carney Landis and Joseph Zubin at the New York Psychiatric Institute; Robert Sessions Woodworth and A.T. Poffenberger at Columbia; and Laurance F. Shaffer, Esther Lloyd-Jones, Kenneth Herrold, and Donald Super at Teachers College. Nevertheless, it was when I came to Garrett that I became involved in the technical field of Pastoral Counseling with Carroll. My years in the clinic and pastorate contributed to the applications and integration of that training, but it was Carroll who focused for me the technical field of Pastoral Care and Counseling per se.

I gained in three specific ways from teaching with Carroll. First, I took note of his applications of Scripture. I used his books in my classes, and turned often to them for lecture material. However, as I will point out later, our views of Scriptural inspiration and the use of the Bible differed. Second, my early contact with Pastoral Counseling as such came when I taught at Drew Theological Seminary, 1948-49. I brought Paul E. Johnson to lead my classes for several days. Though not trained in psychological counseling, Paul was a philosopher by education, and had taken over responsibility for the psychology of religion and counseling classes at Boston from Carroll while Carroll was still Chaplain at Worcester. This was a disappointment for Carroll, who had counted on returning to Boston sometime to teach counseling. In fact, Carroll related once that he had learned he would no longer teach at Boston when Paul visited Worcester and asked if he could borrow Carroll's notes and bibliography, unaware that Carroll had hoped to fill that chair. Paul's "interpersonal pastoral theology" was very philosophical compared to Carroll's "dynamic psychology."

Carroll had been a founder and leader in the Council for Clinical Training in which seminary students spent time in psychiatric hospitals in the study of "the living human documents." Thus, he brought a more psychiatric emphasis to his teaching, and less a psychology of religion or scholarly focus. Having come directly from a psychiatric clinic to the campus, I found our interpretations of behavior compatible. His emphasis on counseling with students and/or referring them for psychotherapy as one answer to personal and neurotic problems again was compatible to my own orientation. Because of his involvement in what became Clinical Pastoral Education, I became involved.

Carroll and I agreed on the need for a strong, dynamic, personal, Christian experience for the pastoral counselor. He wrote in Pastoral Psychotherapy: the pastor who gains insight into his [or her] own Calling sees that "[one's] identity as a clergyman [sic] is given by the quality and meaning of [one's] religious faith." (1983, p.25)

I like to think that Carroll and I influenced each other mutually. I felt that President Loder had wanted me at Garrett with my background in Learning Theory to expand Carroll's stands in Rogerian and Freudian psychology. It seemed to me that during my years at Garrett, he added a considerable amount of learning theory to his teaching and writing. Since Behaviorism is probably the major product of psychology in the United States, this broadened his influence with students, particularly with those who had psychological backgrounds in college.

I recall the first doctoral student on whose oral defense committee I sat. His research focused on a patient in the hospital where he served as chaplain. His description of her dynamics was strictly psychoanalytic. I asked, "How would you describe the dynamics of this patient from the point of view of Learning Theory?" There was a long silence. I withdrew the question, and asked another from a psychoanalytic viewpoint. He answered it successfully, and the committee passed him. I noticed that later our students could use learning theory effectively.

Despite paralled interests, there were some ideas where we differed. One was our interpretation of Scripture. I regarded the first chapters of Genesis as factual, that is, they describe historic events in the cosmic development of the present astronomy and especially the earth in the way events really happened. I see those days of creation as corresponding very well with the 'evidence' in geology and in the fossils. It probably took four and a half billion years for the earth to reach its present state from the "Big Bang" (or however creation took place). Certainly the Scripture "days" were not measured by clocks or calendars. Therefore, I see no conflict between a conservative view or geological and biological descriptions of the development of all living creatures, plants and insects, the development of species, and eventually homo sapiens.

I belong to an Association of biologists and physicists who believe only in a materialistic cosmos; I also belong to the Institute for Creation Research whose members believe the earth was created in six twenty-four hour days. I find both difficult to believe, but the stages of Scriptural creation fit the ages of the earth.

Carroll understood such "stories" in Scripture as "myths" without historical foundation yet revealing philosophical "truth." He described the story of Jonah, for instance, by noting that Jonah was a "mythological figure," and comparing it with the movie <u>Jaws</u>. We agreed on psychological interpretations of the story: namely, a creative solution between desire and conscience; a wish to control God vs. being obedient to God's call; the need for mercy and forgiveness and for new relationships which make possible a creative solution of human conflicts and conditions.

While I cannot explain many of the weird (by modern scientific standards) stories in both Old and New Testaments, I can accept them as reports by people who were there (at least in some instances) and who described to the best of their understanding what they saw, such as the feeding of the 5,000, the healing of the epileptic boy, and so on. We now know much more about the ability of the immune system, when uncontaminated by AIDS, to heal otherwise terminal conditions, and the power of self-suggestion to affect human behavior. I see the Bible as a theological book with some amazing interpretations of natural law which fit current knowledge and as historically accurate since it makes its own claim of Inspiration.

So, when Carroll argued that anyone who disagreed with this mythological interpretation was "defensive," or had "completely misinterpreted" the history of the Bible accounts, I hold to my own belief and remember that Carroll's interpretation was contrary to a large number of faithful Christians.

Another difference in Carroll's classes and mine came in our choice of the psychological/psychiatric models we used. I see the Rogers, Maslows, and Tillichs as more difficult to use simply because they reflect a "naturalistic humanism." In their neglect of what the Church terms original sin (though I call it "primal sin" because it certainly is not original) or Freud would label "infantile narcissism," they create a fatal weakness and unrealistic optimism about human nature. I used two of my professors, B.F. Skinner and Fred Kellar, or Sigmund Freud, whose agnosticism could be confronted directly, even as pastors and Christian therapists could use their insights. I had my students read Maslow and Rogers with a critique of the subtle a-Christian assumptions underlying their systems.

At the American Psychological Association meetings in Honolulu in 1972, Russell Becker asked Carl Rogers in a large public meeting, "Are you religious yet?" Rogers answered with some anger, "Russ, you know I don't believe in your God." Even so, it would seem that Rogers' early childhood rearing in a conservative religious family and his first vocation of the ministry must have taught him Christian approaches to "unqualified concern and love," though his experiences in psychology at Teachers College Columbia left him with a moral and psychological therapy which always has seemed to me to be "almost" Christian without the actual historical-Christian tradition.

Carroll and I discussed his and my beliefs in the Christian concepts of Deity. At times he seemed to prefer a Tillichian description, for instance, "Infinite," "Ultimate Concern," or "Ground of Being." I had been influenced by Tillich during the years in the Columbia University Seminar on "Religion and Psychiatry" in which he participated. I questioned, within myself, when I sat behind him around the conference table, whether he believed in the Christian God. Leonard E. Wheat's paper on "Paul Tillich's Dialectical Humanism, Unmasking the God above God" reinforced my opinion that Tillich's Ultimate was closer to a god that moves in Hegelian-Marxian fashion from potential unity to actual self-estrangement toward actualized potentiality, which is a non-supernatural God--or humanity. With Carroll, our discussions usually closed with his using terms such as "God," "Christ," and "the Creator" as a symbol of the "Ultimate Being." Certainly Carroll did not fit the Tillich description of Ultimate Being, but I moved even further from The Courage to Be (1952a) to using a clear Biblical language.

Carroll and I both felt sad when students completed their doctorates, left the ministry, and surrendered their credentials of ordination. They were well trained and skillful psychotherapists and marriage/family counselors. We never withdrew our love and friendship when they did this, but we both were convinced that "pastoral" therapy was the highest kind of concern for persons and produced the most profound change in human character.

Lowell Colston and Seward Hiltner (1961) described in Lowell's doctoral dissertation, The Context of Pastoral Counseling, factors which gave the pastoral counselor advantages over the secular therapist. Such factors include: the Church and all it symbolizes, the Christian setting, the expectation of the counselee in the pastoral relationship, the continuing involvement in the congregation for support, the strength of Christian beliefs in moral and ethical guidance, and the promise of eternal life through faith in God.

The stimulus for the above conviction comes from a statement of Carroll's: "A part of the task of Pastoral Counseling and of Pastoral Psychotherapy. . . is that of bringing these potentials in human beings to full realization." (1983, p.297) I heard him make that comment many times.

The Psychological Study Of The Seminary Student

I could not conclude without a discussion of that Study on which Carroll and I collaborated. It began in the minds of Carroll and Dwight Loder. Their application brought support from the Lilly

Endowment, Inc., of Indianapolis, and we secured a second grant from the National Institute of Mental Health of Bethesda, Maryland. I, with Carroll's close involvement, designed the Study, carried out the data collection and computer programs, and wrote the two volume report. The report was planned as the data base for a second volume which interpreted the results and projected two aspects of the study: (1) what personality factors are in seminary students, and (2) the use of psychological testing and counseling with seminary students.

Carroll wrote in the Preface to the report:

> We wanted to know some of the psychological facts about our students as a group, and we wanted to know some undiscovered facts about the tests. . . Obviously this research was grounded in the assumption that the personality of the minister is of great significance for his [or her] work. . . There is a sense in which the Christian ministry is the most personal of all professions. . . the spiritual problems and crises of modern [people] take the effective minister into deep and significant aspects of personality existence. One of [the] resources for this task is [one's] own personality, and the quality of [the] relationship which [one] is able to establish with those to whom [one] ministers. To be a Christian minister in the deepest sense is to be a person whose presence, understanding and love speak of or point to the reality of the presence, understanding and love of God. By virtue of the fact that the [clergyperson] is in a position where [one] may do great good, [one] is also in a position where [one] may do great harm. (Unpublished report, pp.1,2)

Our primary purpose was to uncover the most effective ways of ministering to the troubled student. Seminary students, like all students, brought their personality conflicts to school and parish. If we could discover those emotional and intellectual problems, our students could go to their parishes and homes with healthier and more mature personalities and, thereby, be more effective ministers.

The ever-present problem of student drop-outs concerned Church leaders and faculty alike. If we could find practical ways to locate and help troubled students, the Church and the student would both benefit. We were concerned also about the relationship of intelligence to spirituality. How could the poor achiever in seminary become an outstanding pastor or counselor? Our concern was less with screening students in or out and more with aiding them to become more mature, competent, and spiritual pastors.

As Carroll saw it, "thus far theological faculties have tended to discuss these matters without much information, and some with not a little

58

irritation." (Ibid., p.1)

The Study focused on the psychological tests appropriate for the seminary population. The sample consisted of approximately 1500 students and 350 graduates. Carroll had administered the Minnesota Multiphasic Personality Inventory from his first year at Garrett. His years as Pastoral Counselor at the Hennepin Avenue United Methodist Church in Minneapolis had acquainted him with the development and use of the MMPI in the University of Minnesota studies. Thus, the MMPI became the most used test in our battery.

I added the group administered form of the Rorschach Ink Blot Test; a group administered Thematic Apperception Test; the Ohio State University Psychological Test, Form 21, rescored on our seminary population; the Bender Visual Motor Gestalt Test; the Murray Leiffer Counseling Aid Form; The Theological School Inventory, Form C; the Wechsler Adult Intelligence Scale; and the Gustafson Religious Beliefs Test, all from standard psychometrics and clinical tests.

In addition, I developed a Seminary Incomplete Sentences List (SISL), a Self-Evaluation Check List (SECL), and a Draw-A Person Test. The SISL had thirty stems from standard tests and fifteen stems with a religious motif. Lorge, Thorndike, and Symonds (some of my professors at Columbia) and Rotter and Rhode gave us permission to use their stems without violating their copyrights. (This Sentence Completion test has been used in several seminaries since.) Individually, each test had a rationale as we added it to the battery. Collectively, they offered important information about a specific personality area of our subject's self.

The Second Phase of the Study took us to the Registrar and Faculty for information about students' intellectual capacities. That included such things as: Grade Average at four periods in a student's academic history; Discipline Committee data on students who had appeared before it with violation of rules; Honors and Senior Comprehensive information; as well as sex, age, nationality, degree, field work records, in short, anything that provided information on the student's performance during their education. College grades were secured along with major and minor concentrations, and whether the student was on probation or accepted with qualification. While we looked at the written recommendations, we found little help from them.

We, and other faculty members, added anecdotal information. This data were carefully coded to protect confidentiality. Again, Morris Taggart, our Irish doctoral student, helped develop computer programs, supervised our Northwestern psychology students, and kept me sane.

Carroll and I were interested in finding ways to strengthen students academically and spiritually as well as to diagnose their needs. We wished to help students resolve those personality conflicts which, as

Carroll put it, "would render [them] ineffective in the ministry or in [their] personal life."

The Third Section of the Study was a follow-up with 499 graduates who were out of seminary at least two years but not more than eight. I developed a many-paged questionnaire, which included a standard MMPI Test and a set of questions covering the primary 13 scales. This section included an evaluation by each student of his or her seminary education; what they were accomplishing at the time of the follow-up; and those aspects of ministry which they felt most important for their parishioners and in their own self-evaluation. We asked for permission to contact their district superintendent (or other supervisor) for an evaluation of their effectiveness. There were a number of smaller side studies, one of which was a history and benefit of their previous counseling or psychotherapy during seminary, and another which evaluated student preaching appointments. These were examined to see their effect on their training, which proved to be very good, and on their families, which proved to be disastrous.

I brought to campus a number of national leaders in the fields of psychometrics and statistical design as consultants. Since those were the days before canned computer programs, I had to make programs for our statistics. I learned Fortran I and II for Northwestern's IBM equipment. I worked in the Technical Institute's computer room, first to debug the programs, but also because it was air conditioned and the Garrett offices were not. At First, Carroll thought I was playing hooky, but was quite apologetic when he discovered me slaving over the hot statistics and computer programs in the air-conditioned computer center.

I always found the Northwestern people cooperative. Since the original grant did not include funds for computer work, the Northwestern people were very generous in letting me use the machine at no cost time. Professors Sechrist and Campbell of the psychology department particularly, along with other professors, gave me a great deal of time in organizing the Study.

Carroll kept close watch on these activities, though they were my primary responsibility. When the report was nearing completion, our sharpest divergence surfaced. I interpreted the data to say that seminary students were significantly more stable, altruistic, socially skilled, dedicated to their profession, and of superior intelligence capabilities than the sample with which I compared them. The comparisions were with first year graduate students in medicine, education, the sciences, and with other seminaries. Carroll felt the data must be faulty, or I had misinterpreted it. He felt seminary students could not compare with students in science and medicine. In those days, certain church leaders claimed that these two professions were taking the top students, with the ministry having to take what was left.

I did not disagree with Carroll that our students had many personality problems and that counseling was needed by a significant number. However, I pointed to comparable studies at Harvard and Menningers in Topeka, Kansas,, where 10% of their students were seriously troubled. When I ran comparisons with these other professional first year graduate students, my findings showed that our students were emotionally healthier and more altruistic, among other factors, than these groups. Intellectually, their Wechsler Adult Intelligence Verbal Scales were only two I.Q. scores below that of the psychiatrists in training at Menninger. I also had samples of first year medical students at North Carolina and Minnesota, and the medical school headquarters in Evanston shared data on their general student profiles. It was from these comparisons that I drew my conclusions.

One of the tragedies of my own life occurred when the Study was not published. There is a copy of the two volume work, of 519 pages, in the Garrett Library, the NIMH has a copy, and I have a Xeroxed copy. So far as I know, this research Study contains more information about seminary students than any other in existence, at least about Methodist students in one seminary. It is still locked up in those volumes.

When I left Garrett in 1964, Carroll decided the Study data belonged to Garrett, and I was not to publish it. I have faithfully kept to that decision. Harold Duhling of the Lilly Foundation had indicated that Lilly would subsidize the printing, probably from a University Press. They did so with William Douglas's Study of Ministers' Wives, as well as the Dwight W. Culver and Keith R. Bridston study of Pre-Seminary Education and the Making of Ministers. Nevertheless, our Garrett Study remains unpublished. I hope someday someone will conduct another study on the Seminary Student, using this research and its test data as a base.

One of the most valuable portions of the Study, however, was to me, the time we spent with the students going over their test results. There was time for interpretation, questions, and discussion as to the tests' meanings. In the nearly 25 years since the study was concluded, I have had many students come to me with appreciation for the information Carroll and I shared, which they used to better order their lives. The intelligence tests helped students plan for better educational goals and better study habits. The personality tests pointed to more effective ways of maturing intellectually and emotionally. The psychiatric diagnostics often uncovered emotional and mental symptoms, which resulted in the students entering counseling or psychotherapy. The religious beliefs test informed them as to their theological structure and areas of major pastoral interest. Each test had a purpose. Many students express gratitude that the seminary thought enough of them to be thoughtful about their personal lives. We both were grateful for the patience and willingness of our students to participate.

I could say the same of the administration and faculty at Garrett. They were friendly, cooperative, and supportive, even when many could not understand why I insisted on such careful procedures which took so much time. Ink blots and Thematic Apperception Themes, to say nothing of the 550 questions on the MMPI, seemed to many faculty "nonsense" when the students could have been studying Bible, Theology, and Christian Education. In the end, however, the faculty was quite cooperative, especially after the Faculty Retreat at which Carroll and I explained the rationale of each test in detail and described what it told us and the student. Some faculty even took the tests themselves.

Two Personal Recollections

Recently, I noted that my original membership plaque in the American Association of Pastoral Counselors was signed by "Carroll A. Wise." In one of the first letters I wrote him, before coming to Garrett, I spelled his name "Carol." On our first visit, when I think he was making up his mind as to his recommendation that I come to Garrett, he tactfully and gently let me know that he spelled it with two "r"s and two "l"s. "Carol" was a girl's name. He never referred to this again.

Epilogue:

As I look back now, from the vantage point of nearly twenty-five years, I will always regard my six years at Garrett with Carroll as great years--exciting, wearing, growing, learning, maturing, rewarding. With their high and low moments, they were very worth while overall.

Those years, with their close contacts with students, were precious for me. Friendships with faculty and seminarians have continued through the years, and Ruth and I treasure those personal relationships. Going from Garrett to the Iliff School of Theology at the University of Denver, then to Anderson School of Theology in Anderson, Indiana, and, after becoming professor emeritus, three years at Asbury Theological Seminary in Wilmore, Kentucky, were tremendously fulfilling periods. Through those years the private practice of counseling and psychotherapy kept my teaching immediate and appropriate, germaine to the needs of hurting persons. The coming from an hour with a person suffering with an Anxiety Neurosis, to the classroom to talk about The Christian Answers of Faith to suffering persons, kept my teaching seasonable. Again, Carroll and I agreed on this timeliness of clinic and classroom.

I often wished during those Garrett years that Carroll and I had been able to spend a summer month apart, working out our distinctive approaches to the teaching of pastoral care and counseling. Though this is seldom granted to pastors or professors, I always felt that he and I would have gained more mutual brotherly regard for each other, benefitting both ourselves and our students. Many of our assumed differences would have been unmasked as differing approaches to common conclusions. After Carroll retired and served as Director of Pastoral Counseling at Lutheran General Hosptial, he accepted the invitation to be a resource leader at my National Institute of Mental Health Workshop for Clergy at the Anderson School of Theology. We had a good day together, and his visit overnight in our home reconstituted some of our earlier warmth.

I hope our students felt these positive aspects of the relationship between Carroll and me, and have applied the insights we tried to teach to their own personal lives and those of their parishioners. We took, quite literally, Christ's concern for suffering persons and, especially, Jesus' admonition to his disciples to "feed my sheep" in serving the Kingdom of God. We wanted people to minister in the most effective and efficient way possible.

I will always be proud to say, "I taught with Carroll Wise."

THE LEGACY OF CARROLL WISE

John E. Hinkle, Jr.

The Clinical Years

Carroll Alonzo Wise had his eyes set on parish ministry throughout all his years of training.[1] (Moss, 1976b) In light of that fact his presence, influence, and impact at Garrett Theological Seminary in Evanston, Illinois, are somewhat remarkable. In early days of ministry, Wise indicates that he had no thought of seminary teaching as a career. His pursuit of doctoral studies at an early period in his career was carried out at the instigation of the superintendent of the hospital where he was appointed in 1931. Carroll pursued those studies as a means for increasing the effectiveness of the hospital ministries in which he was engaged at the time. (Ibid., p.24)

Not that Carroll was anti-intellectual as some would later argue. Rather, he perceived his future in terms of the work of hospital and parish ministry. True, Carroll vigorously opposed the use of intellect as a means to dominate and control human emotional and religious life. He states,

> . . . while I could appreciate the intellectual formulations, I wanted more. Intellectual formulations point to something deeper, only we must follow where they point and not short-circuit the process. It is futile to intellectualize about "love" or "faith" and not deal with the barriers to love and faith within the emotional experience . . . The key to it is in the integration of the theoretical and the experiential. This integration means one has the ability to deal with another human being using rational understanding as well as an emotional awareness to help other people help themselves. (Ibid., p.25)

And it was with this "service orientation," i.e., pastoral work, in mind that Carroll resumed his studies in 1931, and completed his doctorate in 1935 at Boston University. While he had no intent to engage in a career of seminary teaching, yet, during that same period, and for a total of 10 years, in addition to his pastoral duties as a hospital chaplain, he taught the course left open when Anton Boisen left New England in 1931, as well as other courses at the B.U. School of Social Work. And, as he himself noted, "I've never been able to keep out of teaching." (Ibid., p.24) While Carroll was never in love with ideas for their own sake, he nevertheless valued, developed, and taught sound theory as a means of deepening and clarifying significant understandings of the human experience and interpersonal relationships.

In 1942, following his ten years of ministry at the Worcester State Hospital, Carroll began work as Director of the Department of Religion and Health of the Toledo Council of Churches, in Toledo, Ohio. (Shackelford, 1986, p.16) A major aspect of this ministry was delivering pastoral counseling services though the Y.M./W. C. A. As matters turned out, this position provided a good transition for him from a mental patient hospital population to a somewhat more "normal" group of constituents with whom to work and counsel. Yet his desire for both parish work and teaching (which was by now "in his blood") spurred another move shortly thereafter to a post in the parish. Years later, in commenting on the move to that Hennepin Avenue Methodist Church in Minneapolis in 1944 as Minister of Counseling, Carroll said, "I wanted to pursue my original intention to do parish work, and. . ." with a twinkle in his eye he continued, "I knew that you couldn't get to a significant seminary teaching post from the Toledo Council of Churches."[2]

Carroll's move to the parish, as a minister of counseling in 1944, provided him with an opportunity to fulfill his original vocational intent, participation in parish ministry. Additionally, it yielded a context which required that he "translate" to pastoral work and the parish setting what he had learned in the hospital and clinic over those thirteen years. He puts it thus, "I went to Minneapolis in '42 and this was my problem: how should I take my years of hospital training, experience, and insights, and use them in the parish as a clergyman? as a pastor?" (Moss, 1976b, p.21)

Retrospectively, it can be seen that this context provided important preparation for later teaching of seminarians and pastoral therapists. He says,

> It became very obvious [to me] that adequate training in pastoral therapy could not be done within an institution for the mentally ill, or for the physically ill, or for any other acute infirmities. It has to be done with people who live in the parish. Pastoral psychotherapy today is dealing with an entirely different set of problems than the chaplain deals with in the hospital. (Ibid., p.22)

One difference that Carroll saw was the rather significant difference between appropriate approaches to "crisis" problems, as are most frequently seen in the hospital setting, and the long term, often entrenched, problems of living that occur in the lives of individuals and families in parish settings. These long term problems require a different approach than the crisis problems in the hospital. He concluded, "Every pastor needs training in crisis counseling or therapy," such as is appropriate to the hospital setting. On the other hand, "we have felt that this is not enough" for parish based pastoral care/counseling. (Ibid., p.23) His first book on pastoral counseling, published in 1951, sets forth what he means by "a different approach." These views about the preparation of ministers, and many more, Carroll brought with him in his appointment to the Garrett Faculty in 1948.

The Teaching Years

Frederick Norwood, a Garrett historian, writes, "Certainly the development of pastoral psychology under the pioneering direction of Carroll Wise marked an epoch in theological education." (Norwood, 1978, p. 147) Wise emphasized attention to ". . .the psychological strength and understanding of the individual minister [or seminarian], in relation to all the stages of development of persons from infancy to old age." He added: "An important facet of the program, both for ministerial [read parish] and advanced [read specialist] training, was clinical training, on-site experience in the pastoral and psychological arts and skills . . . There was no seminary in the country with an approach and concern like that of Wise." (Ibid., p.148)

While the foregoing retrospective statements by Norwood have the advantage of hind sight, along with a certain glow of idealization, opinions at the time were decided mixed, as psychiatrist Carl Christensen notes.

> With the passage of time, however, a dichotomy developed among the students and faculty. About half of each thought that dynamic psychology and psychotherapy were a most important part of a seminary education . . . The other half of Garrett decried such thinking as utter nonsense. The Christian religion was sufficient unto all and complete in itself, they protested . . . I believe that the basic tenets of Christianity and the elementary principles of dynamic psychology are in agreement. Differences exist as to the ways and means of realization, but even these differences are not irreconcilable. (Christensen, 1972, p.90)

Norwood's remarks, as edited by Christensen's observations, set the stage for what follows in this chapter on Wise's impact at Garrett.

The Seminary-University-Psychotherapy Context

Garrett (now Garrett-Evangelical) Theological Seminary was/is a graduate professional school of theology with strong denominational and university connections. Hence, one of Garrett's strengths is the necessity of maintaining a healthy tension and balance between the academy (read academic) model and the professional school model. Vigorous participation in denominational and ecumenical networks and structures is set side by side with an equally vigorous participation in university and academic professional societies. In addition to rootedness in the (now United) Methodist denomination and tradition, as well as ecumenical structures and ideologies, Garrett also participates as equal partner in a joint advanced degree program with the Graduate School of Northwestern University.

This particular ethos provided an ideal context for the refinement,

67

further development, and dissemination of Carroll's learnings and insights about parish pastoral care/counseling on the one hand, and his notions about the development of pastoral counseling specialists on the other (as he himself had developed in a clinical, theological school environment which was set in the midst of and related to a major university, See paragraph one). However, something was missing in the Garrett context, and Carroll set about immediately to find a way to see that it was provided. That missing ingredient was the clinical/psychodynamic dimension.

Let me be clear. Carroll was himself one of the better clinically trained pastoral counselors himself. Still what was needed at Garrett was an "institutional" way of both representing and presenting psychodynamic theory and practice and the implications of that approach for both theological anthropology (the nature of humanness) and pastoral practice. Fortuitously, or providentially, while Carroll was looking for a way to get the psychodynamic/clinical aspect of the curriculum developed, another recent arrival in Evanston (July, 1949), Carl W. Christensen, M. D., a psychodynamically trained psychiatrist, was searching for sources which might refer patients. Carroll and Carl met. And, according to Carl,

> From this initial meeting developed a relationships which has persisted through these many years. In the twenty years (as of '72) of our association, I cannot recall any major disagreements. It has been a continuing privilege to join with Carroll in the development of the pastoral counseling program at Garrett. Patiently, with quiet wisdom, he furthered my education in the area of our mutual concern. Any contributions I have made to the advancement of the education of pastoral counselors and to the understanding of the mental health of ministers derives in large measure from Carroll's enthusiastic counsel. (Ibid., p.88)

From this relationship between Carroll and Carl flowed the development of the "clinical dimension" for which the GTS program of Pastoral Psychology and Counseling became known so widely. In 1952, Carl was first appointed as a visiting lecturer to teach a course in the development of personality. In 1963, he was appointed as Adjunct Professor in the Department of Pastoral Psychology and Counseling. And in 1966, at the Ph. D. level, a "full scale, if fledgling" practicum site was developed in connection with the Department of Guidance and Counseling at Kendall College, a department chaired by James McHolland, Ph. D., an alum of the program. (Christensen, McHolland, and Wise, 1968) (See Ashbrook's critique in this volume.) Additional Clinical Adjunct Professors joined the ranks in the persons of Alfred Flarsheim and Bernard Greene. These, and other like-minded psychiatrists and psychologists, began teaching seminars, providing consultation, and supervising Ph. D. students. In this manner the clinical dimensions of the curriculum were "fleshed out" by Carroll and colleagues.

While this "clinical aspect" of the program worked well more often than not, there were problems. Chief among these was the fact that academic programs built on a cadre of Clinical Adjunct Faculty who are in large measure doing "volunteer work" does not long survive unless a greater degree of "institutionalization" occurs. In this instance, substantive institutionalization did not occur, and the clinically based dimensions of the curriculum did not last much beyond Carroll's tenure. However, the newly created clinical dimension [circa 1968-1978],[3] in this jury-rigged structure, was, nevertheless, present and powerful for a period of some ten years, a testimony to its significance for the students who were benefiting from these efforts.

Thus, Carroll had his context, both received and constructed,consisting of the pastoral/theological, the psychological/empirical, and the psychiatric/clinical.

Impact On Students At The Basic
Professional Degree Level

As one Garrett student on whom Carroll's work had considerable impact, this author would have to say that his own experience of the curriculum as a student during the middle to late '50s on subsequent ministerial practice was quite strong. It may be taken as somewhat representative of many B.D. (now M.Div.) student experiences in the '50s and '60s, and I will use it to serve as an example, but first I cite more empirical data.

Evidence to support the notion that the Garrett curriculum in Pastoral Care/Counseling was helpful to large numbers of students comes from a survey conducted by the Bureau of Religious and Social Research, and carried out by Sam Wong. He surveyed alums who were serving parishes from the '50s and '60s student group. Findings showed that they ranked seminary studies in the fields of Pastoral Care/Counseling and Bible alternatively as the most important and second most important areas of curriculum in terms of perceived benefit to their own pastoral practice. (Wong, 1971; See Houts' chapter in this volume for further commentary on this point.) The survey clearly indicated that Carroll's impact came in part because he mobilized resources into a program that was broader than himself and his own interests.

While I was not one who was particularly helped by Garrett's approach to the study of the Bible in those days (circa 1955-60), due in part to a strong background in Biblical Studies from college, my own ministerial experience in both pastoral and missionary work (in Indiana as a student pastor, '54-'58, in the Philippine Islands, '60-'64) provided strong confirmation for the usefulness of the insights and perspectives of the care/counseling field and related courses. These contributed the most to my effectiveness in the practice of ministry. I think particularly of Carroll having sent me over to Northwestern University

69

(during M.A. studies) to take courses in Culture and Personality in the Anthropology Department. (See Chapter entitled, "The Living Human Experience Across Cultures," in this volume.) The impact of the GTS/NU curriculum at the B.D./M.A. levels was as much a program impact as a personal or C.A. Wise impact. From my point of view it was Carroll and context.

True, Carroll was the first to write on a paper of mine, as he did on many I'm told, "Consider seeing a good counselor." This well intended advice was well received, I might add. It was also true that I found studies in the pastoral care/counseling area the most interesting, enlightening, and helpful--both actually as well as potentially useful for the pastoral ministry in which I was already engaged as a student pastor while at Garrett. While Carroll's contribution to these studies was major, there were other contributors as well.

Jesse Zeigler's course on pastoral counseling opened my eyes to the meaning and power of the experience of empathic listening on self and others. Ruth Wicke's (1953-57) presence as a counselor, and her going to sleep during a session in which she was supposed to be counseling me late one Spring afternoon, provided gentle but persuasive evidence of my own need for personality change. John Vayhingher's (1958-64) complex course on research design opened up vistas of scientific method. Lee B. Sechrest's (NU-Psychology) course on psychopathology enabled me to draw distinctions between "pathological" and "normal" behavior. And Francis L. K. Hsu (NU-Anthropology) moved us beyond simply Western notions of personality theory as a basis for understanding humanness.

I mention these mentors as persons who enriched the context in which Carroll worked, and to which his student's could choose to be exposed. His impact was in part that of a sensitive, insightful, and informed individual who both discovered and created a context in which students could pursue their own interests, putting together resources appropriate to their own interests and needs. Clearly, Carroll's presence and influence at GTS/NU was creating channels and program structures for students in the developing area of pastoral care/counseling.

(See the Chapter by Vayhingher for a further treatment of the development of the Pastoral Psychology Department during the years 1958 to 1964 from the perspective of his own functioning as a professor.)

Impact On Students At The Ph.D. Level

One test of the quality of a professional degree program is its relevance for the practice of that profession. Along with most of my colleagues in the '50s and '60s, I would affirm that Carroll's curricular program in context was most relevant to the practice of ministry. And I wanted more!

By the time I returned for Ph. D. studies in 1964,[4] the doctoral program in pastoral counseling/psychotherapy was firmly established,[5] both in terms of the Department and the Faculty at and through the Joint University Degree Committee which provided the administrative link with the Graduate School of Northwestern University.

Under Carroll's leadership this specialized degree program became one of the finest and largest Ph.D. programs in the country.   Morris Taggert had just joined the Faculty.   Professors from the Department of Psychology at Northwestern, following the leadership of Donald T. Campbell, later President of the American Psychological Association, who described himself as a "cautious yet missionary-minded social/behavioral science methodologist," were participating in the program with enthusiasm.   Campbell wanted to train researchers in the "quasi-experimental" approach to field research.   He found in the pastoral psychology students an eager and dedicated group of researchers.   From his "vision" and leadership, as well as that provided by many of his colleagues in the University, Garrett Ph. D.'s were enabled to produce some of the best "field research" in North America. It would be difficult to overstate the contribution of the Psychology Department Faculty to students in the Pastoral Psychology Department's Ph. D. offering.   (See the chapter by Haight in this volume for more detail on research in the program.   A listing of students, dissertation titles, and years is included at the end of Augspurger's chapter in this volume.)

As an example of the range of student use of NU Faculty, my own course work included: Campbell and Sechrest in the Psychology Department, and Hsu, Ethel Albert, Raoull Narroll, Laura Bohannon, and Robert Coleman in the Anthropology Department.   Other students chose other courses and professors, depending on their theoretical and research interests.   In such an academically rich environment, the student's task was to focus his or her interests in a manner that would allow for meaningful selection of courses as a way to build an integrated individualized curriculum incorporating the values and concerns of the Pastoral Psychology and Counseling specialization.

The richness and variety of these offerings at NU made possible the fulfillment of one of Carroll's basic values, namely, the provision of a context in which students could exercise and develop their own autonomy and identity.   At the same time, the common content of offerings at GETS through the Department provided an experience of professional socialization as well as "core" information.   Courses by Taggert and Wise were supplemented by studies in the theological, historical, philosophical, Biblical, and ethical areas offered in the basic degree curriculum.   Carroll's task was, in part, to assist students in the identification of their weaknesses and to help them structure a program of study which would fit their own special interests.   His impact on students in the role of advisor was often as important as that of

71

teacher.

Through the years Carroll authored five books: Religion in Illness and Health (1942); Pastoral Counseling: Its Theory and Practice (1951); Psychiatry and the Bible (1956); The Meaning of Pastoral Care (1966); and Pastoral Psychotherapy (1983), as well as numerous articles. These writings added immeasurably to his influence here and elsewhere.

During his later years at Garrett, along with Carl Christensen and Larry Holtz, Carroll developed a practicum site for training pastoral counselors in cooperation with Lutheran General Hospital in Park Ridge, Illinois. This service and training site, named the Community Pastoral Counseling and Consultation Center, called its first full-time director, Dr. Bruce Hartung, in 1971. Carroll continued his ministry of teaching, supervising, and counseling at the Center following his retirement in 1972.

E. Brooks Holifield (1983, p. 275), in his book, A History of Pastoral Care in America, describes Wise as one of the four intellectual leaders in the postwar pastoral theology renaissance. His leadership within the Faculty at Garrett was no less noteworthy. As an administrator, he developed a Department with a distinctive emphasis in its blending of the pastoral, the psychological, the clinical, and the empirical research dimensions of curriculum, both for practice in ministry and for specialized counseling. As a teacher, he modeled the pedagogical practice of learning and teaching from cases. As a clergyperson, he modeled the sensitivity of presence and a depth of capacity for communication which were at the core of his pastoral identity. As a theoretician, he developed a pastoral theology appropriate to his times, yet one with timeless roots. (See Hessert's chapter in this volume.) As a professional, he maintained the highest standards, and worked diligently to assist in the establishment of a professional association. (See Bruehl's chapter in this volume.)

And through it all, Carroll remained controversial. He was prophet and pioneer as well as colleague, mentor, and pastor. His "absolutely authentic" way of relating was threatening to some, and reassuring to others. He was tough minded as well as tender hearted. He was realistic as well as empathic. He was in touch with both the depths and the heights of human experience. He sought to understand the working of the Spirit of God within the human experience and to communicate with others at that level of being and within that context of meaning. His incarnational-interpersonal-insightful-imaginal/associational manner of being as a pastoral person was spiced with an earthy humanity and an administrative style that was alternatively creative and "crusty." Norwood is probably right. There was/is no seminary in the country with an approach and concern quite like that of Wise. (1978, p. 148) Given this legacy, what would remain?

The Emerging Future

The Department which Carroll had built, and from which Carroll retired in 1972, found itself struggling to maintain the robust programs developed under his leadership. This struggle arose because of factors beyond those of his leadership and departure. For one thing, the massive cultural changes of the late 60s and early 70s were challenging curricular structures and assumptions. The pastoral psychology curriculum was not excluded from these challenges, nor should it have been. In addition, changes in the composition of the student body meant that adjustments were needed in response to this new ethos, an ethos in the seminary that reflected major changes in the mindscape of the broader sociocultural matrix of which the seminary is a part.

However, Carroll's departure did expose the extent to which many components of the program depended on his own associations. While the Department was institutionalized within the Seminary/University setting, the clinical component depended, for the most part, on Adjunct positions and volunteer service. Further, like the University and other academic institutions across the country, inflation was forcing reevaluation and retrenchment in seminary programs. The Pastoral Psychology and Counseling program felt the effects of these financial concerns. Though many other factors could be included, the following examples will serve to indicate that "a storm was brewing" on the horizon that would not abate for some years.

The Legacy--First Steps

To my mind, a figure that was in some ways as "heroic" as the figure of Carroll Wise in the Department was that of his colleague and associate R. Ronald Lee, an alum of the GTS/NU Ph. D. program and the Menninger Institute (Topeka, Kansas), from Australia. Ron came to the Department in 1970 to fill the position which had been vacated by Morris Taggert (1964-70), and became Chair upon the retirement of Wise in 1972. Lee was a brilliant theoretician, an effective teacher, an insightful author, an astute clinician, and an able researcher, as well as being a thorough and foresighted administrator.

Like Carroll before him, Ron began carrying a heavy load of teaching, supervising, and administration. In addition, he began the task of negotiating, revising, and generating new structures in response to the massive sociocultural changes which were impacting the Department and the Program. Norwood refers to this period as Garrett's "Time of Troubles." (1978, p. 223; see Chapter 8 for a full description.) Due in part to these sociocultural changes, the Departmental and Program Legacy, along with Garrett's posture in theological education more generally, was in need of revision. And due to the inflationary pressures on academic budgets, already limited financial resources were even more limited than usual, so there was in fact very little "room to manuever."

Ron took all this in stride. His commitment to the values represented in and expressed through the Department, and his loyalty to Carroll and the Program, knew only the limitations of his own time and energy. Nevertheless, he seemed to have more energy than most. It would be difficult to imagine a more devoted and effective effort than Ron's during his time on the Faculty (1970-1979). In a personal communication to the author, following the Memorial Service for Carroll, November, 1985, he wrote, "As you know, Carroll made a significant contribution to my life, a contribution for which I shall always be grateful. It was mainly based on gratitude that I gave nine years of my professional life to teaching at Garrett. . . "[6]

I joined the Faculty in the Fall of 1972 to participate in The Legacy. At this time a rather large number of Ph. D. students were pursuing studies in Pastoral Psychology and Counseling in the Joint Program. Additionally, the instructional needs of students who were "majoring" in Pastoral Care and Counseling in the M. Div. Curriculum were equally strong. My own interests both in assessment and personnel selection of ministerial candidates and in the application of insights from "culture and personality studies" were thrown into the mix.

Institutional issues from Garrett's "Time of Troubles" continued. President Merlin Northfelt was working hard with students, faculty, and trustees to resolve those issues. The M.Div. curriculum was undergoing revision. A merger with our sister seminary, Evangelical Theological Seminary in Naperville, Illinois, was undertaken. The Northwestern Graduate School began a review of its offerings at the doctoral level, "taking an intellectual inventory" as Dean Clarence Ver Steeg, put it.

In the midst of these major changes, the Pastoral Psychology Field was attempting to be faithful to its mission and to the larger institutional mission of both Seminary and Graduate School. The institutional changes during the decade of the 70s are difficult, perhaps impossible, to portray. Blacks and women were admitted to the program in growing numbers. Katherine Wilcox joined the Departmental Faculty (1976-78) at the end of her career as a Clinical Psychologist. Clinton McNair, a Black pastoral psychologist, taught from 1978 until 1981.

Interlude

The situation in the Department began to change significantly with Lee's resignation in 1979. In my opinion, though he has never said so, his resignation was a final and visible protest against the politicizing of academic standards and personnel procedures of both the faculty and the department by others in the interest of instituting social change on issues other than on academic and educational grounds. Clearly, The Legacy was at risk, not only in terms of program but in terms of the structure of the department as well. Ron could not, and would not, bear the burden for its demise. He had worked for too many years, at an incredible pace, to sustain it. He could not bear seeing it destroyed. So, as this author sees it, he resigned in protest.[7]

The Legacy--Next Steps

I became Chair and purveyor of The Legacy, but with considerable reluctance. The Department was in acute distress. The Legacy was in jeopardy due to personnel changes, institutional adjustments from the merger with Evangelical Seminary, and curricular revisions which were being mandated by the University through the Office of the Dean of the Graduate School.

With me in the Department in 1979 were Emily Demme Haight, Clinton McNair, and Emma Justes. McNair was in his second year, Haight in her first, and Justes was just coming on board. Flarsheim and Christensen continued to do some Adjunct Clinical Teaching, but were retiring from the Program due to the pressure of other involvements.

Thus, in addition to postponing other career directions which were in my mind, accepting leadership of the Department at such a time seemed foolhardy. The dilemma was that there was no one else to continue The Legacy. Was this a message from God...or what? Still, I did have a few ideas about how to proceed, so on the basis of a set of conditions (sine qua nons, as it were), I accepted the responsibility of the Chair, and with it, The Legacy.

New Directions--The Clinical Dimension And The D.MIN.

By this time my own thinking was moving strongly in the direction of transferring the clinical aspects of The Legacy into a training structure that would be more or less permanent, and into the hands of professional clinicians in combination with professional academicians. Since AAPC (American Association of Pastoral Counselors) standards were based on a combination of theory (operationalized in terms of academic degrees) and practice (hours of therapy, supervision, case work, etc. in the clinic), it seemed that these two dimensions properly could be "married" through a program which would link the classroom and clinic in a "joint program structure" analogous to the program structure between GETS and the NU Graduate School.

Further, under the able and persistent leadership of Professor Douglas Wingeier, GETS had developed a contextually based Doctor of Ministry Degree program which would provide an "ideal" degree structure for the linkage of clinic and classroom. Finally, Adjunct Faculty at the clinical sites (pastoral counseling centers) were available from among our own and other Ph. D. graduates. The issue of quality control of research and teaching at the clinical sites would not be problematic. It seemed to me that if there were interest in such education/training on the part of individuals who had already done their "novice preparation" as pastoral counselors, such an approach would make sense.

Testing The New Vision

These ideas were tested in a paper presented at the Centers and Training Conference of AAPC in Savannah, Ga., in 1981, and later published in the Journal of Supervision and Training. (Hinkle, 1981) Subsequently, a member of the AAPC Centers and Training Committee was invited to GETS for an initial consultation concerning the development of such a degree program. Conversations were held in a similar site visit with Marvin Taylor of the Association for Theological Schools.[8] As a part of this process, a formal proposal was prepared by the D. Min. Committee, presented to the Faculty, by the then Acting Dean, Tyler Thompson, and approved by a unanimous vote. Next, the newly appointed Dean, Carl Marbury, met with an invited group of some 20 members of AAPC for further consultation. As a result, the program was launched. The concept, as originally set forth, was implemented.

Institutionalizing The Legacy In A New Form

GETS, in partnership with co-operating AAPC accredited pastoral counseling training centers, was offering a Doctor of Ministry Degree Program with specialization in Pastoral Counseling/Psychotherapy. It was easily the most demanding such program available. Member Level Equivalency in AAPC was regarded as the standard for ENTRY, with Fellow Level Equivalency as the standard for completing the center/clinical side of the training. It was also intended, that persons having completed both the clinical and the academic training could apply for Diplomate, at such time their clinical and supervisory skills warranted such an application. By voting for this program, the GETS Faculty and Administration committed themselves to the preparation of a continuing flow of leadership into the Pastoral Counseling Movement.

Experience with the program, however, has shown that the levels of competence described have, thus far, been more of a vision than a reality.

Certification And Accreditation (ATS and AAPC)

While this new program was first envisioned by Hinkle, in consultation with Wingeier, rather than by Wise, and while it was carried forward by many others, the Program did, in fact, represent a new vessel for the old/new wine of The Legacy. The clinical/professional dimensions of The Legacy had new and more permanent programmatic life. Journeyperson pastoral counselors could be prepared clinically in a more appropriate and "in depth" manner, and in greater numbers, to a higher level of quality as counselors, in the pastoral clinical setting, while the on-campus classroom could provide the continuing emphasis on empirical research and theory development, as well as the necessary interface between the historical, Biblical, and theological dimensions, and all this with the academic rigor appropriate to doctoral level degrees. The format insured clinical as well as academic competence. The AAPC

Centers and Training Accreditation Review Committee, following a site visit, recommended approval of the program to the National Committee, and it was done.

The Legacy of the (Wise) professional model Ph. D. was re-incarnate in the new GETS/Counseling/Training Center Joint Program Structure of the D. Min. in Pastoral Counseling/ Psychotherapy. A half-time Faculty position was devoted to the development and co-ordination of the new program. Haight was designated Track Co-ordinator. Under her able administration the program developed with vigor and validity.

Demise Of The "Old (Departmental Form Of The) Ph.D. (GETS/NU)

The demise of that aspect of The Legacy, soon to be known as "the old" Ph.D. Program, came over the next three years. Under pressure from the NU Graduate School, the Faculty moved from offering seven departmental Ph.D.s, to a single Ph.D. in Religious and Theological Studies with four foci, under a newly formed Graduate Council of GETS Faculty. The Adjunct Faculty for the "old Ph.D. Program," Carl Christensen and Alfred Flarsheim, retired. What remained was completion of the work on some 12 to 15 dissertations by students from that era. As of this writing those have been completed; the days of "the old Ph.D." are gone.

A New Ph.D. Or No Ph.D.?

And what of the possibilities provided at the Ph. D. level in the new Graduate Council structure?

A comment by Professor Peggy Way, Vanderbilt School of Theology, Nashville, in an address to the National Convention of Clinical Pastoral Educators in Minneapolis, MN, concerning the contexting and interfacing of pastoral counseling with the other theological and social science disciplines has stayed with me. It was, in my mind, a "naming" of a major weakness in the old approach to the Ph.D. The Departmental Ph.D. was just that, in my view: a program that was largely encapsulated in the Department, at least in terms of adequate interface with the other disciplines of a theological curriculum. Speaking to this issue, Way had pointed out the need for ongoing contexts of dialogue between the pastoral and the academic disciplines. This notion of contexts for ongoing dialogue was, in my view, a key to the future. As it happened, the new Ph.D. structure could provide just such contexts.

A second notion that was equally important, from my point of view, in connection with the question of "A new Ph.D. or no Ph.D.?" was that AAPC and the Pastoral Counseling Movement were in desperate need of theory development which could meet the canons of both the academic (theological school and graduate school) and the social science communities. The "old (Departmental) Ph.D.," which was based on the scholar/practitioner model, seemed to come up short on both the scholar and the practitioner sides. True, pastoral counseling was focused on an epistemology which begins with observation of the "living human document" as its primary data source, and that is a proper beginning. Yet work is sorely needed at the level of the nomothetic, as well as the idiographic, approach to "living human documents." Hence the scholar/practitioner model has something of a weakness in that it does not allow for full specialization on each side. If the GETS D.Min. fleshes out the practitioner side of the equation, I reasoned, then a new form of Ph.D. could flesh out the scholar side of the dyad, especially in the interface with the theological and social science disciplines in terms of theory, research, writing, and teaching.

With these insights, as Chair of the Department, I began to work on the development of a new, broader, and more appropriately interfaced Ph.D. It seemed to me an excellent opportunity, perhaps one that would not recur in many years, to structure in a program of study at the Ph.D. level that would allow for, and perhaps help provide, continuing and significant theory building which could benefit both the specialization of pastoral counseling (AAPC) and the general ministries of the church as the pastor seeks to provide care and counseling to persons in need. In this way, The Legacy could be carried on through new structures and a new, phase appropriate, mission of the Department.

The New Ph.D.

Clearly, it was a new day and a new vision. Program restructuring, curriculum revision, and personnel selection have been woven together into a new fabric from 1980 to 1986. In 1981, the new Pastoral Counseling/Psychotherapy Track had been inaugurated in the Doctor of Ministry Program. By 1983, the new shape of the Ph. D. Program was emerging. The Department was part of the Focus titled Religion in Society and Personality. In 1986, a practicum structure for meeting clinical program pre-requisites for the Ph. D. was approved by the Faculty. At the M. Div. Level, Introduction to Pastoral Care is one of the required courses in the Basic Degree Curriculum.

New Personnel For A New Degree

By 1981, the Department was in need of a senior scholar to work with and further develop the new Ph. D. Program. James Barbour Ashbrook, formerly Professor of Psychology and Theology at Colgate Rochester/Bexley Hall/Crozer, joined the Department. He brought a legacy of his own, as well as an awareness of and appreciation for The Legacy for which the Department had become known. His long involvement with a theological faculty and the theological/pastoral disciplines, his "track record" of research, writing, teaching, supervision, and clinical/consulting work, and his recently focused work on theological promise in brain research made him the "ideal" candidate for the new context.

The New Shape Of The Department

It was a "heady" mix, combining the Pastoral Theology focus provided by Justes, the Pastoral and Empirical emphases of Haight, and the Culture and Personality approach of Hinkle, all in the context of The Legacy. Ashbrook's distinctive emphasis on the neurotheological aspects of human functioning constituted an entirely new dimension, but one which had multiple connections with The Legacy. Additionally, he contributes to the academic interface through his membership on the Graduate Council, having established himself as a valued colleague on the Faculty.

More recently, Edward P. Wimberly and Lallene J. Rector have come to the Faculty and the Department. Wimberly has brought a special interest in the dimension of spiritual values and inner healing through story and re-storying, which is anchored in "the tradition and the Black Church." Rector's orientation to the phenomenological as a source of knowledge, and her commitment to the traditions and forms of empirical research, provide for an extension of The Legacy in terms of Carroll's original and continuing interest in a phenomenologically based epistemology when combined with empirical research.

The Beginnings And Current Outcomes Of The Legacy

The Lieffer's note that "[in] 1948 a significant new teaching field was introduced in the curriculum (of Garrett) with the coming of Carroll Wise as Professor of Pastoral Psychology and Counseling." (Leiffer, 1987, p. 110) This new teaching field was "...a significant addition to the curriculum . . ." (Ibid.) By 1987, this "teaching field" was composed of five full and part-time Faculty on campus, and 12 Adjunct Faculty in Pastoral Counseling Centers stretching from Alaska to Texas, from the District of Columbia to Iowa and Arizona. The Legacy of C. A. Wise is alive and well. As Ashbrook notes in the Preface of this volume, the continuities between the work of the present and the emphases of the past are clear. But what of the future?

What Now?

Carroll Wise was a man who wanted no imitators. Just as he "carved out a path" based on the realities of human experience and Christian ministry to that "humanness" as he saw it, his pioneering spirit and eager curiosity were such that his legacy calls for continuing development in terms of the realities of human experience and Christian ministry as they are revealed to those who follow. Faithfulness to The Legacy means a continuing re-working of the fundamental insights which are to be gleaned from an authentic humanness, a caring Christian ministry which benefits from those insights, an authentic openness to the phenomenology of human experience, an on-going appropriation of The Tradition in both personal and pastoral functioning, and a continuing institutional restructuring based on current understandings and insights.

Carroll once said, "I learned from Elton Trueblood that discipleship is a form of idolatry, unless it is directed at Jesus Christ. And I believe that with all my heart." Those who knew him deeply can attest that his attitudes, words, and behavior support his contention that he did indeed believe it. In so believing and behaving, he demonstrated that he was himself a true disciple, a servant of all who knew no master save one, the Lord, Jesus Christ.

Consequently, his former students, colleagues, constituents, and friends honor him not by imitating him, but by taking what he gave and finding ways to make it our own . . . and then giving of ourselves to others. We do so out of a past that is rooted and anchored in The Legacy, in a present that is significantly different from, yet continuous with, the ethos that yielded that Legacy, and toward an unfolding future which has only begun to see the deep and far-reaching consequences of The Pioneering and Partnering Legacy of Carroll Alonzo Wise.

His scholarly, spiritual, structural, pastoral, therapeutic, tutorial, and personal gifts continue their lively activity through those who now carry The Legacy, each of us in his and her own way.

NOTES

[1]". . . another thing I find amazing is that all through my training years I was going to be in a parish. But I've only been in a parish for four years. I've never been able to keep out of teaching." (Moss, 1976b, p.10)

[2]Private conversation, Fall, 1976.

[3]Ron Lee writes, "There were functionally two Ph.D. programs in pastoral counseling, the one prior to 1969, and the one from 1969 to 1978. The early Ph.D. program was institutionalized and incorporated into the Ph.D. program which continued after 1978, the latter was not (at least not until 1986 when provision was made for a combination of the academic-clinical program once again through G-ETS and the Masters Level Ramp Program--author's comment). The early Ph.D. program in pastoral psychology and counseling had as its goal the training of teachers for seminaries and church related colleges. Evidence to support this thesis comes from the pattern of student admissions into the program and graduate employment patterns. The one Ph.D. student in pastoral psychology admitted during the 1950s, and eight admitted from 1960 until 1968, taught, at least for a time, on the faculty of a theological seminary or at a Methodist college. Places taught were Garrett, Duke, Boston, Iliff, St. Paul's (Kansas), Vanderbilt, Queens (Belfast), and Kings (Brisbane).

In 1969, with the admission of six students, the program made providing of leadership for AAPC and developing pastoral counseling centers its major goal. From 1969 until 1978 the program admitted 43 students. The clinical dimension was strengthened by adding experienced psychiatrists as adjunct professors and stressed supervision." (Personal correspondence, 9-07-87)

[4]Carroll initially rejected my application for Ph.D. studies, and would have continued to oppose it except for the influence of Lee Sechrest, a professor in the Department of Psychology at Northwestern University, who was a former member of my Masters Thesis Committee (1959-60). Lee knew my work in the Philippines well (1960-64), as Carroll did not. Lee was quite interested in the culture of the Philippine Islands, having done research and writing in and on that culture.

[5]The Ph.D. program in Pastoral Psychology and Counseling was by this time moving into the "scholar-practitioner" phase with a combined emphasis on the clinical-academic orientation, a movement that reached maturity in 1969, according to Lee. My own assessment is that the "scholar-practitioner" model was, in fact, in place by the 1966-67 academic year when the Kendall Practicum Site was developed by McHolland, Christensen, and Wise.

[6]Lee, Ronald R. Private correspondence, 12-18-85.

[7]Lee was also eager to get on with his first love, the clinical practice of psychotherapy. By this time he had stayed well beyond his original commitment of five years. He nevertheless acknowledges, "I thought by leaving when I did the timing would clearly indicate protest over the undermining of standards, and this would be of some help to the whole institution."

[8]At the end of this consultation the ATS Representative said, "There are two problems with the progposed program. The entry and performance standards are too high. It will be too expensive. Students will not enroll." Experience with the program has shown that this judgement about standards and costs has not been accurate. Students and centers have participated in record numbers. While standards and costs remain high, so does the quality of student experience in the program structure, as well as the number of student registrations.

The Limitation of the Older Medical
Model in Training Pastoral Counselors

James B. Ashbrook

Christensen, McHolland, and Wise (1968) described the initial Garrett
graduate program in pastoral counseling. At that time I was asked to
critique it in an editoral for The Journal of Pastoral Care. What follows
is my analysis at that time. I suggested that the model illustrated the
strength and weakness of current development in the field. From the
vantage point of twenty years later we can see how Carroll's "Legacy,"
which Hinkle traces so skillfully, has incorporated those kinds of
concern, as well as going beyond them. The current D.Min. Specialty
Track in Pastoral Counseling/Psychotherapy reflects the movement's
"coming of age." We continue to utilize interdisciplinary collaboration,
but AAPC is maturing rapidly in making our own particular identity as
"pastoral" therapists explicit.

The strength of that first program embraced (1) the supervised
experience of evaluation-disposition and some ongoing therapy with
people presenting themselves for help, and (2) the intense didactic
focus on the psychodynamic formulation of character structure and
conflicts in order to understand the person. For that purpose the
program utilized a college counseling center, which benefitted both the
college and the graduate program, and the combined professional skills
of psychiatrist and psychologist (although McHolland is also a trained
pastoral counselor).

The weakness of the approach, and this applied to what most of us
were doing, was the limitation of the older medical model. By the older
medical model I mean: (1) a clinical setting in which individuals are
usually "patients," often "clients," but seldom "persons;" (2) a
hierarchically ordered staff with a trained physician at the top and the
social science oriented people at the bottom (with the religious
professional almost always a fifth wheel); (3) a primary focus upon
etiology and the development of pathology with only secondary
consideration given to current functioning and personality strengths; (4)
a lifting of the individual out-of-context rather than dealing with him
[or her] within context; (5) a failure to sharpen the meaning and
dynamics of the role of "pastoral" and world view of "religious"; and (6)
a primary emphasis upon rehabilitation rather than prevention, a
pattern incidentally which was being radically reversed in terms of
community psychiatry and mental health. (Instead of getting people to
come to clinics, clinicians are going to people in the communities where
they live and work.) We [pastoral counselors] have allowed ourselves to
be locked into a restricted world view and a limited methodology, in
part, because we find it more manageable.

The authors of the paper concluded that pastoral counselors should be trained most desirably by clergy rather than secular professionals. Such a conclusion, in my opinion, reflected conceptual confusion in that they were training "pastoral counselors" in a setting and via a role model that was not "pastoral." I did not object to their approach, in fact encouraged it, yet they failed to construe its assets and liabilities. The candidates functioned, as far as I could infer, as counselors or psychologists without awareness or utilization of the role of pastor, on the one hand, and without exploration of the implications and experience of not being religious professionals, on the other. No indication was given of the meaning and use of Christian vocation, which was the assumption for the psychiatrists serving as adjunct professors, as it expressed itself in professional responsibility and experience. The authors were locked into a traditional one-to-one interviewing process that failed to utilize context, strengths, and prevention.

Despite a formal recognition of the issue by references to the training's contributing to "a total theological education," "not being trained to function as quasi-psychologists or psychiatrists," or "the attitude is that of ministers doing psychotherapy," there was no operational expression of the concern. To give such sophisticated attention to evaluation-disposition in a college counseling center was implicitly to establish that function as primary. That a candidate became skilled in the area was not the point. The latent consequence would be his [or her] retardation in those areas that ought to be [one's] special strengths. These are: an awareness and use of the dynamics of structures and contexts; the cultivation of personality strengths; a mobilization of community; the meaning of religious role models; and the expectancy limitation-possibility of an explicit religious context.

If Biblical-theological understandings are not simply useless abstractions, then they have a contribution to make in understanding and strengthening human becoming. If all human experience expresses and reflects universal structures of personhood, then clinical experience has a contribution to make to Biblical-theological understandings. Yet in the approach as outlined at that time in the mid 1960s, nothing came through of the two-way street between universal formulations and concrete expressions. The theological background was acknowledged, then forgotten. The experiential foreground was acknowledged, then restricted. The dynamic gestalt of shifting figure/ground was absent. The result was a too fixed figure and a too charged ground.

To think theologically is to think with precision about God's relationship with [human beings]. Since theology deals with "the-truth-about-God's-relationship-to-[humanity]," we must be asking continually: what is this situation telling us about God's relationship to [people] in general, to me and to this person with whom I am working in particular? To think Biblically is to think with integrating themes and orienting images from the Bible. These express ways God has acted in relation to [humanity] and lead us to ask continually: What does the story of God's saving activity, as told in the Bible and understood through tradition, tell us about what God might possibly be doing here-and-now?

Thus, beyond the clinically oriented questions as outlined in the article, I argued that we needed to press on to ask: What is the truth of this situation? What does it mean to be responsible in this situation? What do we intend to do and what are we perceived as doing? What does our style of responding "say" about our ultimate concern?

Answers to such questions require contrasting contexts, contrasting role models, and contrasting world views. To collapse the training of pastoral counselors into a secular setting with secular professionals was short-sighted. To restrict that training to a "religious" setting with "religious" professionals would be incestuous. Because [humanity] is a multidimensional being, the biological, the psychological, the sociological, and the religious dimensions are all potentially present and often actually operating in any particular configuration. To fix on one dimension only is to misunderstand the human person. Because insight and responsibility cut across disciplines as well as are focused within disciplines, adequate training of pastoral counselors requires the active involvement of a variety of persons with a variety of skills and a variety of orientations. To fix on one profession only is to miss the human community.

The concerns of this brief editorial critique of the Wise Ph.D. program twenty years ago have been shaped by Hinkle and the Department into a more adequate institutionalized ideal. The particulars are elaborated in the preceding essay. What Carroll so carefully planted we are harvesting.

PART II

PASTORAL IDENTITY

EXPERIENCED REALITIES

The initial section presented Carroll as a person and the ways in which his impact was institutionalized in the preparation of ministers for pastoral care and pastoral psychotherapy. In the next three sections we shift to examine specific emphases within that complex of convictions and issues.

Those who only heard **about** Carroll--and were disconcerted by his impact--often held the image of him as someone who had sold out his pastoral identity to the bankruptcy of Freudian psychoanalysis, at worst, and the dillutedness of Rogerian non-directive therapy, at best. Nothing could be further from the truth. Donald Houts addresses that issue of whether Carroll "undermined or underlined" parish pastoral practice for the sake of an uprooted, cut-flower (to use an image which Elton Trueblood employed in another connection) specialty in pastoral counseling which could not maintain itself. Those who knew Carroll were not likely to fall for that stereotype. If any residue of doubt remains, Houts sets the record straight.

Wise modeled the caring pastor. Further, in his classes and through his books he constantly addressed the issue of meeting people at the point of their need. As convinced as he was as to the validity of a conflicted view of human motivation (i.e., Freudian), Carroll was even more committed to the grace of compassionate forgiveness, the centrality of love, and the relational quality of the Spirit of Christ. In a limited, though impressive, survey of 16 graduates of Garrett between 1948-52, who remained in parish ministry, Houts found overwhelming appreciation for the way in which Carroll opened their lives to the lives of their people. The single most persisting theme was the personal warmth with which Carroll taught them to "listen" to people, especially to the reality of their feelings, the affective reality which operated more powerfully in their lives than any and every conceptualization. He imprinted them with a sense of awe of the human psyche.

Perhaps the actual ground of such awe, was Carroll's insistence on the crucial role self-knowledge played in a pastor's life. In the parish setting, more than in the specialist's office, transferential entaglements could play havoc with relationships. Without an adequate acquaintance with the ins and outs of one's own psyche, the pastor was most likely to find himself or herself caught up in conflicted relationships with parishioners. Wise's pastoral identity underlined the sine qua non of parish ministry requiring expertise in interpersonal relationships.

The phrase "human experience" sounds evocative of "human" reality, yet Homer Ashby explores the cultural captivity of that phrase in Wise's use of it, as well as in the way most white pastoral experts have used it. He rightly articulates the way we are made actively to shape the meaning of our experience. He skillfully shows how the counseling context allows both dependency and responsibility in a manner that leads to "mutuality." He movingly conveys the "inner meaning" of what matters to individuals in specific examples. Moreover, he reminds us all that what we understand to be "human experience" must be enlarged to take into account the black experience.

More pointedly, the black experience is one of "otherness," that is, an experience of spiritual transcendence in the midst of oppressive circumstances. That sense of freedom provides "a recognition of and a living through the suffering toward the experience of the sacred." Ashby draws upon contextual and liberation theologies that critique Western, male, whiteness as "the" norm of human experience. Other cultural context and cross cultural approaches are required.

However, Ashby warns against a too rapid universalizing of such comparative experience. An analysis of cultural contexts can lose "both the uniqueness and the sacred power of the liberation symbol." This relativizes rather than particularizes "experience." He takes the reader from experience as universal to experience as deeply contextual. More specifically, the black religious experience is characterized by "rhythm" or "expressiveness"--that which runs through the whole of black culture. He shares the center of black expressiveness with specific examples of pastoral care in which religious symbols carry us to the deeper meaning of experience. Thus, the experiential approach of Wise's, which strengthened the ego, offers blacks an affirmation of their own particular context and offers whites an insight into human vitality in an "other" culture.

While continuing to focus on "context," John Carr places "Care" in the perspective of what he calls "an evangelical ministry." He avoids "the psychological reductionism" which minimizes the healing power that can come from connecting personal stories of suffering with the story of God's journeying with us in our suffering. He equally avoids a "theological reductionism" which loses personhood in suffering by an overemphasis on particular texts, particular acts, or particular exhortations. With a couple embroiled in "terrific arguments," he illustrates how a sensitive pastoral response of "You two sure have a strange way of making love" can address both the individuals and their fear.

Carr identifies basic components in pastoral care that make the "context" genuinely "evangelical." Those are: theological use of the roots and resources of belief; psychological use of the "learning about human functioning" from the various scientific disciplines; and "the recognition and authorization of the Body of Christ" that pastoral care is "a ministry of the Church." From this base he sketches an "emerging epistemology for pastoral care," one that can enable people to restructure their perceptions of themselves, the world, others, and God. The approach, drawing upon the contributions of Donald Capps, includes a sense of wonder which accords Scripture "a unique place as a determinant of belief and practice"-even as it recognizes the "flawedness" of our understanding. In addition, the approach sees science and the healing disciplines as "allies" in pastoring and in trying "to understand the created order." Carr contextualizes this evangelical epistemology in an account of a pastor and a pastoral specialist working together to bring healing to a couple--and family--which had been torn apart from themselves, their church, and their support systems as a result of an "affair."

Paul Hessert moves "the contextual" issue further "toward a theology of pastoral care" by probing the dialectic between "innocence" and "experience." Drawing upon Wise's distinction between "utilitarian religion" and "genuine insights," he examines how utilitarian religion legitimizes our cultural structures of what constitutes "reality." A view which devalues the present as "non-ideal" takes on "the culture's burden of time," which looks to a time "when" something good will occur. In contrast, a view which idealizes the present takes on "the burden of guilt," which blames everyone or every period for our imperfections. Utilitarian religion confuses "the ideal 'reality'" with "God's creation and plan." Innocence accepts that ideal, even at the cost of "inner suffering."

An awareness of "limits," however it confronts us, challenges conventional "reality." Hessert shows how "the Gospel of Christ "crucified" cuts off every cultural solution to suffering. The "core" reality of the pastoral role is that of a dead Messiah, and the resurrection, which lies beyond crucifixion, "is not within the safety and certainty" of cultural structures. In contrast to innocence, "experience" means "awareness of life outside . . . [the] reassurance and legitimization" of every culture. Experience comes when insight uniquely integrates "feeling with understanding" in faith. Such "emotional apprehension" makes "the sacraments of baptism and eucharist . . . central to pastoral care."

"Pastoral identity," in essence, is a particularized, contextualized, culturally transcending "reality" in which we are joined to each other and to Christ.

PARISH PASTORAL PRACTICE: UNDERMINING OR UNDERLINING?

Donald C. Houts

The book (Mowrer, 1961) had been published 13 years earlier. The lively dialogues from the journals were past, and the polemics which had been carried on in pastor's schools were largely forgotten. However, as I sat at lunch with O. Hobart Mowrer that winter day in 1974, his impression of Carroll Wise as one who sold out the Church and the tradition to the Freudians and the client-centered therapists was still evident if subtle. It had persisted--although expressed in a dignified and somber fashion, befitting a luncheon guest. To discover a disciple of Carroll Wise who was deeply interested in the Church and in theology, and who had experienced Wise very differently from himself was apparently a surprising turn of events to the distinguished retired professor, who later offered me many signs of friendship, prior to his death in 1984.

Later conversations with Seward Hiltner and with Orville S. Walters, M.D. had a similar flavor. Certainly each of these three men has contributed to the dialogue between religion and the behavioral sciences. Each is worthy of our appreciation and understanding. Each had been critical of Carroll Wise, primarily because of his identification with Freud and psychoanalytic presuppositions, assumed to be antithetical to those of Christian theology. Nonetheless, it is my studied conclusion over the years that Carroll A. Wise stayed closer to the Church and to the parish ministry (both out of personal experience and profound personal values) than others who preferred to live in the world of intellectual and philosophical thought, and to critique the movement from a study. He represented a truly unique balance of practiced clinical judgment, sense of context, vast personal experience across the spectrum of human need and tragedy, with a special gift for exciting response in theological students, and a striking ability to integrate theological and psychological perspectives. It is this special character of the man that I now examine.

With such a personal bias, it did not seem proper to simply share that opinion, however convincingly I might make the case. I began the task by re-reading relevant portions of his five books. Several such passages are quoted in this paper. I was in no position to conduct an analysis of questionnaires from those who both remembered Carroll as mentor and were also deeply involved in parish ministry. I used alumni records to locate a sample of 16 clergy who graduated in the years 1950-52 who had spent most of their professional lives in itinerant parish ministry.

My letter requested a response to only one question: "How has your own parish ministry been affected by your exposure to the teaching of Carroll Wise at Garrett--both through his writings, his classroom leadership, and perhaps more subtle ways as well." The discussion which follows is based on the responses received from 14 persons who also gave permission to share their comments. Thus, the task has been more like sharing with old friends and a time of personal reminiscence and reflection than a formal preparation of publishable material. Hopefully, the informality and the liberal use of quotations from both former students and from Carroll's five major writing efforts will complement rather than confuse and will allow the reader to reflect on her or his own experience.

Listening Skills

The single most frequently mentioned impact of Carroll's teaching for those who responded to my inquiry came back consistently in words like these:

> He was the one who opened my eyes to 'listening' and why listening is so important in understanding another person and so needful in the counseling process. Whenever I catch myself playing god with my know-it-all answers for a counselee, the image of Dr. Wise drifts across my memory with the gentle reminder to listen, listen, listen.

> His case study approach got us to listen long enough to other factors in the client's life . . . I have learned as a talker to listen with intensity, which gives me insight and rest from having to say something.

> To learn to listen is to give people space to be, without drawing judgment. That approach to counseling made me ready to hear and see much more than I might otherwise have seen.

> He helped me . . . to be a better participant in the listening side of dialogues.

> From him I learned the value of listening and understanding, two marvelous qualities for a parish pastor and former district superintendent.

> What I kept was the wonderful ability to listen to people and to let them know that I heard what they were saying.

While several informants acknowledged that they subsequently found important help in other more varied approaches to counseling and psychotherapy, they uniformly seemed to recognize that learning to listen is more than a simple and obvious technique. They began to see that their own anxiety was often behind their need to speak prematurely and to give answers before they had heard the story of their parishioners. When one considers the vast spectrum of readiness among theological students for learning technique and the choices one must make in a very limited classroom opportunity, it becomes more obvious why Carl Rogers and E.H. Porter were so attractive as mentors for specific training. The techniques were easily learned and, according to my informants, long remembered!

Client-centered therapy has taken its licks from pastoral psychotherapists and from many critics across the psychotherapeutic spectrum. Those who remembered Carroll's classes in the late 40's and the early 50's remember the favorite indoor sport among seminarians was a constant mimicking of the technique. In a play written for the annual school banquet, one wag recalled:

> Oh, I counsel non-directive.
> Of group process I'm protective.
> I'm as person-centered as a man can be.
> When I preach the people swoon
> And say I always quit too soon.
> I'll be as great as Harry Fosdick, wait and see!

While the technique became a whipping boy, two observations easily might be missed. The first is that when one is equipping inexperienced people to be sensitive to people in the parish, one necessarily picks a strategy that is easily learned and one which in Carroll's words: "Never does any harm." Thus, the critique of "Rogerian" methodology by specialists from a psychotherapeutic bias seems particularly inappropriate when applied to the generic, basic-training intent for which the method was quite ideal.

A second observation is perhaps more subtle, but in some ways more important. In teaching groups of lay pastors over the last ten years, I have seen that woeful lack of training, anxiety, and naive zeal are frequently factors which cause many inexperienced pastors to talk too much and to trust their verbal answers far more than experience warrants. The capacity to listen intently and actively is a first defense against premature judgments and simplistic "answers."

When one is listening, the focus is on understanding and appreciating the intent of the message and the message sender. It is therefore difficult to listen at that level without first laying aside one's own pre-judgment, one's conclusions, and one's own answers. It is precisely in this process of learning to listen effectively that one also learns to set aside pre-judgments and not commit to them prematurely. The new data almost certainly make one's impressions and stereotypes obsolete and one's neat solutions increasingly ambiguous and sometimes irrelevant. It is a rich religious discovery when one finally learns that parishioners hold both the seeds of self-destruction and of healing within themselves, and that the pastor's role is more often to establish a climate for hope and faith and growth and to enable patience by our own posture and example.

Carroll Wise was well aware that the inexperienced and the zealot are both tempted to speak out of their anxiety and their need. Learning to slow down--to listen--therefore became for countless students the best protection against pre-judgments and snap solutions. No wonder there were those who rejected the listening techniques so quickly and vehemently. In all probability, such motives are still present. This essential learning, if practiced consistently, continues to sensitize the consciences (if not the mechanical practice) of clergy today. One suspects that there are many practiced specialists in pastoral care and counseling who would do well to remind themselves to listen to each other with the same intensity, energy, and openness with which they presumably meet their clients!

The importance of this issue and its centrality in Carroll's mind is caught in the following quotation:

> The point which we would emphasize here is that it is not listening in itself that is important. It is the attitude with which a person listens. The counselee will catch the attitude of the counselor, whether it be positive or negative. Much harm can be done by listeners whose reactions to what they hear are negative. (Wise, 1951, p.83)

Wise reminded his students that "the emotionally mature religious worker will be able to allow the person freedom to work out his or her own religious faith." (Ibid., p.220) So it was that one of our informants indicates that Carroll's courses "prevented me from giving premature advice to hurting souls who came seeking help." While several of these informants indicated that they later abandoned a strictly non-directive approach with their parishioners, in retrospect, they all seemed to appreciate that it was safe, productive, and a dramatic corrective to a common inclination to dominate and overcontrol. Even more dramatic is their common reflection on the importance of "being with" parishioners and the developing of a consistent mood of sensitivity and openness to hearing their stories fully.

Feelings

A second theme which registers strongly in reading comments from parish-oriented respondents is symbolized by the word "feelings." Here are examples.

> I suppose Carroll Wise, more than any other person, helped me to balance the cognitive and affective stance in life. My original leanings, after college and into the seminary, were highly cognitive in terms of philosophical and theological underpinings. At seminary, under Wise, I was able to see and understand the affective side of our

orientation and to appreciate that most of our cognitive decisions are essentially affectively based. That meant, at least in part, in my preaching I dealt with controversial issues from the perspective of trying to understand those whose behavior was giving me difficulty. This was particularly helpful to me when I was quite active in the anti-Vietnam role in the late 60's and early 70's. Somehow, it was helpful in the congregations for people to know that I was trying to understand where everyone was coming from rather than flaying away on a negative track.

It was Carroll Wise's insistence of gaining deeper and deeper insights into human nature and behavior and his insistence on focusing on the feeling level of the client which was essential to employment of any other approaches. . .

It (training under Carroll Wise) sent me out, not only with an appreciation for the importance of accepting people as they are, including all of their feelings, no matter how distasteful or irrational, but with an understanding that the reality of that acceptance communicates the grace of God.

"How do you feel about that?" was a common sarcastic retort of student after student in courses taught by Carroll Wise--particularly in introductory courses. The emphasis was hardly accidental. Carroll was himself very conscious of the tendency of an academic environment to encourage intellectualization and inadvertently to allow it to become a primary mode of defense against intimacy among many highly educated persons. His references often made that suggestion as in the following:

As the pastor turns . . . attention from the intellectual content of such conversations to the feeling that a person is expressing, you will find the situation becoming one of real creative interest. (Ibid., p.170)

In a more profound way, he saw the emphasis on feelings as the language by which to approach the parishioner's sense of meaning of an event--a different and perhaps deeper level of perception, upon which the person was apt to base a response. This emphasis is clearly expressed in the following quotation: "As the minister enters the sickroom, [one's] primary interest should not be in the specific illness or symptoms of the patient, but how the patient feels about [the] experiences."

Carroll Wise was not afraid of feelings. His intense and sometimes provocative manner could elicit strong feelings from students, as for instance when he started classes in group therapy by simply rearranging chairs in a circle and offered no overt structured leadership whatsoever! He had strong opinions and was embroiled frequently in controversy. For all of this, his advice to students was germane: not just to look at events but to see how people feel about them and recognize that there is a subjective reality experienced by each person involved.

Wise was incurably religious. Mildly iconoclastic, he nonetheless was a "closet pietist" in the sense of having a deep and pervasive personal conviction about the Church and the world. His emphasis was always more personal than communal, but the implications of his emphasis on personal feelings were more than subjectivity and navel gazing. As late as 1983 he wrote:

> Many have set the self up as the highest value . . . for many [programs of self-development] have become false gods. These have missed an essential aspect of genuine religious faith, which is, however, not opposed to the growth of the self . . . A central message of Jesus was that people find their real selves as they commit themselves to the Ultimate Source of life, God. (Wise, 1983, p.288)

When one contemplates the relevance of applying these insights to life in the parish, a truly reflective person cannot miss an application such as those reported above by our informants. To be in touch with the feelings of parishioners has everything to do with managing conflict and power struggles within the parish. Emotions are very relevant to the transitions of the pastor from one parish to the next, and with routine parish decisions which affect deeply-held values or status issues. In addition, the pastor who is in touch with feelings--his or her own and those of family--is not often shocked by serious and sudden marriage or family crises. The pastor who minimizes these issues neglects not only pragmatic sensitivity to individual parishioner differences in perception and response, but also neglects a symbolic way of addressing the important function of helping them interpret and find meaning in their lives.

Know Thyself

Theologically, it is of profound importance how the pastor deals with "distasteful" or "irrational" feelings. At the heart of Carroll's own practice lay a conviction that grace can be transmitted in human relationships as easily as can law and judgment. It became for Carroll, and those of his generation, a central issue that the way pastors choose to relate to their people carries a powerful message of God as either harsh and judging or as compassionate and forgiving. Thus, the choice of a Carl Rogers rather than a Frederick Thorne as a model was purposeful and consistent with the intent to choose a method of full acceptance of feelings to carry a theological message of redeeming grace. Apparently some students caught that message clearly!

> Carroll Wise enabled me to appreciate, in a way that I had not grasped before and in a way that has been helpful to me ever since Garrett, the human side of the equation.

> As I reflect about it, I see Dr. Wise as a lively, gentle human being--completely at ease with himself--one who was not trying to impress others either with his overwhelming practical experience or academic expertise.

> During class I remember Dr. Wise said that no one has any business serving as a counselor until he/she has gone through the experience of being a counselee. It took some time for that idea to sink in and for me to muster the courage to make the decision to seek a counseling relationship. . . Though Dr. Wise did not do the counseling, he was the catalyst, for which I am grateful.

Carroll's roots in the clinical pastoral education movement had from the very beginning deeply influenced his perception of training for students. He was constantly balancing what he could do in the classroom with the need for further supervised clinical experience and for some kind of individual counseling or psychotherapy as might be needed. I cannot recall that there was ever any pressure to get into counseling, as such. I only recall the continued references to the need for self-discovery and the fascination I felt with his own awareness of hidden motivators, unconscious influences, and different levels of the self. It was a fascinating journey he proposed and invited. Case histories constantly unlocked mysteries and awakened awe and reverence toward the human psyche and the prospect of ministering to persons at such a level of intimacy.

Carroll was fond of speaking to the "blockages" of individual pastors which inhibited their fuller and deeper involvement in ministry. He would surely have agreed with the observation of Otto Kernberg regarding a common feature of many clergy treated at the Menninger Foundation:

> These clergy had a great need to be loved and admired by others, and a curious apparent contradiction between a very inflated concept of themselves and an inordinate need for tribute from others. . . In addition, their personality difficulties make them unable to tolerate intimacy and closeness. (Kernberg, 1970)

Wise puts it pointedly:

> The pastor must be very careful about reading into the person's words [one's] own personal feelings and ideas. [One] must be

sufficiently free from [one's] own need to project that this is avoided. This means that the pastor must listen to [oneself] to catch feelings, defenses, fantasies, and motives in [oneself] that may be reflected in [one's] responses. . . Every pastor, even for the general work of the ministry, needs a deep understanding of [oneself]. (Wise, 1983, p.158)

In an earlier work he writes of the importance of a vital Christian experience in the making of a pastor:

It is an experience which gives the person a solid sense of identity before God, and therefore before [others]. It is an experience which leads [one] to openness toward [oneself] and [one's] own motivations rather than to a projection of [one's] anxiety, guilt, or hostility onto others. At [one's] age [one] cannot be expected to have achieved a fully mature love, but [one] has a sense of [one's] need for growth in this respect. [One's] experience of forgiveness is still progressing. [One] has not yet arrived. (Wise, 1966, p.119)

Most would agree that specialists in pastoral care and counseling need to have a therapeutic experience and a significant period of supervised clinical work to be more in touch with their own inner resources, as well as their inner blocks and unconscious unresolved conflicts. The observation seems obvious that the intimacy in which the counselor works one-on-one or in small groups makes others highly vulnerable to being victimized by the pastor's own unresolved issues. While in the quotation above Wise recognizes considerable need for this self awareness in the parish, a still stronger case could be made from my vantage point as one who counsels exclusively with parish pastors and their families. A transference phenomenon is still a trap and enticement to pastors who are not adequately facing their own issues and dealing with them forthrightly. Few of the extra-marital affairs and violations of pastoral integrity are on the basis of cold, calculated cynical use of others. They happen, for the most part, to needy persons who rationalize their situations and then suffer intense and overwhelming guilt for transgressing their own personal values--quite aside from the ministerial convenant.

There is a sense in which the structure of the pastoral counseling office gives greater protection than the permeable and moveable relationships within the parish. The pastor operates more on a free-lance, saddlebag, off-the-cuff, informal basis, which for many clergy makes it more critical to know their limitations and to police themselves, as well as to find resources for their own healing.

Several judicatories have adopted a requirement of a quarter of clinical pastoral education prior to full ordination in the denomination. While these judicatories are still few in number, it seems clear that none are moving away from that requirement because of its importance for the functioning of parish clergy.

In a recent survey of nearly 2,000 United Methodist pastors, (Orthner, 1987, pp.13ff) the single most obvious recognition of those clergy was the need for more supervised clinical experience beyond the classwork they were provided in pastoral care and counseling. It may well be that parish clergy are beginning to assert themselves in demanding more opportunities for a dimension which continues to be missing in any depth from their professional education.

Parish Pastoral Care

Carroll Wise was never reluctant to make claims about the centrality of pastoral care in the work of ministry. "Pastoral Care is not an adjunct to the ministry; it is the very core." (Wise, 1966, p.12) He goes on to paraphrase the Corinthian letters by saying: "For whether a [person] preach, teach, conduct the affairs of the Church, or engage in any other pastoral activity, if [that person] has not love, [one's] ministry is nothing. This is the central problem of the pastoral ministry today." (Ibid., p.3) Wise is very clear and unequivocal in stating that "the meaning of pastoral care is that we must be able to enter into and suffer with those whom we seek to help. . . Not that [one] relieves them of their suffering, but in suffering with them and for them in love, [one] makes it possible for them to find the redemptive answer in love. . . Finally our ministry is not our ministry, but the continuation of Christ's ministry in us through his Spirit. . . It is a living model of the Spirit, and this is the Spirit of Christ. It is in this Spirit that the true pastor fulfills [one's] calling." (Ibid., pp.6,7)

His classes and his textbooks are replete with additional illustrations of the sense in which pastoral care is essential to effective ministry in its every aspect. "The pastor cannot preach in a condemning manner and show an accepting attitude in a pastoral or counseling situation. There is room for considerable discussion of the relation of this approach to preaching, religious education, worship, and other activities of the minister." (Wise, 1951, p.168)

Behind the emphasis on pastoral care as ministry is the repeated emphasis on building pastoral relationships.

> The basic purpose of calling is to develop and maintain a close pastoral relationship with the people in the parish. While elements of this relationship get established through the other contacts, they deepen only as the pastor has the opportunity to sit down with another person and quietly talk with him [or her]. (Ibid., p.169)

> The pastor should not expect that every call will produce a conversation about significant problems. Many calls will not do this. However, all calling that is carried through on these principles will produce between the

pastor and [one's] people a deeper relationship of confidence and understanding that will make [one] emotionally available to them at any time when a crisis may occur. (Ibid., p.171)

In working with the bereaved, it is particularly important for the pastor to understand that much of [one's] value lies in the personal relationship which [one] is able to establish, rather than in the ideas that [one] can give. Persons are saved from acute emotional pain through relationships more than through ideas. Patience and gentleness are very necessary. (Ibid., p.216)

It might be said that Carroll was too timid in seeing many situations beyond the average pastor's skill and for which he counselled referral. Given the level of sophistication and the inconsistency of guaranteed levels of functioning, this was probably sage advice, even though it earned him considerable criticism from those who felt he sold out religion to the evil forces of psychiatry and particularly psychoanalysis. Hobart Mowrer was only one among several who voiced this stern criticism. As we have seen, however, it often has been persons with the strength and vitality of Wise who dialogued effectively with those who spoke adjacent languages, and for the sake of serving humanity, he would continue to insist on that dialogue.

While several of our informants broadened their views towards psychotherapy models after leaving the seminary, none seemed to regret their introduction to more than one level of therapeutic intervention represented in a client-centered approach by clergy and in a dynamic psychology deeply dependent upon Freudian insights. In the words of one informant:

I am sure it was through him I gained an understanding of the importance of counseling in the life of ministry and how crucial pastors can be as 'first stops' for people with psychological problems.

What can one say except to appreciate that Carroll was a specialist with a great deal of training as a specialist and considerable pride in that role. At the same time he recognized that most of his students were not headed in that direction and his frequent references to his parish experience at Hennepin Avenue Church and his use of verbatim case material from student parishes constantly established the parish as an exciting arena for pastoral work. Furthermore, he always appeared to be very clear that pastoral counseling was not some kind of step above pastoral care but simply a specific 20th century embodiment of an ancient manifestation of faithful discipleship and servanthood.

Role Model

One of our informants puts the impact of Carroll as a role model so eloquently that almost any further discussion will seem a distraction.

> . . . my experience with Dr. Wise, both in the classroom and in his writings, was that his presentations were always biblically and experientially oriented. That is to say, though he was not a proof-texting expert, the reader/listener had no doubt of his Christian foundation and orientation. Likewise, his counseling wisdom and skills were the result of his own counseling experience; the life-situation case studies and illustrations sharpened the focus of his principles. I have found this to be a sound basis not only for my own counseling work, but also a solid foundation for preaching, for administering the program of the Church, and for developing a service of worship week after week.
>
> Beyond that, Dr. Wise was one whom I could go to with personal problems . . . He was able to respond in terms of the sitatuion and was not bound by what I took to be his theory . . . The care and openness which he taught, I believe, still stands me in good stead, and was the foundation of what I try to do now with the foundation he gave me. . . And perhaps that was the best thing I learned from him.
>
> Dr. Wise was truly my role model.

Another pastor who has spent his entire ministry in a specialized ministry of pastoral care indicated in a private conversation that it was partly through the excitement of the ideas, the opportunity for self-exploration, and the vision of ministry that he valued Carroll Wise. In addition, he was grateful for the intense personal relationship involved in having experienced him as a personal therapist, but even more fully it was in seeing the role model of a man who represented strength and compassion, a sharp mind and a sensitive spirit which finally gave him a model around which to fashion his own personal integration.

Carroll Wise was very mindful of the leadership potential of the pastor's visible influence in the parish.

> The pastor, as the leader of the fellowship, has a major opportunity in promoting this sense of community. Through [one's] relationships with . . . people [one] can help them to feel accepted or unacceptable, in fellowship or isolated. The kind of relationships which [one] as a person creates will be a symbol to [one's] people of the kind of relationship which God offers them. [One] can

103

mediate to them something of the love of God, or something of fear and divisiveness. And a pastor who has achieved in [oneself] the confidence of fullness will help [one's] church to become whole. (Wise, 1956, p.131)

As much as Carroll Wise worked with graduate students and in his retirement years invested himself in a pastoral counseling center, he was always interested in the role of religious practice in assisting healthy personal development. He refused to consign the work of ministry to psychopathology and spiritual malaise.

> We have also indicated the function of religion in the development of personality, and the ways in which religion may function to produce illness or health. In the light of this, the role of the [clergy] in being primarily in the field of prevention and secondarily in the area of cure should become clear. (Wise, 1942, p.257)

Summary

Perhaps two summary statements will represent our small sample with eloquence.

> David Roberts described Carroll's book [on Pastoral Counseling] as being 'deceptively simple.' He indicated that it carried within it the very heart of effective pastoral counseling. . . Beginning parish work . . . I discovered that probably the most practical course that I took at Garrett was in pastoral counseling as taught by Carroll Wise. It provided an extremely useful beginning point for the parish pastor. . . . At this particular point I would have to say that the influence of Carroll Wise has been extremely significant in church work.

> He seemed sincerely concerned for each of us, that we be in touch with who we are, and that we be genuine in our relationships with others. That has been a guiding force in my life and in my ministry. . .

I have attempted to be faithful in portraying the free-form data which came in response to a simple request in the form of a letter. What is remarkable in reading through those careful and thoughtful responses is to pick up themes which are in no sense guided by a set of specific questions. The impact of Carroll's teaching upon the parish practice of those surveyed seems directly proportional to the impact of life upon life. The intensity of their relationships was certainly reflected in the depth of the responses. Just as he would have insisted, the relationship is more powerful than the rules.

Upon reflection, it becomes self-evident that all of these central issues except one were shared fully by parish pastors and specialists in counseling. It is only with regard to the relevance of the parish as primary arena that these pastors conceivably might disagree with the pastoral counseling specialist, and even that is doubtful. One is pressed to the conclusion that where ministry is faithfully practiced, within the faith tradition, and where meanings are shared within the faith community, and where the individual practitioner is true to his or her calling as believer/theologian/practitioner, even though our settings and uses of time are quite different, our ultimate responsibilities and our calling are the same.

In the light of the judgments of some contemporaries and others who have become involved in the field of pastoral care and counseling too late to know Carroll Wise on a personal basis, these words of his might well be a final word on the subject of parish pastoral practice. The reader must by now have decided clearly whether Carroll Wise's work undermines or underlines the heart of that historic theological and ecclesiastical task of pastoral practice.

> The [clergyperson] has a unique contribution to make to the problems of personality and of culture, but this contribution may be made only through the development of the methods of the [clergy] to the place where they are adequate for present day needs. Of course the problem is deeper than methods. The [clergyperson] must have a living faith to express through [one's] methods. (Wise, 1942, p.257)

Carroll's most lasting bequest is perhaps the same for both parish clergy and for pastoral care specialist--a keen sense of awe and mystery about God and life by way of our own identity as wounded healers. Such compassion cares always. Such humility never seeks disciples.

PASTORAL COUNSELING AND THE BLACK EXPERIENCE OF OTHERNESS

Homer U. Ashby, Jr.

Even a cursory analysis of Carroll Wise's work reveals that human experience lay at the heart of his thought as a pastoral theologian. Wise does not explicitly define what he means by "human experience." By reviewing his major writings, though, we can construct a working definition of human experience that is consistent with Wise's thinking.

In Religion in Illness and Health, Wise locates the hub of human experience in the dynamic relationship of the human organism with the environment and the relationship of the organism within itself. Thus, human experience occurs concurrently as an encounter with persons and events in the world and an integration of those encounters within the self. The relationship between the organism and the environment is not uni-directional. That is, the interaction between person and environment is not solely that of the active environment impacting upon the passive organism. Instead, Wise argues, the opposite is true. The organism first acts upon the environment before reacting to it. (1942, pp.77-78) Before we react to persons and events in the world we engage in the processes of receiving, perceiving, and organizing the persons or objects we have encountered. These active initiatives involve the mechanism of the ego which integrates the external and internal dimensions of human experience into a total organismic response. That response is what Wise identifies as our personality, "Personality is the expression of the life experience of the total organism." (Wise, 1951, p.19)

Religious symbols are crucial features in this integration process. They provide the means for expressing realities that reside within the experience of the individual. Whether these religious symbols are stories, works of art, rituals, places or ways of being, they convey meaning which gives understanding and power to human experience. Most often these religious symbols and their meanings are formed into a Weltanschuung or world view from which a way of life or reaction pattern develops. With this Weltanschuung, persons possess the creative possibility to fashion lives of meaning and purpose. (Wise, 1942, p.119)

Wise indicates that the failure of persons to participate in the creative possibility of human personality can have dire consequences. "The inability of personality to function positively according to the laws of its own being leads to illness in one form or another." (Wise, 1951, pp.32-33) For Wise, the two factors that block the positive function of personality are a lack of human freedom and a weak integrating ego.

Human freedom is a derivative of free will. Free will, while a condition of human creatureliness, is more than a gift from God which we passively received. "Freedom is the experience of being able to engage spontaneously in creative work or creative human relationships." (Ibid., pp.22-23) Freedom, thus defined, can lead to a mature self and a mature faith marked by responsibility and mutuality. In the counseling process individuals experience acceptance for the freedom to convey their experience in terms of its meaning as well as the freedom to exercise their autonomy. The counseling relationship is one in which "the person becomes a self-determining agent in so far as this is humanly possible." (Ibid., p.51) A weak ego distorts reality and inhibits the creation of healthy relationships with others. The function of counseling is to strengthen the ego so that it can mature and face things it has not been able to face. Finally, in the counseling relationship the person is allowed to be both dependent and responsible which leads to mutuality.

In highlighting the dominant theme of human experience in Wise's pastoral theology, two other critical dimensions emerge: the counseling relationship, and religious symbols. Wise warns pastoral care practitioners that technique is secondary to the counseling relationship. He is interested in what happens between pastor and counselee; how they experience one another. The counseling relationship is of vital importance not only because it is the vessel that carries the processes of communication, integration, dependence, freedom, and mutuality, but also because the counseling relationship offers the opportunity to receive the liberating power and gracious mercy of God. The counseling relationship is a precursor for a wholistic and salvific relationship with God. (Ibid., p.83) That is, the freedom and creative renewal promised in the Gospel are experienced in the relationship between pastor and person. "Pastoral care is the art of communicating the inner meaning of the gospel at the point of a person's need." (Ibid., 1966, p.8)

How is this inner meaning conveyed? By what means does one experience a relationship with God? Such meaning is most often conveyed by means of religious symbols. As persons seek ways of naming, understanding and claiming their experience of themselves and the world, pastors become "signifiers"[1] who offer through their person and the counseling relationship symbols that mediate between sacred and profane. These symbols are religious symbols because they point to a transcendent reality beyond immediate experience. And they mediate between the sacred and the profane by illuminating profane experience (pen-ultimate reality) in the light of sacred experience (ultimate reality).

A brief example from the work of John Patton may be illustrative. (Patton, 1981; pp.161-162; 1983, pp.30-36):

108

Pastoral Counselor: What do you think is going on?   Has anything
in particular happened?

Sally: Well, my aunt died, but that was last week.   That
couldn't be it.   I just can't seem to get down to
work.   It's just like before.

P.C.:   (Not remembering having heard much about the aunt)
Tell me more about your aunt.

Sally: (Sally talks at length about her aunt and the way
Sally's father made fun of her and didn't take her
seriously.)   But she was always doing something for
somebody else.   I didn't really see her that often.   I
don't think that that's bothering me.   I really should
be over it.

P.C.:   Sally, how much do you know about grief? (P.C. gives
a mini-lecture on grief work and suggests that Aunt
Rebecca may be more important to Sally than she is
aware of.   P.C. encourages her to tell him more about
Aunt Rebecca.)

Sally: It's so unfair.   She was killed taking a blind woman
across the street. (Gives details of the accident.)

P.C.:   You sound angry.

Sally: I am.   I don't see how if there is a God, he could
allow this kind of thing to happen.   I don't know
what I believe anymore.   Do you think I should talk
to Jim (the pastor who had referred her)?

P.C.:   It depends on whether you feel he could tolerate your
doubts.   Why don't you stay with it here for awhile.

Sally: (Talks about what a bad world this is and asks why
things like this happen.   She gets further into her
anger and wonders if her husband can tolerate it.)
Why bother living, why work, why do anything?

P.C.:   It's interesting how important your aunt is to you,
and that in all our months together I hardly knew
anything about her.

Sally: She was there when I needed her.   Whenever my
mother wasn't there, it seemed like Aunt Rebecca
was. (Details several incidents)

P.C.:   It sounds like she helped make you who you are.

Sally:	(Seeming to ignore the last comment) You know, I went through her house after she died. I wanted something of hers. I took some of her violets. (She smiles) Aunt Rebecca could never get them to bloom.
P.C.:	I suspect you have more of her than you are aware of.
Sally:	(Again smiling) Aunt Rebecca and I are the only ones who know how to make my grandmother's caramel cake.
P.C.:	Another way you are like her. I hope you'll give me a piece of that cake sometime.
Sally:	I will. (Reflectively) Before I went to the funeral, I was in her house, and she made a cake like that-- just the day before she died. I ate three pieces of it. It was so good, I could hardly get enough. (Silence)
P.C.:	I imagine you know a bit more now about what Holy Communion means.
Sally:	(Cries softly for awhile and then smiles)
P.C.:	Thank you for letting me know her.

In this brief vignette Patton's client is experiencing the grief and pain of the loss of her aunt. Part of the grief and pain is bound up in the never again to be experienced sharing of special times and special secrets. When in the counseling relationship Patton introduces the symbol of Holy Communion, the shared experiences are let loose from their prison of pain and misery to a new possibility of celebration and cherished remembrance. By means of the counseling relationship, the relationship between Sally and her aunt becomes laden with new meaning. The counseling relationship becomes an occasion for the gift of new life; a reflection of God's liberating power and mercy.

Black Experience

This all too brief synopsis of Wise's pastoral theology sets the stage for an examination of the experience of Americans of African descent. Is the "experience" of blacks in America the same "experience" that Wise refers to in his writing? Yes and no. Experience is experience. That is, our engagement with the environment and with ourselves coupled with our attempts to give meaning and purpose to those encounters is part and parcel of the human condition. Whatever race or nationality we are, we all engage in this meaning-making process. (Kegan, 1982) However, there are certain a priori, culturally specific assumptions which we bring to this phenomenon of experience that result in vastly different methods of meaning-making and vastly different perceptions on the meanings derived.

Charles Long is one of the chief proponents of a new methodological approach in the examination of the black religious experience. (Long, 1986, pp.1-9) Long believes that to understand adequately and accurately the black experience in America one must enter into the sacred center of that experience; one must participate in the "otherness" of that experience. Referring to the black struggle for freedom, Long writes:

> they (blacks) came to a knowledge and experienced another reality, a reality not created or given by the Man. This otherness is experienced in the spirituals as God, or as the mode of perception that is not under the judgment of the oppressors. It is equally expressed in the practical and concrete proposals that speak of another space, whether Africa or another geographical location, or heaven. This sense of otherness, or the sense of the other that has arisen out of the black experience, is present when the black communities contemplate the meaning of America as a free society, for if blacks are to be free in American society, this society will indeed have to become a radically different one, an-other place. (Ibid., p.153)

Participation in this other reality has empowered black people to survive in a brutal and hostile environment. This other reality is not an "otherworldliness" which blacks use to deny the suffering of their daily lives, but is participation in a reality that transcends the limiting experience of an oppressive world. Participation in the reality of "otherness" means not the denial of oppression, but a recognition of and a living through the suffering toward the experience of the sacred. One experiences this movement through suffering to sacred salvation in the spiritual, "Nobody Knows the Trouble I Seen:"

> Nobody knows the trouble I seen
> Nobody knows but Jesus.
> Nobody knows the trouble I seen.
> Glory, Hallelujah.

Any discussion of the journey toward the center of black experience requires that the journey proceed in the correct direction. The journey is not outward toward the universal which relativizes all experience beneath it. Instead the journey proceeds toward the center of black being which is particular, unique, and absolute on its own terms.

The community from which I come expressed another attitude, an attitude that confronted the reality of America, not as plastic and flexible, amenable to the will of the human being through hard work and moral fortitude, but a reality, inpenetrable, definite,

111

subtle, and other--a reality so agonizing that it forced us to give up our innocence while at the same time it sustained us in humor, joy and promise. I am speaking of a quality of the American experience which through its harsh discipline destroyed forever a naive innocence, revealing a god of creation--a god of our silent tears--a god of our weary years. This may be called nitty--gritty pragmatism. It is from this kind of history and involvement with nature, humanity, and God that the dense richness germinates out of which profound religious awareness emerges. (Ibid., p.139)

Carroll Wise did not contemplate such an other reality when he wrote about pastoral counseling. Wise's perspective was limited by the basic assumptions, Weltanschuung, and construction of reality that handicapped most pastoral theologians prior to the 1980's. The invisibility of the black experience,[2] the misinterpretation of a hostile environment as benign,[3] and the relativizing of all experience based upon white, Western norms represent features of this limited view.
Recent work in the area of liberation or contextual theology attempts to address these problems by taking the context and experience of blacks and other minorities into account as they devise alternative ways of defining the world. (Roberts, 1987) In discussing the liberation theologies of Latin America, Roger Haight has identified certain general characteristics of liberation theology: 1) the experience of poverty, 2) the experience of historicity (a historical consciousness through which persons can change events in history, and declare the particular historical situation as the departure for theological reflection), 3) the use of social analysis in theologizing, 4) the close relationship liberation theologians see between liberation and salvation, and 5) the identification of love as the essence of Christianity, and that love must be linked with the demands of justice, in particular, social justice. (Haight, 1985, pp.15-24)

J. Deotis Roberts is also interested in moving beyond the provincial view of universal Western theology.

To assert that Western theology is universal is to fly in the face of compelling evidence. It is not universal. It takes a very provincial point of view and attempts to totalize it. The situation now demands that theology first be contextualixed . . . If we reach a universal situation, it must take seriously the several contexts in which theological reflection is being done. (Roberts, 1987, p.13)

In a fashion similar to Haight's, Roberts emphasizes those features of a black theology of liberation which grow out of the black experience in America. First, contextual theology should be more interdisciplinary, using insights from the social sciences, notably social analysis and economic theory. Second, contextual theology should be ecumenical. All sources are to be used, transcending limits of denominationalism, gender, race, and culture. Third, the Bible needs to be pushed to the center of theological reflection. Fourth, the historical perspective which is rooted in the life and worship of the believing community should be the base for theological reflection. (Ibid., pp.16-19)

As far as the theology of pastoral care is concerned, significant steps have been taken recently to address these contextual issues. Edward Wimberly and Archie Smith have written skillfully on the need to include the contextual reality of the black experience when doing pastoral counseling with blacks. Both Wimberly and Smith strongly emphasize the history of black Americans as a major factor in understanding how best to counsel with blacks. (Smith, 1982, pp.13-34; Wimberly, 1979, pp.17-38) From this stress on historical consciousness Wimberly highlights the spiritual values that influence black thought and community life. (Wimberly, 1982) Smith has integrated the historical consciousness into an approach to pastoral care with blacks that combines care of the individual with social action. Smith's third paradigm is a combination of these two traditional approaches. This third approach or paradigm moves toward the empowerment of the individual in the midst of an oppressive social system. (Smith, 1982, pp.39-54)

David Augsburger's Pastoral Counseling Across Cultures also points to the need of the counselor to be aware of the cultural context in counseling. Augsburger encourages the counselor to "seek sources of influence in both the person and the context, both the individual situation and the environment." (Augsburger, 1986, p.20) In his analysis of the cross-cultural issues in pastoral counseling, Augsburger reviews the various ways in which human cultures view the world, value individuality vs. solidarity, identify inner controls and outer controls, live in families, ascribe roles for men and women, make moral and ethical decisions, define the demonic, assess mental health and mental illness, and practice healing. His rich descriptions of cultural differences are an invaluable resource for the pastoral counselor who is challenged by the diversity of persons from different cultures who enter his or her office.

What we see in the writers thus far examined is the evolution of pastoral care theology and practice over the past 40 years. From a pastoral theology whose basic assumptions were thought to be universal and tended to be blind to other realities and the "otherness" of its experience, the pastoral care field is now on the threshold of acknowledging other cultural contexts and being sensitive to working with individuals in light of the realities of their historical situation. Theologians such as Tracy, Cobb, Chopp, Schreiter, and Haight have helped to give these alternative theologcal perspectives legitimization in the West. (Tracy, 1975; Cobb, 1982; Chopp, 1986; Schreiter, 1985; Haight, 1985) The black voices of Long and Roberts have highlighted the major flaw in previous theological perspectives, that of making Western thought normative for all cultures. Smith, Wimberly, and Augsburger have echoed the contextual approach in the practice of pastoral counseling, encouraging counselors to be aware of the

113

particular historical/cultural situation in which persons reside and to work simultaneously at transforming persons and transforming societies.

I perceive a danger, however, in the recent evaluation of contextual theologies and the development of cross-cultural approaches to counseling. That danger is the too rapid movement toward appealing to the universal in analyzing cultural contexts. While acknowledging the importance of contextualization, Haight wants to use liberation theology as a foil for the critique of post-modern Christianity. For Haight, "liberation theology is not just or simply a local theology. Liberation theology has implications for Christianity as such and hence for a more general theological interpretation, and not merely for Latin America or the third world." (Haight, 1985, p.23) The symbol of liberation is used as a lens through which Christianity is being reinterpreted. My belief is that such utilitarian analysis of the liberation theology experience denies both the uniqueness and the sacred power of the liberation symbol.

Liberation theology is an experiential theology first and foremost. It has evolved out of the experience of persons in what Bruno Bettleheim has called "extreme situations." (Bettleheim, 1979, pp.11-18) Liberation theology can be, but fundamentally is not to be used for, methodological manipulations. Too quickly separated from experience, the liberation theme no longer has sacred power. Consequently, it becomes easy for Haight to conclude that "liberation theology is a modern and secular theology." (Haight, 1985, p.23) What has occurred for Haight and other theologians is that the theological task, per se, has taken over center stage, rather than human experience itself, out of which theology emerges.[4]

A similar danger exists in the pastoral counseling discipline. The attempt to be cross-culturally sensitive can lead to a turning away from the deep, rich, and sacred meaning of the contexts in which the particular cultures reside in order to form a pastoral care approach whose methodology is more important than the integrity of human experience. Augsburger urges the pastoral counselor to perceive the universal (like all others), the cultural (like some others), and the particular (like no others) in human behavior. He further encourages the adoption of a cultural relativism perspective. "Cultural relativism is committed to the view that alien idea systems, while fundamentally different from our own, display an internal coherency that can be understood but not judged by our own." (Augsburger, 1986, p.68) And beyond cultural relativism Augsburger suggests a theology of culture for pastoral counseling in which there is a synthesis of universal, local, and individual interpretations of human experience. "A theology of culture must be rooted in multiple cultures corrected by universals and applied by individuals." (Ibid., p.72)

Much of what Augsburger suggests I support. However, the methodological approach appears to endanger the cultural potency of a

114

people's experience.   My concern is that a counselee's reporting of an
experience which is heavily laden with cultural meaning, when viewed
in the light of universal meanings, may lead to interpretations by the
counselor that have little relevance or impact.

I am intrigued by Long's notion of journeying to the center of religious
experience as a way of better understanding the experience of blacks in
America.   This method is suggested by other observors of the black
experience who refer to such centering as journeying to the "roots."
For Pasteur and Toldson, (1982) there are dimensions of the black
experience which can be explored at depth, revealing a unique and
powerful thread that has not only shaped the expressive behavior of
blacks, but has influenced the whole of the Western world.

Rhythm is the thread that runs through the fabric of black culture; it
is therefore at the base of black expressive behavior, evident in the
music, dance, poetry, drama, oratory, folklore, sculpture, and other
expressive forms of the black community.   These gangly, invisible
threads that we call rhythm are the "Roots of Soul."   (Pasteur and
Toldson, 1982, p.4)

This "black expressiveness" is characterized by depth of feeling,
naturalistic attitudes, stylistic renderings, poetic and prosaic vernacular,
and expressive movement.   Methodologically, they examine the black
experience through a reverse hermeneutical lens which is less interested
in relativizing and more interested in particularizing the black
experience.   Instead of viewing the black experience as one of many
cultural experiences that possess universal, local, and unique features,
Pasteur and Toldson are interested in the unique features of black
experience that form a distinctive black expressiveness.

Long and Pasteur and Toldson suggest that truly to understand the
black experience as manifested in religion and behavior one must not
carry the investigation from the particular to the universal, but to
delve deeply into the ways, customs, and expressive acts of black and
African people.   Identifying rhythm as the fundamental behavior
principle, Pasteur and Toldson suggest that the healthy personality of
black people depends upon their capacity to participate in the rhythm
of black expressiveness.   Participating in this rhythm allows blacks to
exist at the sacred center of their being.   In this sacred, rhythmic
center there is power, meaning, and resources for survival.   Indeed,
being alive at the center enables blacks to transform present reality
into an other reality where the restraints, negations, and brutality of a
hostile environment are robbed of power.   Pastoral care with blacks
should be geared toward assisting blacks in being more alive at the
center of their black expressiveness, at the center of their black
experience.

As a chaplain at a large metropolitan hosptial and as a pastoral
counselor, I have had the opportunity to engage with black persons at

this center of their black expressiveness. For me, they have been sacred moments where the power of black expressiveness has been set free for healing and growth.

During a day when I was the on-call chaplain at the University of Chicago Medical Center, a call came over the beeper that a patient had died and the family needed a chaplain. When I got off the elevator at the appropriate floor, I could hear the wailing and sobbing of the family members in the hall. Turning the corner, I saw two young women walking briskly, almost running down the hall, an older woman leaning against the wall, a young man running back and forth between the younger woman and the older woman.

The head nurse approached me and informed me that the 24 year old son of the older woman had just died, and that the emotional outburst was too much for the nursing staff to handle at the time. The nurses did not have enough staff to address all the members of the family as well as care for the other patients. She explained that they were also concerned that the disturbance was upsetting the other patients.

I asked the young man, who was the brother of the two younger woman and the son of the older woman, if he would stay with his sisters while I escorted the mother to a waiting room down the hall. He said he would. In the waiting room the mother cried uncontrollably. I did not say much, but held her hand. Periodically, she would cry out in a loud moan, either calling her dead son's name or asking the question, "Why did he have to die?" Over the next half hour the sisters and brother filed in one at a time and sat down beside their mother, hugging her. At one point the mother got up and said she could no longer be confined in the waiting room. I walked beside her as she paced up and down the hall. After an hour, the family gathered their belongings, thanked the hospital staff, and left.

After they had left, a physician asked to me what I had done. Before I came they had been ready to give the mother a shot to calm her down. I answered that I had not done anything but give them a chance to grieve. Now I would add that I gave them the freedom, space, and opportunity to express the depth of feeling and the expressive movement that were part of their rhythmic way of expressing their grief.

Naturalistic attitudes are those that have an aversion to formality and standardization, promote frankness of manner, display contempt for artificiality and falseness in human conduct, and exhibit sensuality and sexuality without misplaced shame or guilt. (Pasteur, 1982, p.4) Counselors who demand that these naturalistic attitudes be eliminated in order for the counseling to proceed will not keep many average black counselees.

Pauline is a 35 year old black woman who entered counseling to improve her confidence and self-esteem. In the counseling relationship Pauline's naturalistic attitudes sought expression. She has never established a pattern of regular appointments for which she is consistently on time. Frank discussions about men, sexuality, the counseling relationship, and a deep desire on her part for me to tell her "like it is" have characterized the sessions. Pauline's wearing of revealing clothes reflect less upon her "seductiveness" and more on her "style" as a sensual woman.

I have observed that the poetic style of call and response that are evident in black worship can also be found in counseling with blacks. This rhythmic pattern is so set that even when I do not speak, the counselee may continue the pattern. This brief verbatim with a 45 year old black male is indicative of this pattern.

C: Hi, P.J. How are you?

PJ: I'm just fine, Doc, how about yourself?

C: I'm doing O.K. (Pause)

PJ: Yes, Uh-huh, well I called last night because I wanted to remind you of something I wanted to talk about today. (Pause) Yes, that's right. I was hoping we would talk about that argument I had with my wife.

C: The one where you felt like hitting her?

PJ: Yes sir, yes sir. That's the one. Well, I was wondering what made me get so angry. (silence) Well, yea. It got me to thinking about the times my Pappa used to hit my Mama.

P.J. is looking for a response from me. When one does not come, he is not deterred. He keeps on anyway. P.J. is participating in an expressive rhythmic dialogue with me, the pattern of which is altered by my therapeutic pauses. In spite of the break in continuity, P.J. is able to hold on to the rhythm. Prosaic affirmations of interpretations that I make let me know when I have understood accurately the meaning of the experience being conveyed. Expressions such as "Yes, sir. . .I heard that. . .Tell it like it is. . .What you say" are indications that accurate empathy is at work.

P.J., as with many black men I have counseled, is also prone to walking out of the middle of a session. This usually occurs when there is an interpretation which is difficult for them to absorb. Most will return for the next session, but will inform me frankly of why it was necessary for them to leave. Under stress it is often best to take a "walk" as a way of relieving the stress and to prepare one's self for engaging the interpretation at a later time.

117

The earlier critique of Carroll Wise for his narrow cultural vision was not intended to discard Wise's thought altogether as a valuable asset in counseling with blacks. Quite the contrary. Compared with the recent Western apologetics for liberation theologies and the efforts to find cross-cultural approaches to pastoral counseling, Wise's basic experiential approach enables the pastoral care practitioner to enter into that vital center of black "otherness" and release the power that is there.

For Wise, the health of the individual rests upon the capacity of the individual to affirm and be connected to his or her own experience. Conversely, the inability of personality to function positively, according to the laws of its own being, leads to illness in one form or another. When Wise speaks of "the laws of its own being," I believe we can view black expressiveness as part of the natural law of black personality. That is, black expressiveness is part of the black personality and any counseling with blacks must take this factor into account. Moreover, if the counseling process is going to foster health and wholeness, then there must be acceptance of black expressiveness.

Wise identifies religious symbols, constructed into a Weltanschuung, as the means through which the deeper meaning of human experience is conveyed. For Wise, religious symbols are both a means of expression as well as a respository for the realities that reside within the experience of the individual. Experience which is only experience has no meaning. However, when we can find the deeper meaning of experience through religious symbols, then we can participate "in the creative possibility of human personality." Long identifies the symbol of otherness as central to the black religious experience, and Pasteur and Toldson identify black expressiveness as the carrier (signifier) of this otherness symbol. Both the symbol of otherness and its carrier, black expressiveness, comprise the content of a black world view which has shaped a reality that blacks have relied upon to give their lives meaning and purpose.

Wise recognized the importance of focusing the counseling enterprise on the experience of the individual. Before focusing on intra-psychic dynamics, or providing insightful interpretations from the counselor's perspective, he demands that we first encounter the person in relationship; to understand who that person is in the conveying of their experience. With the black counselee the experiential approach is crucial; for it not only allows one to enter into the other reality of black experience, it also encourages the release of black expressiveness for empowerment, healing, and meaning-making.

Finally, Wise's emphasis on the counseling relationship is crucial for successful and effective counseling with blacks. The counseling relationship is the medium through which the black counselee receives the encouragement to claim his or her exerience in words, gestures, attitudes, and rhythms that represent the other reality in which blacks live.   The strengthening of the ego, which Wise views as essential in the counseling relationship, is particularly necessary in the care and counsel of blacks.   To live in two worlds, relating to two realities, is a difficult and sometimes dangerous experience.   In 1903, DuBois noted both the existance and the danger of a double consciousness in The Souls of Black Folk:

> The Negro is sort of a seventh son [or daughter], born with a veil, and gifted with second sight in this American world, a world which yields no true self-consciousness, but only lets one see oneself through the revelation of the other world.   It is a peculiar sensation, this double consciousness, this sense of always looking at one's self through the eyes of another, measuring one's soul by the type of a world that looks on in amused contempt and pity...two souls, two thoughts, two unreconciled strivings, two warring ideals in one dark body, whose dogged strength alone keeps it from being torn asunder. (DuBois, 1982, p.45)

It is the strength of the ego that enables persons to maintain a cohesive self.   The ego also enables persons to perceive reality correctly and to make appropriate judgments about what is perceived. The strengthening of the ego is vital in counseling with blacks in light of the need to live in two worlds and to maintain a sense of self-worth and self-determination in the face of the white world's efforts to reject, oppress, and judge the black world as "less than" itself.

When Carroll Wise wrote, he did not have the liberation struggle of black people at the forefront of his mind.   However, his basic experiential approach has much to offer to blacks in their particular contextual situation.   The affirmation of experience, the use of symbols for shaping reality, the strengthening of ego, and the encouragement of freedom in self-expression and self-determination are vlauable aspects of a pastoral counseling theory that blends well with the black experience of otherness and the psychology of black expressiveness.

NOTES

[1]See Long, (1986, pp.1-9) for a more detailed description of the role of signifiers.

[2]In none of his major works on pastoral care and counseling does Wise address the issue of counseling with ethnic minorities, even though he does address the specific topic of transference and countertransference, in the experience of female pastors in his last book. (Wise, 1983, pp.212-214)

[3]Wise assumes a benign environment that is open to experiencing the individual, aknowledges the presence of the organism, and will contribute to its health.   However, the experience of blacks with the larger societal environment is a completely other experience.   The environment in the larger society is hostile, ignores the presence of blacks, and inhibits self-determination.

[4]Identifying religion as the continual quest for the meaning of human experience, Long writes, "But even if one is to have a theology, it must arise from religion, something that is prior to theology." (Long, 1986, p.174)

CARE IN CONTEXT[1]

John C. Carr

Although I do not consider myself to be an "evangelical" in the sense that that label is used in North American ecclesiastical circles, I believe that the ministry of pastoral care (including pastoral counseling) is an "evangelical" ministry. Like LeRoy Aden, (1985, p.4) I would describe pastoral care as "proclamation taking the form of love and service."

It might seem rather strange to quote an article on Seward Hiltner in a collection of essays in honor of Carroll Wise. The fact that I am doing so reflects the struggle which I have had, as a Canadian Presbyterian, to integrate Carroll's strong clinical focus, with its implicit spirituality, with the explicit theological emphasis which was at the heart of my initial formation for ministry.

When I indicate my belief that pastoral care is an evangelical ministry, I am attempting to find a middle ground between two polarized theoretical positions with differing perspectives on how pastoring persons should be trained for their ministries of pastoral care. Moreover, and specifically as a Presbyterian, I am concerned to develop a theology of pastoral care which will be continuous with Presbyterian and Reformed traditions about the offices of Teaching and Ruling Elders and the priesthood of all the members of the People of God.

I should say, also, that I am using the word "evangelical" in a way that is congruent with D.T. Niles' definition of evangelism:

Evangelism is one beggar telling another beggar where to find food.

The Polarization Of The Field

At one end of the spectrum there is the position which has been typical of the teaching, writing, and practice of many specialist pastoral counselors and clinical pastoral educators, and of many of the parish pastors and church workers trained or otherwise influenced by them.

For many years, and the trend is gradually being reversed, clinical pastoral educators and institutional chaplains have tended to psychologize religion and almost to rule religious language and practice out of the exercise of chaplaincy except in chapel services. Pastoral care, in Clinical Pastoral Education, has tended to become indistinguishable from the care offered by other helping professionals in the hospital or prison setting.

Pastoral counselors have also tended to practice their ministry in ways which have rendered them indistinguishable from other counselors in

121

the community. Religious language and practice have been noticeably absent in their work, and they have been more comfortable with the language of psychiatry or psychology than with the language of the Bible, of theology, or of the Church. That, too, is changing.

However, CPE and pastoral counseling have participated in the creation of a pattern of isolating pastoral care from the mainstream of the Christian Church's ministry and in the minimization of the use of religious and theological resources in pastoral care. The role of the institutional church in that isolation has been its failure to move into the new territory along with those of its ministers and people who have a vision and vocation for these new forms of ministry.

The other position over against which I am staking a claim for an evangelical pastoral care is one which sees itself as already having occupied the "evangelical" territory. I am referring to the fundamentalistic, conservative, and neopentecostal writers and practitioners in the field of pastoral care.

Some of these place their emphasis on the application of the appropriate text to the particular problem. Others emphasize the importance of prayer and the laying on of hands, sometimes, with anointing, for the healing of emotional or relational problems, or to prevent their emergence. Still others focus on the strengthening of the will through moral suasion, exhorting people who have a problem to repent and set their mind on wholesome goals and objectives, and to use their wills to achieve the same through the practice of holiness.

Pastoring persons who hold to the first position may, tragically, miss the opportunity to apply the healing resources of Christian faith and practice to the human problem. More than that, if the specificity of Christian faith and practice is missing in the pastoral care provided, the sufferer may lose the opportunity to grow in faith as a result of the struggle. There may be no connecting of the personal story of pain and suffering with the journey of faith and with God's care and concern.

It is important that the struggling, hurting one come to know that a pastoring person cares. Several of the Garrett-Northwestern M.A. and Ph.D. dissertations have demonstrated that that kind of ministry of caring and empathic listening significantly can enhance the healing process in the hospital setting. (See John Florell's and Richard Augspurger's essays in this book.) It is also important that the struggling, hurting one come to know directly from the pastoring person the Source of the pastor's care and concern.

It is not just that the pastoring person needs to have a specific identity so as to differentiate oneself from other caring persons. It is not just that pastoral care is apt to get lost in the shuffle if it is not somehow differentiated from other therapies. Rather, the psychological reductionism of some pastoral care may, at least potentially, be contributing to the loss both of health and faith for the persons to whom the pastoral person is ministering.

Pastoring persons who hold to the second position may miss the personhood of those who are experiencing the problem. They tend to be overly concerned with the biblical orthodoxy of the act of healing, or too strongly invested in the potential result of the healing act, to be really concerned with the person or relationship needing healing. Overemphasis at this end of the spectrum is akin to the medical "joke" that the operation was a success even though the patient died on the table. Also, this approach to pastoral care makes the assumption that people have illnesses or problems which must be removed, rather than seeing those illnesses or problems as signs of who the person or relationship is and is in process of becoming.

A brief case history may clarify what I am saying here. This is not an actual case, although it reflects my own pastoral experience and that of some of my colleagues.

George and Mary had terrific arguments almost from the beginning of their marriage. Their making up, after an argument, was just as passionate as their argument. Told about their arguments by a neighbor, a well meaning pastoral person visited with them, reading some passages from the Bible which enjoined meekness and forbearance, even counseling Mary to be subject to her husband rather than giving him a hard time when he would do something which annoyed her. More than that he prayed with them and invoked the healing power of God's Holy Spirit for their marriage. The violent arguments ceased. But something else happened. Mary became depressed. George no longer experienced much joy in the relationship. Their sexual activity came to an end. And George died of a massive cardiac arrest in his early 50s.

Did healing really take place as a result of the pastoral intervention? Of course not. The pastoral person was insensitive to the function of the violent arguments in this marriage. It was one of the ways, certainly a maladaptive way but nevertheless their peculiar way, of keeping passion alive in their marriage. It was a sign of their fear of deeply felt positive passion, but at least it was better than no passion at all. That was what needed to be addressed by the pastoral person. Or, rather, it was George and Mary, in their fear, who needed to be addressed. One of the ways in which I enter such a system is to say something like: "You two sure have a strange way of making love."

The evangelical approach which I am positing falls between the two positions of psychological and theological reductionism. It affirms three basic components in pastoral care.[2]

    1. It is **theologically** responsible.

2. It is **psychologically** responsible.[3]
3. It is a **ministry of the Church**.

Whether it is carried out in the parish, in a hospital, in a prison, in a pastoral counseling center, or in any other context, it seems to me that these are essential elements if pastoral care is to be an evangelical ministry.

Theological responsibility involves exploration of personal and denominational theological roots and resources for and with the other to whom one is ministering. It involves constant reflection on one's own personal and denominational theological roots and resources. That process involves pastoral persons, and those to whom they minister in mutual growth:

1. in theological and biblical knowledge,
2. in understanding the meaning of faith,
3. in depth of spiritual experience, and
4. in capacity to articulate that understanding and to live at deep levels.

Psychological responsibility involves openness to learning about human functioning from the social sciences, medicine, and the other disciplines concerned with the wellbeing of persons and relationships. It involves willingness to learn about people from people, to listen, to be present, to be open, to be aware, to be enough in touch with what is going on in oneself that one does not confuse it with what is happening in the other's life. It involves willingness to frame hypotheses about the meaning of events in people's lives and relationships and to test those hypotheses in the practice of ministry. It involves openness to affirming that which is confirmed and discarding that which is not supported, so that emerging truth may be available for healing and growth and for theological understanding and exploration.

Finally, pastoral care needs to be **ministry of the church**. Whether it is carried out in the traditional context of the parish, or in other settings such as those in which pastoral counselors and chaplains work, it needs the recognition and authorization of the Body of Christ. That recognition may be accorded denominationally or ecumenically. Nevertheless, it is essential to the practice of one who defines her or himself as a pastoring person. That person may be ordained to the ministry of Word and Sacrament, or to the eldership, or designated as a diaconal minister, or recognized as a lay person with special gifts and a vocation to this ministry.

I am, here, articulating a "high" view of the Church. In doing so, I am not intending to support the heresy that God's saving and healing activity are confined to the operations of the institutional Church. God does work outside the institutional Church or, to use Calvin's term, the Visible Church. However, I am articulating the ideal because

I believe that it is important for those called to new and creative ministries in the world and in the Church to seek endorsement of the Visible Church for those ministries as a way of testing their vocation. If we applied this principle more consistently, it seems to me, we would have fewer schisms as a result of the emergence of new movements and charismatic individuals in the Church. I am, of course, making the large assumption that the Church Visible will remain open to new possibilities and to trying new ways of being the Church, that the Church Visible will continue to live out the **reformatus reformandus** principle.

Emerging Epistemology For Pastoral Care

I am strongly attracted, in my attempt to clarify an epistemology for pastoral care, by the hermeneutical approach of Donald Capps. (1984, p.4) Capps focuses on the literary forms of the Bible, particularly the lament, the proverbs, and the parable. His thesis is that a given literary form makes possible certain kinds of divine revelations or disclosures and precludes others. The goal of pastoral care is the restructuring of the person's perceptions of self, world, and others, including God.

Capps rightly points us to the value of the lament form as it relates to pastoral care with grieving persons. The goal is to comfort, and the structure of the lament is admirably suited to that goal with its elements of address to God, complaint, confession of trust, petition, words of assurance, and vow to praise God (e.g., Psalms 13, 54, 102, 121). Psalm 13 is a particularly poignant example.

> How long, O Lord? Wilt thou forget me for ever?
> How long wilt thou hide they face from me?
> How long must I bear pain in my soul,
>   and have sorrow in my heart all the day?
> How long shall my enemy be exalted over me?
> Consider and answer me, O Lord my God;
>   lighten my eyes, lest I sleep the sleep of death;
>   lest my enemy say, "I have prevailed over him;"
>   lest my foes rejoice because I am shaken.
> But I have trusted in thy steadfast love;
>   my heart shall rejoice in they salvation.
> I will sing to the Lord,
>   because he has dealt bountifully with me. (RSV)

This biblical form can inform the grief counseling process, giving it shape and direction. Yet it is just as important with this form, as with the form of Elisabeth Kubler-Ross's description of the grieving process (denial, anger, depression, bargaining, acceptance), not to try to fit persons forcefully into the form. In both instances, the form may help the pastoring person and the sufferer to understand the process through which they are going.

Less valuably, I think, Capps points to the proverb form as a model for premarital counseling which he describes as an instance of moral guidance. Although moral guidance involves communicating the accumulated wisdom of the generations which have gone before, it errs grievously if it does only that. Moral guidance in general, and premarital counseling in particular, needs also to focus on helping the persons clarify the values by which they are choosing to live already, to the end that they may then choose whether they will continue to live by those values or will incorporate different values and follow new ideals.

I agree with Capps about the value of the parable form in marriage and family counseling. Parables, for the most part, deal with the broken, distorted, and otherwise troubled relationships of the children of God in the kingdom of God. They can be an effective mirror, for us, of the particular relational distortion in which we may be caught in our marriages, in our families, or in the church family. They can provide us with considerable energy for change in our way of being and in the structure of our relationships. Moreover, they help us contextualize the change process as an aspect of life in the kingdom of God.

There are many other forms, for example, confession and thanksgiving, which can give shape to pastoral care, if we have allowed both the form and the content to sink into our personhood through our own thinking and feeling of the text's Word to us. The Word then becomes available for our spontaneous response to persons because it lives in us.

Capps (1984) describes four basic principles for the role of biblical and theological knowledge in pastoral care. I agree with three of these, propose a modification of the third principle, and add a fifth. First, I summarize his principles.

1. **The Principle of Relevance.** It should be obvious that whatever use is made of the Bible or theology in pastoral care, that use should be relevant to the particular needs and circumstances of the person being helped. In my own practice, I often feel a text or a biblical story or a theological concept rising up within me. Although I trust my capacity to connect with others with a minimum of distortion on my side, I always check myself out when that happens by asking myself whether the biblical or theological material is coming into consciousness just for my own use, or whether it is emerging both for me and for the counselee(s). One can never be absolutely certain, but it is important to check it out as best one can, and then be open to the possibility that the biblical or theological material has nothing to say to the counselee, at least in that moment of time. That is, it may not be relevant at all, or it may just be relevant for the pastoring person.

2. **The Principle of Sensitivity.** The use of biblical and theological material in pastoral care should reflect sensitivity to the physical,

126

psychological, relational, and spiritual needs and limitations of the other. The material must not only fit the situation; it must fit the particular person or group of persons.

3. **The Principle of Consistency**. Whatever use is made in pastoral care of psychological and psychotherapeutic theories and techniques, that use should be consistent with the disclosive power of the Bible. Psychological and psychotherapeutic theories can assist the pastoring person toward the goals established on the basis of the biblical form. However, the Bible is given the central role in establishing the goals of pastoral care and the shaping of the therapeutic process. I believe, for the reasons cited below, that this principle needs some revision and a new name.

4. **The Principle of the Bible as Change Agent**. This principle says that whatever use is made of biblical and theological material in pastoral care, it should be informed by the pastoring person's awareness that biblical texts have the power to change attitudes. One sees life differently when one sees life from the perspective of God's real presence in the world. Capps refers to this perspective as having an "alien quality" which shakes us out of our usual approach to life's problems, challenging us to take a perspective on these problems which we have not yet considered taking. He points out that this emphasis on the disclosive power of the Bible indicates that, theologically speaking, the pastoring person is working with what Ricoeur (1980) calls "the idea of Revelation."

Capps also suggests that, even when the Bible is not introduced directly into the pastoral conversation, the four principles remain applicable. If the biblical form is only in the back of the pastoring person's mind, and no text reflective of that form is quoted or alluded to, the pastor still wants to be satisfied that the form **itself** is relevant to the situation, is sensitive to the limitations of the person being cared for or counselled, is an appropriate basis for goal-setting, and is a potential change agent. The principles apply even when the Bible informs the pastoring process in a non-verbalized but nevertheless intentional manner.

I find Capps deficient at the point of his apparently limiting God's revelatory power to the text of the Bible. He seems to be saying that there can be no experiencing of God's transformative power apart from the use of Scripture either as an element of the pastoring process or as determinative background in the mind of the pastoring person.

It seems to me that this is a subtle form of theological reductionism which needs to be treated with care just because the reductionism is so subtle. What is needed is more affirmation of the value of the psychological, social, and biological sciences, in and of themselves, as vehicles for God's saving and healing activity among us, and as instruments of God to inform and deepen our knowledge of God and of

127

the processes by which faith is strengthened and spiritual growth takes place.

Affirming Capps' principles 1 and 2, I present a revised third principle which I call the Principle of Correlation.

3. **The Principle of Correlation**. My revised third principle involves the clarification of the fit or non-fit of "science" and theology.

On the one hand, we have psychological, psychotherapeutic and systems intervention theories and techniques, and the knowledge which we have about human wholeness, illness, and the healing process, from the various sciences. On the other hand, we have that which we know about the human condition and about redemption and healing from our theological reflection on Scripture and the development of Christian doctrine.

Simply put, the dialogue between science and theology may yield benefits for theology in terms of opening the eyes of the (pastoral) theologian to biblical truth not previously understood and for science in terms of its pointing to hypotheses about the way it is in the world which science hitherto has missed.

In this view, truth is seen as unitary, and as something which can be apprehended by us creatures to a limited extent. Scripture is still accorded a unique place as a determinant of belief and practice, but it is acknowledged that our best attempts to understand and interpret Scripture are flawed. Science and the healing disciplines are seen as allies to the pastoring person in the task of pastoral care, and in pastoral theological reflection. Theology is seen as an ally of science in its responsibility to try to understand the created order, even when science denies the existence of the Creator.

Yet then, I add a new fifth principle, not forgetting Capps' intervening fourth principle of the Bible as Change Agent, that is as having unique revelatory power which is released by the activity of the Holy Spirit, often in ways which we do not understand.

5. **The Principle of Wonder**. I have spent 8 years in full-time parish ministry, 5 years in post-graduate studies with a strong "clinical" component and continuing part-time parish ministry, and 12 years in the specialized practice of pastoral counseling and training of others, during which time I have also been involved in ministry to congregations on an interim basis.

Many times, in the course of those 25 years of professional ministry, I have experienced the feeling of "wonder" as moments of healing have also become moments of deepening spiritual experience for me or for the other to whom I am present in ministry.

128

Sometimes the healing (emotional or relational) was a response to a specific "religious" stimulus introduced by the other or by me. Sometimes it was a response to an awareness or a technique derived from one of the "scientific" healing disciplines. Occasionally, the source of the healing or awareness might be classified as antithetical to the biblical and theological traditions of Christianity, for example, explosive anger or involvement in a non-marital sexual relationship or in drugs or in criminal activity. I am not advocating any of these as a pastoral counseling technique. However, I know that, where sin abounds, there grace may abound also. (See, e.g. Romans 5:20 - 6:1 ff.)

Pastoral care is "evangelical" when we are open to the "wonder" of God's healing presence in the process, however that happens. So often, treasure comes in earthen vessels. (II Corinthians 4:7) The Gospel may even become real in the midst of an apparently hostile environment. Yet we should not be surprised at that. After all, that is the kind of environment into which the Good News came 20 centuries ago.

A Case In Point: Care in Context

The theoretical principles described above are illustrated in the case story which follows. The story is about a fictitious couple named Robert and Janice, but it embodies details and themes from the lives of several of the families to whom my colleagues and I have ministered during the past few years.

Robert and Janice are Presbyterians, baptized as infants, confirmed in their teens, married by Janice's minister father in their early 20s, themselves the parents of baptized, church-school-attending children aged 12 and 10. Robert teaches Church School and Janice is an Elder. The whole family is in Church every Sunday, the kind of family one might expect to see pictured on the worship bulletin for Christian Family Sunday, with happy, shining faces and voices uplifted in song.

Then, something happened. For several weeks in a row, Janice was missing from her customary pew on Sunday, and did not attend the regular monthly meeting of the Elders. Robert and the children began arriving at the last minute on Sunday, and dashed out right after the Benediction. One of the Elders drew this change of pattern to the attention of the Pastor, and she scheduled a late-evening visit with the couple as soon as possible. In the visit, the pastor learned that Janice had been having an affair with a neighbor, also a member of the church, and had stopped coming to church after Robert found out. Their home had been filled with recrimination, guilt, anger, and tears. Both had threatened to leave. In one heated exchange, Robert had slapped Janice across the face. They were at their wits' end to know what to do next, and had not known where to turn for help. Needless to say, the children, even though they did not know the details, were markedly upset, and that upset was showing up in their schoolwork and in other distressing behaviors.

The pastor listened and encouraged them to share their feelings. She tried to facilitate a decision about their relationship. But she also worked on facilitating a commitment to professional counseling at a pastoral counseling centre.[4]

The pastor might have chosen another course of action. She might have sided with Robert, taken the matter before the Elders, and recommended that Janice be suspended from the office of Elder and from Church privileges. She might have laid a lot of texts on Janice as a reproof of her behavior and as a call to a return to fidelity in marriage, with repentance. In a similar manner, the Pastor might have followed such a plan of action with the other "guilty party."

However, the pastor was guided in her response both by her training in a unit of Clinical Pastoral Education and by her theological reflection. She had thought a great deal about the ways in which "sin" impacts on human beings in general and marriages in particular. One of the Scripture texts which was important for that reflection was a passage in Jeremiah (31:29) and Ezekiel (18:2):

The fathers [or mothers] have eaten sour grapes and the children's teeth are set on edge. (RSV)

The verse suggests that Janice's affair was a product of the brokenness in her personality formation in her family of origin. Some system theorists would also understand that the affair was a sign of the brokenness or deadness in the marriage relationship, and a cry for help and healing. Neither Jesus nor the Old Testament prophets would have ignored the moral or ethical dimensions of the situation, and neither can the parish pastor, the pastoral counselor who worked with the couple, or the pastoral theologian seeking truth in the pastoral context. We will review more about that later.

The pastoral counselor who worked with Robert and Janice encouraged them to face themselves and each other with honesty. He helped them to clarify their unmet needs and wants, especially, their unexpressed feelings which had accumulated over the years, building a rock-hard emotional barrier preventing the deepening of their relationship. Robert eventually was able to own and acknowledge his insensitivity to Janice's feelings, wants, and needs, and Janice accepted responsibility for not having worked as hard as she might have to make those feelings, wants, and needs known.

They came to understand the affair as a symptom of the loss of integrity in their relationship with each other. They asked forgiveness from each other and from God for what they had done to themselves and to each other, and committed themselves to living out their relationship at deeper levels. They realized that, in what had happened, God was calling them to deeper levels of relationship. God's

Word, the Gospel revealed in the affair, involved a summons to deeper levels of integrity and intimacy in their relationship.

Throughout the counseling, the parish pastor stayed in touch with the couple and with the pastoral counselor. With their permission, she attended the Staff Case Consultation at which the pastoral counselor presented his assessment of Robert and Janice. That assessment included a summary of the data gathered in a couple of sessions of work with the couple, and of the psychological and relationship instruments which they had completed in an endeavour to focus the issues needing attention. The parish pastor provided useful information for the formulation of a therapeutic plan, and the pastor's participation in the Case Conference helped her to clarify ways in which she and the congregation could further facilitate the healing process.

The process was not a smooth one. After one particularly stormy session, the couple threatened not to come back. It seemed to them that things were getting worse instead of better. Because she knew what the pastoral counselor was trying to do in his work with Robert and Janice, the parish pastor was able to encourage them to return to counseling. She told the other Elders that Robert and Janice were having a rough time in their marriage and that they both needed to be relieved of their responsibilities in the congregation for a while. There were immediate offers to fill in for them. The Elders went out of their way to express warmth and encouragement to the couple and their children. Their individual lives and their relationship were lifted up before God in prayer during the devotional period of the monthly meeting of the Elders and in their private devotions.

The counseling with the couple involved a focus on what had been happening in their relationship with each other and an exploration of their individual life stories, with connections drawn between the one and the other. During that part of the process, the pastoral counselor drew their attention to the Jeremiah-Ezekiel passage about "sour grapes."

They almost had to be forced to talk about some of the matters they were afraid to share with each other. Sometimes the counselor had to speak the words for them. They explored the Ephesians 4-6 and Colossians 3 passages about marriage, integrity, and anger. They were encouraged to pray with and for each other and, hardest of all, for the other marriage which had been "pulled into" theirs.

As might be expected, it was extremely difficult for Robert to express any care or concern for "the other man," except in terms of hoping that he would be able to get his marriage back together so that there would be no threat to Robert's marriage. First, however, he had to pour out his anger in the direction of an empty chair with a pillow on it to represent Janice's former lover. And it was only after it became clear to him that the man was no longer a threat to his own marriage

131

that Robert really was able to pray for him.

The counselor and the parish pastor worked together to get the other couple into counseling, but that effort was unsuccessful until the breakthrough in Robert's ability to pray for the man. Almost "miraculously," at that point, the man came to the pastor, broke down in her study, asked for pastor's help in owning up to his wife about the affair, and eventually entered into marriage counseling.

As the counseling with Robert and Janice moved toward resolution and recommitment, the counselor asked them to bring the children in for an extended session during which the children's feelings about what had been happening in the home were explored.

That helped to revive the children's anxiety about what was going on, and they also contributed insights and awareness which facilitated further healing and growth for their parents. Some of what the children had to say was very painful for Robert and Janice to hear. Like their parents, the children discovered at a greater depth than they had experienced it before that they were part of a community, the Christian Church, which really cared about them.

The moral and ethical dimensions of situations like this cannot be ignored. Through the counseling process, sin was acknowledged on both sides, responsibility was taken, forgiveness was asked for and received, and reconciliation achieved. These things might have been accomplished through a "moralistic" approach, that is, through condemnation by the parish pastor of a specific act, the adultery, but the likelihood is that that would have been at the expense of the marriage.

The story illustrates how the Church can maintain a high sense of morality without becoming moralistic, and thus be more effective as an instrument of healing and reconciliation. That high sense of morality is grounded in the fact that God came to us "while we were yet sinners," and that God loves us without any other condition than that we love others as God has loved us.

Recall LeRoy Aden's statement quoted earlier about pastoral care being "proclamation taking the form of love and service." He also writes that

> only as we are addressed by the Word and are able to embody it in a living relationship does it 'move over the face of the waters' (Genesis 1:2) and recreate. In terms of pastoral care, this means that grace and forgiveness must be incarnated in acts of service in ways that are appropriate to the situation. In this sense it is a very human act, even though it is prompted by what God is and does for us and not at all by our inner goodness. (Aden, 1985, p.83)

In pastoral care, as in preaching, we are both faithful and effective when we are bearers of the Living and Loving Word who is Jesus Christ, in and of Himself the Gospel, the "Good News."

This case story was first used by the author as the core of a sermon to colleagues in ministry (Teaching and Ruling Elders) at the opening service of a Church Synod. One of the effects of the sermon was that an increasing number of ministers and elders began referring people to the pastoral counseling center of which he is Executive Director. Another was that a number of scenarios similar to that of the case story began to surface in the congregations of the Synod. Some of these resulted in the kind of resolution described above. Others ended in unresolved pain for the families and for their congregations.

Postscript

There is a story which Edward Schillebeeckx (1981) borrows from Martin Buber, in which the latter puts the following words in the mouth of a rabbi.

My grandfather was paralyzed. One day he was asked to tell something that happened with his teacher--the great Baalschem. Then he told how the saintly Baalschem used to leap about and dance while he was at his prayers. As he went on with the story, my grandfather stood up; he was so carried away that he had to show how the master had done it, and started to caper about and dance. From that moment on he was cured.

The Gospel will be real in pastoral care if the pastoral care provider has experienced its healing power in her or his own life. Pastors need training in the "art" and science of making the Gospel available for those to whom they minister. Yet prior to the acquisition of such talent and knowledge they need to experience its healing power for themselves.

NOTES

[1]This essay, in an earlier draft, was presented as a lecture to the faculty and students of Knox College, Toronto, on March 7, 1986.

[2]I am indebted, for the concretization of these principles, to my colleague and good friend, the Rev. Sidney J. DeWaal, Ph.D., pastor of Third Christian Reformed Church, Edmonton, Alberta, Canada. In their present form, they reflect my own elaboration and clarification, previously described in Practice of Ministry In Canada, Winter, 1986.

[3]I am using the word "psychological" in an inclusive sense. I intend it to include sociology, psychiatry, systems theory, and the various other disciplines which study the person individually and in relationship.

[4]Most of those who write about pastoral counseling in the parish encourage parish pastors to refer when counseling extends beyond 4 sessions. Parish pastors who get involved in doing long-term counseling will tend to neglect parish responsibilities, and will tend to get into

issues which, for the most part, they are poorly equipped to deal with and which may lead to relationship distortions which impact negatively on the pastor-parishioner convenant and on the life of the congregation. The author's doctoral research (Carr, 1980) indicated a negative correlation between the number of hours which a parish pastor spends in counseling and the traditional signs of success in a congregation's life such as membership growth, increasing contributions to missions, etc.

INNOCENCE AND EXPERIENCE:
TOWARDS A THEOLOGY OF PASTORAL CARE

Paul Hessert

In his book Pastoral Counseling, Carroll Wise (1951) contrasts "utilitarian religion" with "genuine insight." "Much of our utilitarian brand of religion seeks to help people by protecting them from the necessity of a profound change through giving easy answers to external situations." (148) It hides unhappiness. (2) Insight, on the other hand, is "the emotional apprehension of reality. . . Insight results in the conscious, intellectual formulation of what has already taken place on the deeper dynamic levels of personality." (119) The transition between "utilitarian religion" and "insight" is marked by pain. Consequently, the attempt to help people move from what is the essentially repressive nature of "utilitarian religion" to insight involves "the most poignant kind of suffering." (48)

In this identification of two religious "stances," Wise parallels the observation of the English poet William Blake. In his Songs of Innocence, Blake asked in all gentleness, "Little Lamb, who made thee?" However, in Songs of Experience, which turns from the lamb to the tiger, the question becomes "What dread hand dare frame they fearful symmetry?" The God disclosed by the fearful symmetry of the tiger belies (and underlies?) the benevolence disclosed by the lamb. These two "stances" of innocence and experience offer two channels of reflection helpful in formulating a theology of pastoral care. How is the pastoral counselor's understanding of his or her role in counseling shaped by innocence on the one hand and experience on the other?

We shall begin by examining the relation between innocence and "utilitarian religion."

Utilitarian Religion

"Utilitarian religion" is comparable to what Berger and Luckman referred to as the legitimatizing role of religion. "Utilitarian religion" supports the culture's structure--not only its habitual practices and institutional organization but its language, values, and sense of reality as well, and defines the individual. People tend to see what they are taught they will see, to hear what they are taught they will hear, and to respond to a "reality" they are taught they will confront. In these matters they are taught more by the cultural assumptions, presuppositions, and routines which constitute their human environment than by formal schooling. "Utilitarian religion" maintains the larger structure in which and through which we define and seek our own identity and well-being. It consolidates, affirms, and maintains "meaning."

Self-identity and well-being, on the one hand, and social "reality" in the widest sense, on the other hand, are interdependent. Our indiviuduality is socially defined. In turn, we understand society in terms of our individuality: society is an aggregate of individuals. (Other societies, however, may understand themselves as made up of tribes or clans, ethnic groups or "nations," or economic strata rather than individuals. Individuals, for them, may be merely representative members of one such group or another.)

It would be easy to think of utilitarian religion as merely religion in the service of the individual or social group with which the individual identifies--blessing and sanctifying self-interest. However, the role of utilitarian religion is not primarily to legitimatize the idiosyncrasies of what individuals understand their self-interest to be from moment to moment. Rather, utilitarian religion legitimatizes the structure of "reality"--the context of dependable identities, relations, norms, and values within which individual as well as group life is possible. As Ernest Becker put it, it staves off death. "Much of our utilitarian brand of religion," Wise writes, "seeks to help people by protecting them from the necessity of profound change through giving easy answers to external situations." (148) How easy the answers are rests on subjective judgment, but the form of answers, of one degree of sophistication or another, remains. A major function of utilitarian religion is to provide answers of both the understanding and The behavior sorts.

This legitimatizing of the cultural structure appropriates and redirects the language and concepts of historical religions. It also uses, virtually interchangeably, the self-consciously secular language generated by the public fear of sectarianism and by the sectarian embrace of secularism. In this way, organized, historical religions meld with utilitarian religion as perhaps a more particularized or focused form of the same thing-- the culture in essence or at its best.

Our Cultural Structure

The larger pattern of our own culture's structure defines reality by the ideal. Platonism long ago may have been abandoned as popular metaphysics, but its core assertion, "The ideal is the real," dominates the lives of people who have never heard of Plato, much less read any of his dialogues. What remains of Platonism is the pervading sense of the imperfection and deficiency of the present, at once joined to and separated from the ideal by time and guilt. "Reality" is a complex of should-be's set over against existing but disintegrating ought-not-to-be's. This means that the present may become a "throw-away" world whose significance is denied in preference for a perfect ideal world. In another sense, the present is taken for the ideal world by wishful thinking which both valiantly and pathetically overrides or disguises actuality in the guise of the ideal or absolutizes the present as the ideal.

136

To reject the present as non-ideal and deficient is to shoulder the culture's burden of time. The ideal waits for something to trigger its realization: "once adolescence is over," "when we are married," "when the children are all in school," "when I get my promotion." To idealize the present by taking it as the ideal is to take on the burden of guilt, for the intrusive signs of falling short of the ideal focus on individual failure in thought or effort. These burdens of time and guilt are endemic to the culture. What is not projected toward the future is laid on people as guilt for manifest imperfection. It is culturally essential that blame be fixed for imperfection, and if in our psychological sophistication we are shifting the fixing from individuals to historical circumstances, which we try to address in social and political action, we are still affirming the structure of the culture.

This means that many problems individuals have are structural in origin and nature. These structural problems of time and guilt qualify and reshape whatever more personal problems may be encountered. For example, at the same time a person may be burdened with the immediate pains of an unsatisfactory marriage, he or she is also burdened with the ideal marriage, set above any actual relationship. Feelings of dissatisfaction derived from the ideal must be dealt with along with the pain of actual betrayal or abuse. In this vein, Wise suggests that the pastor who counsels married couples "may need to discard many preconceived notions of what constitutes a happy marriage." (185)

Utilitarian religion compounds this built-in structural problem by making the culture's ideal "reality" God's creation and plan. It is characteristic of utilitarian religion that God and the culture's ordering of things cannot be separated. To question the structure is to offend God: to serve God is first of all to accept and embrace the structure. The cultural structure is thus inviolable and sacrosanct, not imposed by some arbitrary external enforcer but by the mind and imagination of each individual. Utilitarian religion does not rule out change but contains change within established patterns: there are rules for both revolutions and conversions.

Innocence

Innocence is living in fundamental harmony with this cultural structure. It is to accept life on the terms the culture provides. Innocence is not to be free from problems, but to identify problems and to solve them as the culture specifies. Such cultural credos as "Science will find an answer," "Our democratic political structure will meet the challenge," "If at first you don't succeed, try, try again," "God will give you what you want," "A larger appropriation will solve the problem," "Extended therapy is called for," characterize innocence. Innocence is to accept the ideal definition of reality even though this acceptance means at least inner suffering. Innocence is to live within the perimeters that utilitarian religion blesses.

The Boundaries Of Innocence

At times, however, an awareness not subservient to the cultural order breaks into life--awareness of limits to cultural "reality," questions about its adequacy and validity, doubts about the truth of utilitarian religion and its God.

This awareness may be merely that other people, or people at other times, see or have seen life and its setting and purpose quite differently than we characteristically do. Such awareness may be evoked by travel or the study of history. Learning another language, especially one outside the European family of languages, may bring it on. Even though getting inside another "reality" may be far from complete or even profound, it may be enough to disturb the ruts of habitual thought, action, and feeling. Yet even this awareness of other viable cultures or sub-cultures remains within the realm that utilitarian religion, now seen in broader terms, legitimatizes.

More provocative and insistent are the crises which challenge the culture's ability to contain and explain awareness of its limits. Job loss, health failure, drug and alcohol addiction, marriage crisis, retirement, economic collapse, natural disaster, war--these more seriously challenge the claimed sufficiency of a culture's "reality." Finally there is death, the fundamental negation of the individual and the ultimate challenge to cultural constructs providing life with meaning.

Utilitarian religion is the culture's ultimate resource in trying to repress this awareness of limits which it designates as negative experience. It offers assurance that encountered problems are not to be taken too seriously because "all things are in God's hands" and "God is there to help meet our needs and solve our problems." It approaches deep questions as though they were only rhetorical. Wise speaks of the "neurotic trait" of trying to eliminate problems from consciousness, not from reality. (34) Utilitarian religion commandeers historical religions for its own purpose of legitimization--which means that religion is understood generically as intended to alleviate crises, certainly not generate them. Because of the confusion between utilitarian religion and historical religions, cultural doubts extend to the doctrines of historical religions. Thus, the person wrestling with family problems may open discussion with a pastor with, "I can no longer believe in God."

By far the most threatening challenge to the whole enterprise of assurance is the historical Gospel of Christ crucified. To hear this Gospel is not to be released from the chafing awareness of limits but to have that awareness pushed beyond its limits. The Gospel of Christ crucified cuts off the possibility that some other culture or sub-culture might provide the solution to the problem which is generic to culture itself. The significance of Christ crucified lies beyond both the accidents of first-century history (Roman-Jewish relations, for example, or Judaism's interparty tensions, or even the personal dynamics of certain individuals) and the sustaining myth of the hero (within which utilitarian religion would keep it). Christ crucified highlights the fact that the cultural (that is, all cultures') hopes for salvation (read, meaning, significant relationships, actualized ideals of peace and justice) are seen destroyed. Not deferred--awaiting actualization by the magic abracadabra of time, or the potent alchemy of guilt--but cancelled.

In place of culture's sometime, but not quite yet is the Gospel's today, now; and in place of the culture's management/manipulation of guilt is the Gospel's offensive proclamation of forgiveness. The Gospel is not that a man dies under tragic circumstances which are nevertheless overcome by inspiration and willpower--affirming what we all believe-- but rather that Christ, the very agent of justice and deliverance is humiliatingly put to death. "Our own hope had been that he would be the one to set Israel free" (Lk 24:21, JB).

Hearing always has a context. The context within which the Gospel is heard is the void opened by loss. It is not the assured possessors who hear but the poor. All loss, from disappointment to death itself, is caught up in Christ crucified: the Messiah is dead! Here the escape route through some other culture is cut off. Salvation does not lie in Judaism as against the culture of imperial Rome, nor in the heady asceticism of Qumran as against the official temple cult, nor in the excitement and violence of Zealotism as against the prudent accommodaters. By extension, we may say it does not lie in the possibilities of various contemporary subcultures and political movements. The Gospel begins with the news of the dead messiah and until one hears this one can hear nothing further of the Gospel.

What lies byond crucifixion as resurrection is not within the safety and certainty of the cultural structure or within the divine support of utilitarian religion. Cultures may be built on or incorporate notions of immortality. (Wise writes, "On the whole ministers have tended to deny much of the pain of bereavement by putting a stress on the doctrine of immortality." [206]) However, cultures cannot comprehend--that is, take within their boundaries--resurrection. Resurrection does not rest on the resources of the culture but on the power of God who is not the deity of utilitarian religion. To help people hear this Gospel and act in its reality (not ideality!) is the core of the pastoral role.

Experience

In contrast to innocence, experience is life lived in profound awareness of these limits--not the limits of the actual in relation to the ideal, or the limits of the temporal in relation to the eternal (for "infinite" and "eternal" are categories of the cultural structure). Experience is awareness that life extends beyond its cultural definition precisely where that definition makes reference to infinity and eternity. Experience is awareness of life outside the province of reassurance and legitimization provided by the culture, outside the security of an order on which "practically everyone" agrees, especially the "authorities" and "experts."

Innocence may be expressed in certain doctrines of providence where everything is incorporated into a rational plan and purpose: "The accident happened to me so I would not leave home at just that time." "God took her because God needed her more in heaven that we did on earth." Experience, on the other hand, questions whether any plan, seen or yet to be discovered, can explain and justify life's events. Experience's questioning is not of some facet within the culture that seems out of place but which can be fitted in the structure. Experience questions the whole structure itself.

Faith and Unbelief/Unfaith

Experience may be the occasion (not the cause!) of faith. Faith is not a category of the culture (though the culture attaches the word to an inferior sort of knowledge--we "accept on faith" what we are not absolutely sure about but have sufficient reason to think and act as though it were certainly so). Faith is not the rehearsed beliefs of the culture, not the doctrinal form of utilitarian religion. Faith is to accept life as more uncertain than our worst fears imagine it and more beautiful than our most intense longing can suggest and both at just that point where our accepted consolations and legitimizations show themselves bankrupt. To experience faith is to ground life in the God beyond cultural credos.

Nevertheless, experience may be the occasion (not the cause!) of unbelief or unfaith. Unbelief is opting for security rather than trust, or embracing despair as refuge from uncertainty. In experience, a person confronts the "choice" between faith and unfaith, but it is no simple, purely rational, voluntary act--a delimited conscious decision. The element of choice is immured in the complex of past history, conditioning, nameless memories, abiding presences, clear ideas, rumors of angels, and hints of eternity.

The role (not merely the comments or questions) of the pastoral counselor may be a crucial element in this complex in suggesting that beyond assurance, especially self-assurance, there is the province of faith. Wise speaks of the counseling relationship as the pastoral relationship intensified temporarily for dealing with a problem. (45) Yet it is just here that the counselor is on dangerous ground--above all because the counselor is not in control of the situation, recognizing that to gain control is to rule out faith by letting the situation slip back into innocence. The success of counseling within the area of innocence may be its failure in the area of faith. The danger is to both client and counselor. Many counselors find their professional practice pushing them into experience, whatever it may be doing for the clients. The accompanying anxiety may lead the counselors to seek their own security by successfully guiding clients within the safe channels of innocence.

Wise speaks of "the neurotic need for helping people" (199) referring to a person's attempt to deal with--or obscure--one's own inner conflict. But even wholesome helping--that is, in culturally approved ways and with culturally approved motivation--maintains the dynamics of innocence. One might object, in this same vein, that the transition from experience to faith is a matter of proselytizing. However, proselytizing and "conversion" are all too often merely options which innocence offers. The transition is rather a matter of depth and veracity and pain.

Pastoral counselors confused about their role may accept their social definition as agents of the culture responsible for restoring or maintaining its structure. Then, pastoral care comes to mean individualizing cultural resources for particular cases. It entails restoring the individual's capacity to cope--that is, to live and act within the cultural structure. It returns the individual to the culture from which "negative experience" threatened to alienate him or her. The confused pastoral counselor may attempt the theological venture of making <u>Christ</u> <u>crucified</u> safe by setting it within a divine <u>providential</u> plan along lines suggested by cultural wisdom. Christ's death is seen as reinforcing the patterns of justice of the human community (someone must die!). "Utilitarian religion" focuses on world-maintenance. Many pastors, teachers, and laity understand this to be their primary religious concern.

Wise calls this difficult movement from experience to faith "insight." "Faith is insight." (156) Insight stands over against the resources of utilitarian religion. It is not an intellectual formulation of a new world-view (insight is not to be confused with explanation) (155), but a unique integration of feeling with understanding. To reach insight is to have passed beyond the need to cover and disguise life in order to put up with it.

We might indeed define insight as the emotional apprehension of reality, both internal and external, with sufficient clarity and intensity that a person becomes aware of [one's] growth and achieves freedom to make further changes within [oneself] and in [one's] relationships with other persons. Insight results in the conscious, intellectual formulation of what has already taken place on the deeper dynamic levels of personality. In the counseling process, many rationalizations are brought up, looked at and given up, as the feelings behind them are worked through. (119)

Theologically--to use the expression of Philip Watson, one of Carroll

141

Wise's colleagues--insight is to "let God be God."

In this struggle for insight, and not merely helping people deal with their problems, pastoral counseling is no mere adjunct to the parish enterprise but its focus. It is no haven from the hard theological work of the pastor but makes that theological task all the more necessary. Unless pastors understand the difference between the Gospel of Christ crucified and raised and the multiple verions of "believe and prosper" or "believe and be reassured," which utilitarian religion affords, their leadership in relation to the Gospel can only be fortuitous. Their guidance is the chimeral resource of a chance misunderstanding which accidently may contribute to some client's insight.

Christ crucified, however, resists the intellectual formulation to which Wise refers. (119) If the vital issues are not resolved with intellectual answers, (1) and if there may be a divergence between a person's genuine religious attitudes and one's consciously accepted intellectual theological formulations, (10) then the affirmations of "Christ crucified" must be made in some way other than merely doctrinal formulation. This "other way" must nevertheless embody the full profundity of the emotional apprehension of reality. Wise writes, "The qualities that belong to emotional maturity and the qualities which are exemplified in Christ are very close, if not identical." (43) Yet if they are to be identical, if the image of emotional maturity is to be drawn from Christ and not from the prevailing myth to which the culture limits us (the gentle teacher, the revolutionary, the ecstatic healer, to cite a few examples), then the source of that image must be the Gospel itself, always beyond its cultural appropriation.

If this principle is to be received by an "emotional apprehension," then the sacraments of baptism and eucharist are as central to pastoral care as to the other foci of evangelical concern--worship, education, social action, and the like. The sacraments embody and celebrate that core-- the reality of Christ given, crucified, and raised. In this remembering and reenacting the individual and the community are inseparably joined to each other and to Christ at the very fountainhead of insight and faith.

NOTE

Bracketed numbers in the text of this essay refer to pages of Carroll A. Wise's (1951) book.

PART III

CLINICAL CONCERNS

FROM EXPERIENCE TO DIALOGUE TO INTERPATHY

From his Weslyean roots--that is, "first-hand religion" and "the highest in intellectual and emotional standards"--Carroll Wise encouraged others "to explore the ways theology and psychology become friends or foes." We can do this by developing "a coherent system of thought about both disciplines." Within this frame of making "psychological and theological presuppositions both explicit and coherent," Leila M. Foster explores the relationship between the two disciplines via specific clinical situations. After respecting **and** rejecting oppositional and separatist positions, she espouses an interactive relationship between them. More pointedly, they are "different ways of looking at the same experience," even as science uses "phenomenology and measurement" and theology uses "meaning and commitment."

With a glimpse of antagonistic theories and theorists, Foster speculates on a possible--and surprising--affinity between Barthian theology and a behaviorist psychology. More constructively, she sketchs Tillich's critically appreciative relationship with psychoanalysts and deChardin's similarity to Horney, Rogers, and May. Her essay on "the separate but interactive roles of theology and psychology" furthers the pattern which Wise exemplified.

Carl W. Christensen takes issues of clinical concern from the speculative level of Foster to the personal dialogue and professional collaboration Wise and he developed as a pastoral counselor and a psychiatrist. His autobiographical and biographical recollections describe the sharing of corned beef sandwiches, photography, and what mattered to them philosophically. Carl traces their mutual enrichment via concern with "the clinical aspects of religion rather than . . . theological speculations." Thus, "a belief in God," the understanding of "love," and even "the sacraments" could be used by persons in the service of their psychopathology. As the development of ego psychology challenged the assumptions of Carroll and Carl, both practitioners modified their concern from an emphasis on assessing pathology to a focusing on optimizing a person's potential.

Significantly, Carl traces how excellence in serving and training became institutionalized. However, the roots of that blossoming are found quite clearly in the "compatibility" of two professionals who spent more than three decades collaborating. That they could do so--and did-- came, according to Christensen, from their "sense of ego identity." Each was secure and clear about who he was as a person and as a professional. "The central core of our collaboration," Christensen concludes, "was the fact that we were able to achieve a balance between the religious and the psychological." They valued each other and each other's insights.

Beyond that personal collaboration, Richard G. Bruehl analyzes Carroll's participation in the formation of the American Association of Pastoral Counselors. This was, according to him, "the professional developmental theme in [Carroll's] life." Wise integrated psychological insights into pastoral work with missionary zeal, energy generated by his fight "for credibility against opposition from many quarters." Within the zeitgeist of social gospel activism, Wise stressed a holistic understanding of the individual, that is, "a transformation in the total self experience."

In tracing Wise's professional pilgrimage, Bruehl informs us of the conviction--the hermeneutical frame--which so many in pastoral counseling and psychotherapy learned from, or shared with, Wise. That conviction was an understanding of the dynamic "needs and conflicts of the hurting 'well'." Carroll saw the need for a specialized ministry apart from institutions for the mentally and the physically ill. Consequently, he worked for a professional organization other than the Association of Clinical Pastoral Education to accredit the specialized ministry of counseling. Thus, Dick sees Carroll's final book on Pastoral Psychotherapy (1983) as a declaration--and witness--that "pastoral psychotherapy had begun to come of age."

In reporting the conflict between Seward Hiltner and Wise concerning the desirability of professionalizing pastoral counseling, Bruehl lets Carroll voice his own convictions about the speciality: namely, that one's pastoral identity arises from "an inner experience from which all authority and personal gifts derive." Carroll's insight into "the nature and meaning of the healing process" found its outward and visible sign in the forming, shaping, and nurturing of AAPC as "ministry."

Allen R. Gilmore takes us from the larger professional arena back into "The Wise Model" of how pastoral counseling centers actually function, or ought to function. He draws upon his own training with Carroll in "the interdisciplinary colleagueship" model, of which Christensen provides a more personal description. From that "ambience," basic characteristics of contemporary pastoral counseling centers derive: a mission of healing to the widest possible community and of reminding the church that "true worship reaches . . . into the brokenness of human beings;" a colleagueship of "respect" and mutuality among the various professionals; the discipline of professionalism, which blends insight from one's own therapy with theory, including a continuing desire to learn through one's career, and in a context of education and training; a living oral tradition, stretching "back to biblical times," which understands itself as "being in the church, but not of the church;" and, finally, a sense of awe and compassion, exemplified by Wise's late life interest in photographing infants and young children.

John E. Hinkle, Jr. takes up a thematic emphasis which was more present in Wise's relationships than in his developed thought. That emphasis is understanding "living human experience across cultures." Carroll lived that cross cultural appreciation, as exemplified in a reminiscence by a black woman student, by communicating "through cultural symbols to the point of transcending cultural symbols." John speculates that "Carroll was pointing to the transcendent by means of the transpersonal and transcultural" approach to relationships, which was one of empathic participation rather than analytic observation.

Cross cultural dialogue requires an empathic "passing over" from one's own culture into that of another's culture and then reflectively "coming back" to one's own culture with new understanding. Wise shared the monocultural limitation of his time, but as "an enlightened monoculturalist." In other words, according to Hinkle, although the transcending involved ego boundaries, the approach opened the way for a transcending of culture bias as well. Because Carroll was not privileged to encounter "another" culture, he remained somewhat encapsulated in the Western, self reliant, individualistic view of optimum personhood.

Hinkle helps us recognize our own cultural bias. He describes how a Balinese's "individualizing transformation of [his or her role in the drama of life] into [one of] personhood would amount to a psychotic episode" from their point of view. It is "the role and the drama that are the 'real' thing, not the self." Pathology for them constitutes normalcy for us, and normalcy for us constitutes pathology for them. As a result, John moves beyond a critique of Wise's monocultural enlightenment to a constructive sketch of our developing "multicultural perspectives." In essence, the method enlarges "empathy" into "interpathy," a "feeling with" and a "thinking with" another's world view as though it were one's own. Ethnographic questions carry us beyond individual, and even systemic, questions to "genuine dialogue . . . . across cultural boundaries.

148

THEOLOGY AND PSYCHOLOGY: FRIENDS OR FOES?

Leila M. Foster

Carroll Wise was a teacher, scholar, and theologian in the Methodist tradition of a first-hand religion, Scriptural Christianity, and a standard of perfection. From his Wesleyan roots, his emphasis on the importance of experience and his role as a founder of clinical pastoral education are understandable. His writings reflect his appreciation of the significance of Biblical insights for our lives today. His students can attest to his encouragement in seeking the highest intellectual and emotional standards.

Also out of that Methodist tradition, he extended his hand of fellowship to students and colleagues of other theological and psychological persuasions. Study in his program at Garrett Theological Seminary was a rich opportunity for exposure to different viewpoints and schools of thought. He encouraged his students to explore new ideas and to understand the new experiences that awaited them in the parish and in the hospital as they began their ministries. It was not enough for students to have great feelings. Analysis of what their experience meant in theological and psychological terms was essential so that they could communicate it to others.

It was the destiny of Carroll Wise to live and work at a time when an upstart science of psychology came on the scene to challenge the reign of theology. It is not surprising that a teacher of pastoral psychology and counseling in a seminary should encounter conflict and misunderstanding. Yet he did not choose the simplistic solution of siding with psychology or theology over against the other. He encouraged his students to explore the ways theology and psychology become friends or foes, and to adopt for themselves a coherent system of thought about both disciplines.

Too many students and practitioners in the helping professions lack such a coherent system of thought covering both psychology and theology. Too many ministers still look on the scientific study of human beings and the application of scientific findings regarding human behavior as irrelevant to their work--though implicit in their sermons, their dealings with others, and their self-understanding is an underlying and unrecognized psychological theory. Too many mental health professionals disclaim theological persuppositions in their work--though with the current study of the role of values in the therapy process and in scientific research it may be difficult increasingly to claim a strictly "scientific" basis for their opinions without recognition of the underlying assumptions on which their science is based. Indeed, recent attention to the concept of "paradigm change" in science shows how often statements made in the name of science have underlying principles that go undisclosed for long periods of time (Kuhn, 1970).

149

Of all the helping professionals, the pastoral therapist, who claims expertise in both psychology and theology, should be most aware of the relationships of the two disciplines. Carroll Wise, as practitioner, teacher, and writer did much to shape the profession of pastoral therapy and to establish the need to make psychological and theological presuppositions both explicit and coherent.

What is the Relationship Between the Two Disciplines?

There are many answers to this question--not just one. Freud tells us that science is the only meaningful description of reality, and that religion is an illusion. Vitz (1977) has described the political and economic benefits to psychology in terms of government supported research if psychology can claim for science territory formerly held by religion.

Dietrich Bonhoeffer (1953), whose father was a psychiatrist, can write in his letters from prison that "psychotherapists practice religious blackmail." (p.212) Bonhoeffer claimed that psychotherapists tell a happy humankind that they are really miserable, but can not face the reality of their misery. Then, when a person is driven to despair through this teaching, psychotherapy is offered as the salvation.

Between these two value judgments regarding the worth of psychology and theology lies a middle ground occupied by persons who acknowledge that both disciplines are useful. How then are the two disciplines related? There are at least three alternatives:

1. Psychology and theology describe different processes.
2. Psychology and theology not only describe different processes but also some of the same processes.
3. Psychology and theology describe the same processes.

Persons who opt for the third alternative have two further alternatives:

a. Psychological and theological descriptions mean the same thing.
b. Psychological and theological descriptions represent different "languages," which cannot be equated in such a simple manner.

Let us see how the choices for these alternatives might work out in specific situations. Let us suppose that two young people feel troubled about their sense of identity. One seeks answers through the church and the means of grace it recommends--worship, prayer, service to others. The other enters psychotherapy with a psychologist. Let us further assume that both young people deal with their identity problems that caused them to begin their search for self understanding, and they both achieve a healthy personality and the same understanding of themselves in relationship to God. Thus, by definition, we have held constant the reality that is being described. Yet the minister and the psychologist may use quite different words or symbols to describe that reality. Is healing the same as salvation? Is acceptance like grace? Is insight related to revelation?

For persons who adopt the first alternative (psychology and theology describe different processes), the fact that our two young people gained a better understanding of God at the same time their personalities improved may be purely coincidental. Outler (1954) has argued for a clear division of labor between the psychotherapist and the minister, though he does see room for a "synthesis of goals" in the two fields of endeavor. Pope Pius XI (1929) drew a sharp distinction between the natural and the supernatural processes in the encyclical on Christian education.

But what is worse is the claim, not only vain but false, irreverent and dangerous, to submit to research, experiment and conclusions of a purely natural and profane order, those matters of education which belong to the supernatural order; as for example questions of priestly or religious vocation, and in general the secret workings of grace which indeed elevate the natural powers, but are infinitely superior to them, and may nowise be subjected to physical laws, for "the Spirit breatheth where He will. (pp.55-56)

It is interesting to note that Roman Catholic scientists have been able to interpret this statement as eliminating from their consideration the supernatural, but have proceeded to study all human processes in a way that is closer to the third alternative, though the Pope's encyclical seems to reflect the position of the first.

The second alternative is that the languages of the two disciplines describe not only different processes but also some of the same. Those holding this view might argue that prayer is a process that only theology can describe, and that free association in psychotherapy is a process that only psychology can explain, but that church attendance is something about which both theology and psychology could contribute knowledge. Prayer would be outside the province of psychology because it involves God. Free association in psychotherapy, which involves only human beings, is not the concern of theology. Church attendance might be considered within the province of both, for while it is a human activity, it is related to the human being's contact with God.

Persons adopting this second alternative would find useful the definition by Strunk (1959) of psychology of religion as "that branch of general psychology which attempts to understand, control, and predict human behavior--both propriate and peripheral--which is perceived as being religious by the individual, and which is susceptible to one or more of the methods of psychological science." (p.110) Implicit in this definition is the assumption that not all human behavior will be perceived as being religious or will be susceptible to psychological methods, but that some behavior will meet these qualifications. Meadow and Kahoe (1984)

151

also describe a division of labor between the disciplines with some middle ground.

Those who would use the symbols of theology and psychology to describe the same processes avoid the problem of drawing boundaries among the various disciplines to carve up the territory of human activity. The boundaries attempted under the first two alternatives do not seem realistic. They appear to engender border skirmishes or even all-out war between the disciplines and lead to unsatisfying and unrelated descriptions of pieces of human experience. Why should the phenomenon of prayer be off limits to study by psychologists? Why should theologians be stopped from saying something about the changes achieved in psychotherapy? The third alternative avoids this partitioning of human activity.

Within the third alternative, at least two options are available. It is possible to maintain that the truths of psychology and theology are both of value and are both the same. For example, Bowers (1963), a psychiatrist with a significant practice among the clergy, maintains that the psychological truth in a patient who has undergone a successful analysis and the theological truth found in the best teachings of the patient's religion "will coincide when both are translated into a common language." (p.30) Berger (1979), while criticizing such a "reductive possibility," also notes its popularity:

A different language is provided by psychology. What the religious tradition "is really all about" here is . . . mental health or wholeness of the individual . . . And, of course, there are as many subvarieties of this as there are different forms of modern psychology and psychotherapy. As in all these translations, the procedure can be very sophisticated or very crude intellectually. (p.115)

The second option in the third alternative would not provide for the translation of psychological and theological truths into a common language, but would recognize the two kinds of truths as two "languages" describing the same reality. Hordern (1964) gives the example of a scientific explanation of the mechanical causation involved in a game of billiards and a description of the game in terms of the strategy of the players. The language of the force necessary to move a ball and the decisions about which ball to hit next both derive from an analysis of the same game. However, the two descriptions of the same game cannot be translated into a common language, yet the two descriptions are both true. Hordern maintains that "theology and science are two different language games answering different questions and fulfilling different functions in life." (p.153) This position appears to be in harmony with the theories of theologians like Barth, Niehuhr, Tillich, and Teilhard de Chardin.

Still another variable is the effect these disciplines have on each other.

Hiltner (1962) notes the contrasting views of Barth, Niebuhr, and Tillich.

> Positions like Karl Barth's regard any wisdom that may come from the cultural disciplines as purely preliminary. In contrast, positions like Reinhold Niebuhr's believe such knowledge is important and worthy of systematic study; yet the findings are felt to be related to theology only externally. Paul Tillich goes further, holding not only that theology must take psychology seriously but also that no relevant modern theology can deny the contributions that psychology has made to it. In this sense, psychology does affect theologizing internally as well as externally. (p.251)

Tillich's position appears preferable in its recognition that one reality is being described and new truth in any field will affect the other fields. For example, when scientific discoveries led to improvements in golf balls and golf clubs, then golf courses and strategy had to change. The popularity of golf and the development of new courses have stimulated research regarding equipment. Another illustration of a change in thinking about the way to play a game can be found in football. When throwing the ball became more popular than drop kicking it, the shape of the ball, the rules, and the strategy changed. Psychology and theology also interact in as thorough a way as Tillich proposes.

Since the disciplines perform different functions, it is not surprising that they make use of different tools. Science uses phenomenology and measurement; theology, meaning and commitment. The theories of psychology and theology are descriptions of the same reality from different disciplines that make use of different tools of observation.

Individual Theories: Friends or Foes?

Although acceptance of psychology and theology as different ways of looking at the same experience avoids any necessary conflict between the two disciplines, individual theories within the two may enhance or clash with each other. Since schools of thought within a discipline are often in conflict with each other, care must be taken in developing a coherent psychological and theological approach not to mix theories with different presuppositions that clash.

Many examples can be given of antagonistic combinations. Barth surely would object to mixing his theology with any secular metaphysics or with a psychology such as the existential psychotherapy of Rollo May that has explicit philosophical assumptions. Niebuhr has expressed dissatisfaction with the psychology of Freud and Karen Horney and with ontology which contaminates the Christian understanding of humanity. Tillich would have trouble with behaviorist psychologies in which human behavior is the sole focus of attention, and he would have problems with a philosophy which ignored either being or existence. Teilhard de

Chardin rejected Freud's pessimistic view of the human fight against civilization. In attempting to describe the evolution of the universe, Teilhard apparently felt no need to limit himself to a philosophy of language analysis. The Hindu who seeks to lose identity an all pervasive All might find it difficult to reconcile the theories of Self Psychology or ego identity. The Moslem striving for submission to Allah might be troubled with the concepts of freedom and the fully-functioning person advanced by Carl Rogers.

In spite of this recital of antagonistic theories, more harmonious combinations are possible. Would Barth find any philosophy or psychology compatible with his doctrines? Since analytical philosophy rejects metaphysics but seeks to provide a tool through language study, this tool can be of use to theologians who are concerned about the danger of an ontological system that distorts the kerygma of revelation. As for psychology, Barth acknowledges that this discipline can serve a useful function if it is not tainted by metaphysics.

In view of this limit, we might speculate on how Barthian theology would mix with a behaviorist psychology. Both Barth and the behaviorists have been accused of treating human beings like robots-- though for Barth; humans are God's robot. Does Barth think of God activating a helpless toy and then turning that toy loose in the world with the wonderful power God has instilled in it? Do behaviorists think of humans acting in determined patterns so that all the world needs is a group of scientists to set the patterns for the next generation? While these caricatures may not do justice to the full concept of humans in these systems of thought, they may highlight a likeness which would provide a basis for coexistence. Perhaps, Barthian theology, analytical philosophy, and behaviorist psychology could live together peacefully so long as they ignore metaphysical presuppositions and keep away from arguments about their significance relative to each other.

While Niebuhr is as much concerned as is Barth to preserve the integrity of the picture of human beings that is given to us in the Christian faith, Niebuhr appears more receptive to insights from other disciplines. Perhaps he would be willing to accept any insights of philosophy which do not distort the Biblical message. He can praise Tillich for his exploration of the boundary between metaphysics and theology, though he points to the dangers one can meet in this territory. His selection of psychological insights is based on their value to the doctrine of human beings found in the Bible. Niebuhr believes that Erik Erikson's analysis of the human situation is preferable to Freud's pessimism and Horney's optimism.

Of all the theologians we have been considering, perhaps Tillich has been the most concerned about fostering good relationships between the disciplines. He has recognized the transitional state of philosophy at the present time and the problems created by this situation for both theology and psychology. He seems open to insights from both existential and process philosophers.

In an article entitled "Autobiographical Reflections" (1964), Tillich tells of his interest in the relationship between theology and psychotherapy and his personal friendships with analysts and therapists: "I do not think that it is possible today to elaborate a Christian doctrine of [humanity], and especially a Christian doctrine of the Christian [person], without using the immense material brought forth by depth psychology." (p.19) He was on a first name basis with Karen Horney and gave the Tenth Annual Karen Horney Lecture before the Association for the Advancement of Psychoanalysis in 1962. Rollo May dedicated a book to him.

Yet Tillich does not gloss over the areas of potential conflict between the two fields. Erik Erikson (1964) reports this conversation with Tillich:

> Before he left Harvard, Paul Tillich in a conversation expressed uneasiness over the clinical preoccupation with an adaptive ego which he felt might support (these are my words) further attempts at manufacturing a [humanity] feeling so adapted that it would be unable to face ultimate concerns. I agreed that psychoanalysis was in danger of becoming part of such vain streamlining of existence; but that in its origin and essence, it intends to _free_ [people] for ultimate concerns. For such concerns can begin to be ultimate only in those rare moments and places where neurotic resentments and where mere adaptation is transcended. I think he agreed. (pp.605-6)

On the other hand, therapists have expressed discomfort with Tillich's implication that complete healing takes place only when human beings are in a right relationship with God.

de Chardin presents a theory of the universe which includes theological, philosophical, and scientiric contributions. His theology would mix well with some of the ideas of process and existential philosophy. The universe is in process of moving to the Omega point, and we are in process of becoming something ultra-human. Our decision and our freedom are important elements in this process. These concepts would blend well with Horney's emphasis on our potential for healthy growth to self-realization and her stress on the effect of environmental factors. She, too, looks at the history of humans and finds encouraging signs of progress toward an ultimate self-realization. Rogers has described humans as enhancing their species. May also has emphasized the "becoming" process and the significance of our decisions in constituting our world.

Certainly these examples are not exhaustive. It is encouraging to find that many schools of thought within each discipline are reaching out to others across disciplinary lines in an appreciation for the contributions and the problems that may arise in formulating a coherent description

155

of the universe. Two Roman Catholics, Jesuits, who have written recently on thie topic are Kiely (1980) and Meissner (1984). Two Protestant writers are Van Leeuwen (1985) and Koteskey (1980). Anthologies such as the one edited by Malony (1983) can be found. These books are in the tradition established by Carroll Wise in his Religion in Illness and Health (1942), Mental Health and the Bible (1956), The Meaning of Pastoral Care (1966), and Pastoral Psychotherapy: Theory and Practice (1980). Wise was one of the first to interpret the disciplines of psychology and theology to others in his work, his teaching, and his writing:

Some students of these two fields, psychiatry and religion, have been impressed with the fact that they wrestle with many common problems. Others have emphasized the conflicts. Here we are concerned with their positive relationships. Not that we can identify psychiatry with religion. They are not the same and should not be forced into any common mold. But the insights which they bring to the problems of life should be looked at together and be understood in the light shed by each. To the extent that any science throws light on human life it is not foreign to the spirit of the Christian faith which seeks the truth leading to freedom. (1956, p.vii)

The contribution of Carroll Wise is his formulation of the separate but interactive roles of theology and psychology and his provision for his students of opportunities to grow in an experience of theological and psychological self understanding.

PSYCHIATRY AND CHRISTIANITY: A COLLABORATION

Carl W. Christensen

Psychiatry and Christianity share an interest in, and, devotion to, the individual person. This essay will be addressed to that mutual concern as it pertains to a professional collaboration between a pastoral counselor and a psychiatrist. In a sense, the essay is biographical and autobiographical as it deals with aspects of the professional lives of Carroll A. Wise, the pastoral counselor, and myself, a psychiatrist. Carroll, a Methodist minister, was a pioneer in the counseling ministry. I am a psychiatrist whose professional life was mainly devoted to the religious. This essay starts with our first meeting in August of 1949, when fresh from my psychiatric residency, I wandered into Carroll's office and introduced myself.

After the preliminary niceties, we began, cautiously, to explore each other's religious beliefs, psychological orientation and what we could do for each other. As it developed, this first meeting was a positive experience for both of us. We liked each other. Indeed, we agreed to meet again for lunch and further conversation. Gradually, over a period of time and the ingestion of a number of corned beef sandwiches, we began to discuss matters of more immediate concern, particularly minister's doing pastoral counseling. At this time there was no thought of any collaboration, at least on my part. I was, simply, looking for a source of patients and Carroll was looking for a resource to which he could refer patients. This was indeed a happy coincidence. Thus, pragmatically, the relationship began. Thus, it continued until terminated by Carroll's death many years later.

Early we discovered a mutuality of interests, a similarity of concerns, and a likeness in our thinking which, subsequently, led to a collaboration that deepened over the years of our working together. In retrospect, much of what we both accomplished was dependent upon that relationship and its influence on our lives. In those rare instances of disagreement we usually found it was semantic rather than anything profound. Our ethic, morality, goals, and thinking were remarkably similar throughout the years of our relationship. We even shared a common interest in photography.

The fact that Carroll was a minister, specializing in pastoral counseling, was intriguing to me since I had no idea what a pastoral counselor was or did. This ignorance was typical of the helping professions at that time. It was assumed that all ministers counseled with their parishioners. But this was held in short esteem just a little above the giving of advice. Carroll, in his quiet non-judgemental way, accepted my ignorance and began my education in pastoral counseling. This process was not formal but rather "ad lib" as we became involved in case discussions. We discovered that our basic religious faith was similar. Carroll was involved overtly in the practice of his religious faith in the structure of the church. It took me several years before I began to appreciate the significance of his religious faith and its influence on his counseling. Once I stopped condemning the Christian religion as an expression of super-ego, therefore, pathological, I was able to think about basic Christian doctrine in terms of its mythology and practice. I became involved as a psychotherapist and teacher of pastors. Rarely did Carroll and I discuss each other's religious faith, but we did explore the influence of religious faith on the person and on pastoral counseling. This resulted in Carroll's publishing several books and articles on the subject, which he shared with me. The editing of these writings gave me insight into his thinking and stimulated my own. Thus, my professional writing also concentrated on the use of religions in illness and in health. I also wrote a number of articles on the mental health of ministers, which Carroll edited. Both of us were concerned with the clinical aspects of religion rather than with theological speculations.

Our attention first focused on the ministerial student's personal faith. We were also concerned about his mental health and advocated that pastoral counselors successfully complete their own therapeutic experience. This concern eventually broadened to an interest in the Christian emphasis on healing. Eventually it led to a consideration of the faith of a patient. Was it pathological or not? What made the difference? These concerns served as the focus about which our teaching and clinical practice crystallized. In time we realized that the superficial trappings, the pomp and circumstance of the rituals, and even of the sacraments were of superficial interest. We focused on the fundamental beliefs and their use. It came as no surprise that the universal Christian faith was similar regardless of the denomination of the believer.

One of the most psychologically significant beliefs, which we tended to accept as normal, was a belief in God. Agnostic and atheistic beliefs were also accepted as normal. In all instances, however, we were not concerned with the belief itself, but were interested in the possible pathologic use of the belief in the person's life. Frequently, this would alert us to seek and be aware of other evidences of psychopathology. As we continued to study the assessment process, we became aware that the person's definition of the word "love" frequently was significant in revealing hidden psychopathology.

Subjective feelings described by the person during the assessment process alerted us to the possibility of major psychopathology. We learned to pay attention to the person's dependent needs, especially, how they were satisfied. Being aware of these dynamic factors determining or influencing a person's behavior helped us evaluate students seeking a degree in pastoral counseling. Later, these concepts were useful in assessing missionary candidates.

With increased emphasis on ego psychology we changed the goals of the assessment of the missionary candidates from prognosticating whether a particular candidate would have a psychotic episode in the field to suggesting the candidate's optimum placement in which he could realize his potential as a missionary. This shift in emphasis affected the clinical practice of pastoral counseling and the didactic teaching. We modified the strictly psychoanalytically oriented approach to that of modern concepts of ego psychology.

With the passage of time our mutual interest in psychotherapy led to thinking of pastoral counseling as being psychotherapy practiced by a minister, therefore, being no different than psychotherapy as practiced by the other healing professions. However, we also believed the religious dimension added a "faith" factor which, in the Christian religion, was an important adjunct to the techniques of psychotherapy.

Naturally, this led to a consideration of the emphasis on healing as a part of the Christian heritage. How did healing occur? How did the religion of the therapist effect his function as a healer? Was he the healer or simply a vehicle through which healing could take place? How did the faith of the patient effect the healing process? These and similar questions were matters of some concern early in our working together. We discussed these things and continued to ingest quantities of corned beef on a Kaiser roll.

In 1952, we initiated the Garrett Seminars on Psychology and Religion. These seminars were by invitation only and were limited to the Garrett Theological Seminary faculty and selected psychotherapists from the community. This seminar met monthly for more than ten years. Discussion was rife and often heated. I don't recall that we ever solved any of the problems with which we struggled, but they certainly stimulated our thinking and consciously or unconsciously influenced our practice. Specifically, these meetings had some direct effects upon Carroll and myself. They encouraged us to re-evaluate our curriculum as they questioned and challenged our practice. It was this direct stimulation which prodded us slowly to modify our thinking about the training of pastoral counselors from the orthodox psychoanalytic stance to that of the ego psychologists.

As we taught counseling skills to the ministers in the Master of Divinity program at Garrett Theological Seminary, both Carroll and I agreed that any didactic program must be rooted firmly in a clinical practice which was congruent with the theory being taught. One of the major difficulties, early in the program, was the lack of a consistent source of clinical material. The Garrett student body offered a potential source of clinical training, but there were many reasons for students not to treat students. We had considered establishing a pastoral counseling center at the seminary which would be available to the public-at-large. Although an occasional patient was seen at the seminary, this practice never flourished nor was it encouraged.

159

Later, the opportunity was presented to initiate a counseling program at Kendall College, Evanston, Illinois. Our students would work with Kendall College undergraduates under the direct supervision of the Department of Pastoral Psychology at Garrett. While better than nothing, it had the immediate limitation that the case material lacked the diversity necessary for well rounded clinical experiences. Despite this lack, the program limped along until 1963 when a doctoral program in pastoral counseling was inaugurated.

This doctoral program was the realization of one of Carroll's ambitions--to make the training of pastoral counselor's equal to that of clinical psychology and psychiatry. It was realized through the combined work of the Department of Pastoral Psychology at Garrett and supported by some of the faculty who were participating in the Garrett Seminars. The degree was a combined degree of the Graduate School of Northwestern University and Garrett Seminary. It elevated pastoral counseling to a profession instead of it being an incidental function of the ministry. Perforce, most of the work of crystallizing this degree fell upon Carroll's shoulders. My responsibility was to recruit a couple more psychiatrists willing to work in the program. The Ph.D. is still in effect at Garrett, although it is one emphasizing the theoretical while the definitive professional program based upon a clinical practice has shifted to the Doctor of Ministry in pastoral counseling.

In 1970, Carroll, who was an accredited Supervisor in Clinical Pastoral Education, was invited by Rev. Lawrence Holst, Director of Pastoral Care at Lutheran General Hospital, Park Ridge, Illinois, to participate in their Clinical Pastoral Education program. He gladly accepted. Shortly, with Larry's approval, I was involved as a consulting psychiatrist. In a remarkably short period of time there were so many requests for out-patient pastoral counseling that it seemed logical to establish such a program. To Carroll this opportunity offered the possibility of satisfying two of his fondest fantasies--the establishment of a pastoral counseling center as he envisioned it and an adequate source of clinical material for the training of pastoral counselors. He was eager, as was I, to get it going. Accordingly, we did.

In 1971, with the approval of the Board of Directors of the hospital, the Community Pastoral Counseling and Consultation Center was inaugurated. Carroll was its first director and only staff counselor; Larry was liaison between the Center and the hospital; and I was the consulting psychiatrist. Although I would not be seeing any patients seemed reasonable, if I was to consult, that I be on the hospital staff, which I joined. The Center flourished and, in time, other counselors were added. Carroll and I spent time discussing the qualifications of staff counselors, determining the practice of the Center, and organizing the details of operating both a service and training Center. While these have been modified over the years in keeping with changes in practice and education, the basic ideals, values, and standards have

160

been maintained.

In time the clinical program was expanded to provide a clinical experience for pastoral counselors in training at other seminaries. This program also has developed into a three year certified practicum. Each student is supervised by a senior staff pastoral therapist, and his or her progression through the program is determined by the Education and Training Committee.

In keeping with the interest in the healing aspects of the Christian religion, an Interdisciplinary Case Conference was established early for the students in training. While this was recommended by the American Association of Pastoral Counselors, it was foremost in the thinking of Carroll resulting from the discussions of the Garrett Seminars on Psychology and Religion. This Interdisciplinary Case Conference is an attempt by the Institute (somewhere along in time the name of the Center was changed to the Pastoral Psychotherapy Institute) to study, directly, the "pastoral" in pastoral counseling. Participating students present a personally significant religious experience and a segment of a counseling session which illustrates a therapeutic incident. The Seminar attempts to correlate the two, if possible. Throughout the years the correlation has been tenuous, but it has achieved one of its goals-- encouraging the pastoral therapist to consider the import of the Christian religion in pastoral counseling.

In the meantime pastoral counseling was in ferment. About 1961-62, a group of twenty-five or so dedicated pastoral counselors met with the avowed intention of forming a professional association of pastoral counselors to function as an accrediting body similar to those extendent in social work, clinical psychology, and psychiatry. Carroll was deeply involved in this endeavor. It seemed most natural that he invited me to participate in their formative meetings as an observer. At the two meetings I attended, the pastoral counselors were most gracious and listened as I expounded, sometimes at length, on the import of maintaining high standards for membership and qualifications for the accreditation of pastoral counseling centers. This echoed Carroll's determination that pastoral counseling be perceived as equal to the other helping professions. The fact that today the American Association of Pastoral Counselors is a viable respected accrediting organization of pastoral counselors is a continuing source of pride.

Throughout the years the Pastoral Psychotherapy Institute has maintained its close affiliation with the Association. Staff membership in the Institute requires membership in the Association. Members presidents of the Association were on our staff, while others function as chair of various "ad hoc" and standing committees. Carroll served as president of the Association and was awarded the "Distinguished Contributor's Award" as, later, I also was honored.

As I sit writing these memoirs, I am aware that through the years we evolved a very fine counseling center and training institution. In a sense, once started it simply grew because from the beginning it met a community need. But it is also true that it resulted from the successful collaboration between a psychiatrist and a pastoral counselor. Undoubtedly, one of the reasons for the success of the collaboration was compatibility. An important part of compatibility is the sense of ego identity. Each person in a compatible relationship must have a mature sense of ego identity. This is not threatened by the normal interdependency common to all relationships. Carroll was secure in his religious beliefs which he integrated with his psychological orientation. He was a pastor and not a minister playing a role at being a therapist. He lived his faith and practiced it as a part of his counseling. He was therapeutic. I was a psychiatrist secure in the practice of my profession and not a minister. Together we realized our mutual ambitions.

The most important of our goals was to ensure that the training of people to be therapists was the best that could be offered. I believe that goal has been realized as the Institute continues to explore and modify its programs to meet the varied needs of pastoral counseling today. One of Carroll's ambitions was to establish clearly the identity of pastoral counselors as a specific function of the ministry requiring specialized training and experience. No longer is it acceptable for ministers to do pastoral counseling because their church says they can. Another ambition realized was the insistence that any pastoral counseling must be grounded firmly in clinical practice. In many instances the pastoral counselor is the only mental health resource person available in his community. As such, he or she needs the best training that can be obtained. It is a source of pride that graduates from the Institute have gone forth to minister in Alaska, Canada, Australia, Ireland, Africa, India, South America, and other lands.

In retrospect, I believe the central core of our collaboration was the fact that we were able to achieve a balance between the religious and the psychological. Each contributed from their understanding of the human condition and each valued this contribution. The resulting amalgam was a collaboration which utilized the best from each in a manner that respected the individual. The minister was a pastoral counselor, not a psychiatrist. The psychiatrist was not a minister. This accord between psychology and religion as exemplified in this essay demonstrates that the collaboration between the two can result in a clinical practice of psychotherapy utilizing the best of Christianity and of ego psychology. But religion and psychology are simply products of human mentation, and, as such are subject to modification to suit the individual. Therefore, in the final analysis whether they can be integrated into a working amalgam will depend upon the people involved. If they are of good will, accepting and understanding compromises can be effected which will call for collaboration. So it was with Carroll and I, with results that were mutually satisfying and productive.

INNER BEING AND PROFESSIONAL ENCOUNTER:
WISE IN RELATION TO THE FORMATION AND FUNCTION OF AAPC

Richard G. Bruehl

Introduction

In the therapeutic situation, Charles Gerkin (1984) has pointed out, purely objective observation and interpretation are impossible by either client or therapist. Both parties bring to this relationship a world view, specific constructs and assumptions derived from past experience, and the feelings and perceptions generated by the immediate interpersonal setting. Since objective history and interpretation do not exist in pure form, the best one can do is to become aware of his or her biases, and allow for them as meanings are explicated and discovered in the therapeutic process.

Similarly, in writing an appraisal of Carroll A. Wise's participation in, contribution to, and support of the development of the specialized ministry of pastoral therapy and the American Association of Pastoral Counselors, I need to be clear with myself and my reader that I do not come to this task as an impartial observer. Many of the central passions and commitments of Wise's professional life that I came to appreciate as his graduate student (1963-1967) have become so much a part of me that, as I explore this topic, I am never altogether sure what is me and what is Carroll. While I shall not belabor my own experience here, I do need to indicate that my point of view about Carroll Wise's contribution to the AAPC and the specialized ministry of pastoral counseling and therapy is deeply influenced by the fact that I have been a laborer in that same vineyard for some twenty years. I have been part of the "cloud of witnesses" who stood on the shoulders of the giants like Wise, and have, in our various ways, moved the field forward to its present level of development.

Thus I warn the reader that, while I have made every effort to be faithful to the data available to me, what follows is more of a passionate than a dispassionate history. What I hope to demonstrate is that Wise's apologies for and commitment to the specialized ministry of pastoral therapy and his participation in the formation and early development of the AAPC reflects a if not the professional developmental theme in his life. Whether the times create the man or the man the times is an interesting question, which I leave to others to debate. Suffice it to say that, in the development of pastoral counseling and therapy, the AAPC, and Carroll Wise, the times and the man came together in remarkable and creative ways.

The Background

In the author's view, Carroll Wise cannot be understood in any of his personal or professional dimensions without seeing him as a missionary. At times, much to the discomfort of his colleagues, he was a man of great positive and negative passions. While he knew how to compromise, for he dwelt and dealt with difficult political realities all of his professional life, Wise manifested definite points of view. He was seldom afraid to articulate these, and for them would often do battle. But his mission, fueled by his central ideals and values, was at its root a positive and religious one.

Wise's early life was spent in the religiously conservative hills of Western Pennsylvania. (Van Wagner 1986, pp. 158-59) During his adolescence, prompted by the same instincts which later informed his professional life and thought, he grew dissatisfied with the pat answers to life's questions preached and taught in his local church. (Ibid.; Moss 1976b, pp.18-19) He was attracted to Harry Emerson Fosdick through his radio ministry, (Van Wagner 1986, pp. 158-9) and, as a result, began to confront in new ways human life situations and the relevance of the Gospel to them. Later, as a theological student nurtured in the more liberal atmosphere at the Boston University School of Theology, he began to ask still deeper philosophical, psychological, and theological questions. (Moss 1976b, p.18)

Late in his theological school career, Wise enrolled in Anton Boisen's course in the psychology of religious experience and later became Boisen's student at Worcester Hospital where Boisen served as Chaplain. (Moss 1976b, pp.17-21) In his early association with Boisen, Wise discovered that the Chaplains, who operated by the leave of the famous physician and founder of medical social work, Richard Cabot, were expected to entertain and support patients but were not to be personal ministers to them. This approach obtained in great measure because Cabot wholly rejected theories about the psychogenic origin of neuroses and psychoses as well as the possible contribution of emotional factors in physical illness. Hence, Boisen, whose psychodynamic proclivities are well known, had to smuggle psychological reflection into the ministerial training program at Worcester Hospital. (Moss 1976b, p.19)

What seems particularly relevant in this story is that Wise learned early that ministers interested in the integration of psychological insights in their pastoral work would have to fight for credibility against opposition from many quarters, even some of which superficially appeared friendly to the idea. This attitude, in my experience, never totally left him, and provided energy which was later expended in defense of pastoral counseling and psychotherapy. (Wise, 1983)

In a fascinating interview with David Moss (1976), Wise described the tenor of the times in his formative professional years. He pointed to two factors which fired the missionary zeal of those interested in depth psychology and ministry.

First, the work of Freud, the discoveries of unconscious processes

164

and the dynamics of depth psychotherapy were a major factor. The second thing, I think, was the liberal tenor of the theological movement in the church . . . This theological shift, coupled with the social emphasis, affected many of us in a profound way. We were going to make the world safe for democracy. We were going to outlaw war in the 20's. We were going to solve all the industrial relations problems . . . Out of that also came convictions that it isn't enough to change social problems, we've got to do something to help individuals. There is an individual emphasis in the Gospel, and an individual need within life. The old methods of conversion were seen as inadequate. Most of the liberals had moved into the church through the fundamentalistic, conservative conversion process. They went so far in that tradition and discovered a blind alley. They had to move on if they were to grow. They moved on. They moved out of the conservative movement to the liberal movement as their growing edge. So that from that movement the emphasis on the social side was retained in the church. But there was also emphasis on individuals. How can we help people with personal problems? That tied to the whole Freudian emphasis. (Moss 1976b, pp.18-19)

One cannot help but catch the excitement of these beginnings. The zeal of the Social Gospel, depicted by Wise, also caught those interested in pastoral care and counseling. These pioneers began to realize that the insights and procedures of depth psychology were tools which could be used in ministry to help people with their personal and relational issues.

Growing out of this new emphasis on depth psychology and his long experience with Anton Boisen, whom he later succeeded as Chaplain Supervisor at Worcester, were Wise's understandings of the function of religion in human personality. In Religion in Illness and Health (1942), he discussed at length both the positive and negative uses of religion in the psyche. Too often in his pastoral experience he had seen religious symbols and practices used defensively as a way of concealing problems and conflicts rather than solving them. In this book, he also articulated a central theme which informed his commitment to the process of pastoral psychotherapy and was to blossom in later writings. Change in religious ideas, symbols, and experience, he reasoned, could not be separated from change in the entire personality integration of the individual.

Long before "holism" became part of the common currency of the behavioral sciences, Wise focused on the interconnectedness of all sub-systems of the personality. He realized that change in values involved a renewal of the total person. Thus, positive growth toward more functional, lasting, and constructive values to which religion, at its best, points and promotes must be based upon a transformation in the total self experience. Such change, therefore, involves a profound affective shift, a reintegration, and a reinterpretation of personal and

165

interpersonal realities. The process of counseling and psychotherapy offered Wise a methodology, compatible with pastoral identity, in which such change effectively could be mediated.

Clearly in his later writings (1951, 1966, 1983) this theme emerged repeatedly as a focal point and organizing principle. For Wise, movement toward the discovery of creative religious and spiritual values could be facilitated in a unique way through the pastoral counseling and therapy process. It is further clear that to a large extent the very growth engendered and fostered by a therapeutic relationship brings healing to the self which liberates spiritual energy and, if the experience is deep enough, will require the reevaluation of one's world view and relational and ethical commitments. In short, what therapy offers is the opportunity for a kind of "conversion" which is likely to have long lasting effects in a person's life.

In my view, Wise learned a great deal from Boisen about religious experience and, in turn, sought to mediate this experience with others. From my personal recollection, I know that he was against (and passionately so) those who would attempt to deal with and solve these questions at an intellectual level. He felt that the only true answers to life's predicaments are those which are experienced and which, therefore, emerge from the depths of personal reality. In a corollary fashion, those religious and value commitments which derive from the cognitive level only or are imposed by external authority are at best of neutral value or at worst harmful.

With the clarification and consolidation of these ideas and commitments, Wise moved out of the hospital and into the world.

Beyond the Hospital

Throughout his tenure at Worcester, Wise recalled, the insights gleaned from the care and treatment of acutely disturbed persons were viewed also from the standpoint of their applicability to the life problems of people in parishes. (Moss 1976b, p.21) But the question was how could what was being learned about the human being be applied in a broader religious context both in terms of the remediation of problems and, more importantly, the prevention of their development? In pursuit of an answer to these questions, he would serve, in turn, as a counselor at a YMCA and YWCA, a director of a council of churches counseling center, the minister of counseling of a large urban parish, and finally as professor of Pastoral Psychology and Counseling at Garrett Theological Seminary. (Wise 1951, p. x)

What is particularly relevant for us in this pilgrimage is that when Wise came to theological education, he did so with a wealth of experience in the hospital and parish based counseling room. By 1948 when he arrived at Garrett, he had been a specialist pastor for all but four years of his ministry, and had become acquainted deeply with the

166

needs and conflicts of the hurting "well" who populated the parishes and communities in which he served. He knew a great deal about what young seminarians were going to face in their pastoral work; he also knew how ill-prepared most were going to be to meet these challenges. Further, from his experience he knew more than a few things which would be useful for them to know if they were going to try to be of help to others.

His early book, Pastoral Counseling: Its Theory and Practice (1951), reflects the emphasis of his teaching career until the late 1950's and early 60's. Written primarily for the parish minister, it offers a philosophy and approach useful to someone without a great deal of training and attempting to assist people in pain. Only slightly covert is his missionary attitude that parish ministers would do well to focus on counseling in their ministries and to pursue as much training as possible in support of that emphasis. Wise's colleagues, indeed, would often chide him for his implication that ministry was counseling. Though he would never admit to that position, his zeal for being of use to people personally and for helping pastors to be of assistance was never far away. In some sense, it is fair to say that to Carroll Wise, ministry was indeed counseling in the profoundest sense of those terms.

At the time of his appointment at Garrett, Wise could not foresee the full dimensions of the development of the specialized ministry of pastoral counseling and therapy as it was later to come to fruition in the organization of the AAPC. Fifteen years later, however, he had become an enthusiastic supporter of the AAPC, had inaugurated a successful Ph.D. program in Pastoral Psychology and Counseling, and, as we shall see, had become an ardent supporter of the specialized ministry of pastoral counseling and psychotherapy.

Why was this so? This writer's interpretation is that Wise's commitment to the development of this special ministry grew from several different seeds.

First, on the negative side, he had experienced, since his early days at Worcester, resistance to pastoral counseling as a legitimate ministry. In the interview with Moss, previously cited, Wise states:

Basically, the denominations in my lifetime have not been interested in pastoral care. They've been interested in institutionalism and organizationalism and programs of a larger scale. (Moss 1976, p.22)

This statement reflects the years of struggle and conflict within the church and theological education, which supplies the church's leadership, to find legitimation for pastoral care and its individual and personal emphasis. From reading the present material and reviewing my memory of discussions with Wise about this issue, I have concluded that he felt that without a well-trained cadre of clergy, who were committed to the development of pastoral counseling and psychotherapy and would submit to the rigors of the academic clinical disciplines so they could stand side by side with other helping professionals as co-equals, the pastoral care and counseling movement would continue to make only a tangential impact on the church and its ministry. There is much more to pastoral care than Dr. Cabot thought!

Second, Wise decided to support and nurture the growing specialized ministry of pastoral counseling and psychotherapy as a practical necessity. At the time of the AAPC's first meeting in 1962, several hundred pastoral counseling clinics already existed in the U.S. The existence of these services and the uneven quality of the preparation of those operating these ministries (Clinebell 1964) raised for Wise and others basic questions: Who has the right to do pastoral counseling? What kind of qualifications should such persons have? As Wise recalls, these issues, which were flying at the churches at something approaching the speed of light, were indeed "hot potatoe[s]." (Moss 1976, p.22)

While some wanted a certification process to remain under the Association for Clinical Pastoral Education umbrella, it became obvious that pastoral counseling was facing different issues than those confronting CPE.

> There was a felt need of a professional organization to accredit pastors in counseling and to accredit training centers. This brought out one of the basic differences between CPE and training in pastoral therapy. It became very obvious that adequate training in pastoral therapy could not be done within an institution for the mentally ill, or the physically ill, or for any other acute infirmities. It has to be done with people who live in the parish. Pastoral psychotherapy is dealing with an entirely different set of problems than the chaplain deals with in the hospital. (Moss 1976b, p.22)

Wise goes on to state that pastoral intervention in acute crisis, typical of most hospital work, is a different animal, though not unrelated, from working with the individual who has lost hope from wrestling with a problem or a relationship of many years duration.

Finally, Wise supported AAPC because he was convinced that pastoral psychotherapy was an entirely legitimate function of ministry. This conviction he made clear in his final book which he determinedly and joyfully called Pastoral Psychotherapy. (1983) Here he takes the (to me) debatable position that all counseling done by a minister is psychotherapy and that therefore pastors should be as well trained as the secular psychotherapist to do it. (p.8) The fact is, however, that this material is written in such a way as to be of value mostly to persons with the intensive training of the specialist minister, who has the personal therapeutic and clinical experience to apply its wisdom. Whatever the merits of the case, Pastoral Psychotherapy is a declaration to the church, to secular helping professions, to fellow and sister ministers that pastoral therapists are no longer to be viewed as hand holders and purveyors of magic bones and snake oil. Instead, ministers are serious about understanding and dealing with human pain as it becomes manifest in the therapy · setting. For Wise, pastoral psychotherapy had begun to come of age.

Wise and Hiltner

One of the more interesting stories in the lore of the specialized pastoral counseling movement is the difference between Carroll Wise and Seward Hiltner regarding its development and expression in the AAPC. Seward, by virtue of his early leadership in the Council for Clinical Training, the Department of Religion and Health of the former Federal Council of Churches, and his long teaching tenure, at the University of Chicago Divinity School and Princeton Theological Seminary, shaped the emerging pastoral care and counseling movement as much as any other single individual, including Wise. Whatever unfinished personal business may have existed between the two men, (Van Wagner 1986, pp.89-92) it is of more than passing interest that these two giants emerged with such seeming polar positions regarding the development of the new professional organization and specialized ministry. For, while Wise became deeply involved in the AAPC, Hiltner remained opposed to it until his death.

What were Hiltner's objections to the AAPC? In a critique of the organization in Pastoral Psychology in 1964, Hiltner detailed his concerns. His central criticism focused on the certification process which created a specialized minister of counseling. To him, the major need was the accreditation of pastoral counseling centers and not the certification of counselors. (pp.8-9) He was very dubious about "special ministers" who were to be elevated to a unique status of "Pastoral Counselor." Pastoral counseling was a function of all ministers. To create such a special group would weaken rather than strengthen the ministry of the church. (p.11)

Hiltner, in addition, feared that pastoral counselors would, in pursuit of training modeled upon that of other mental health professionals, lose their primary identity as pastors and become merely another breed of bastardized psychotherapists. He contended that although the minister may make use of psychological insights and treatment approaches, the pastoral model was fundamentally different from that of the secular helping professions in that the pastor always represents a fellowship rather than simply working in his or her own name. Further, in the matter of finances, he felt that the pastoral model dictated that no one could be refused service legitimately because of an inability to pay a fee, and that pastors are always to be compensated by a corporate body and never by individuals served directly. This is the "private practice" model of the mental health professions and not that of the pastor. (pp.12-14)

Unarguably, Hiltner was sincere in his opposition to the establishment of what he called the "archpiscopal certified pastoral counselor." He raised points which are hotly debated even unto the present. While many of these issues will not be resolved satisfactorily within the foreseeable future, Hiltner has been of great use to those in the specialized ministry of pastoral counseling precisely for his articulate opposition to our ministry.

Given Wise's deep involvement in the church, his long-time tenure as a professor in a theological school, and his personal and professional history, it is interesting that he supported the concept of the certification of the specialized minister of counseling. Since some of the reasons for his positive response to the formation of the AAPC have already been discussed, only one further aspect of the differences between these two grandfathers of pastoral counseling will be mentioned here. That issue has to do with the pastoral identity of the pastoral therapist about which Hiltner was concerned so deeply.

Wise was aware acutely of the tensions which Hiltner explicated. Indeed, he worked at finding a middle way between the tradition and the models of the secular helping professions. In what to a person with my bias is a remarkable statement first delivered in a speech at the 1967 AAPC convention and later published as an article, he contended that the church had become preoccupied with salvation and neglected, and often despised, the need for healing. (1967) Healing, he says, was left to the medical profession on the one hand and the Christian Scientists and faith healers on the other. The mainline Protestant churches had become bankrupt in terms of their capacity to help in the healing of lives, a process which is inextricably bound up with the search for salvation and reconciliation (p.4).

Wise further takes the position that the pastoral therapist is called upon to live within an ultimately unresolvable identity conflict. Healing is the primary task of the pastoral counselor no matter the context. As a modern healer, the pastoral counselor must be grounded thoroughly in both dynamic psychology and the religious/theological. If one encounters contradictions, intellectual problems or blocks, one must go deeper into the conflict and not seek a superficial resolution by siding with one or the other of these two worlds. (1967, p.6)

He himself says it beautifully:

The central problem the pastoral counselor faces here is his [or her] own identity as a pastor who is concerned with helping persons. For the answer to this problem of discontinuity is not to be found in any theoretical formulation. It is to be found in a kind of dual orientation of the counselor which makes it possible for him [or her] to feel and relate deeply to another person as one who sees life in both its ultimate and penultimate perspectives without the necessity of anxiety of one over another, or the need to manipulate or coerce others from either point of view. Or the answer is to be found in the living identity of the pastor both as a person and a professional worker which permits him [or her] to operate from both perspectives. In such an orientation [one] would understand persons rather than ideas as the focal point in which the ultimate and penultimate meet. (Ibid.)

This statement is vintage Wise. For him, pastoral identity is primarily an inner experience from which all authority and personal gifts derive. Fundamentally for Wise, and I believe he maintained this as a bedrock conviction, the issue of pastoral identity can never be solved intellectually, psychologically, or sociologically. It has to be resolved within the person of the pastor as he or she discovers the gift of healing from within, and, thereby, obtains the power and authority to be of help to others. For both pastoral therapists and their clients a deep mystery always remains in this healing experience. It was this almost indescribable experience of grace, transformation, and integration to which Wise pointed from his earliest days with Boisen to his final statement on the subject. Moreover, it was paradoxically, this belief in the almost unspeakable deep source of healing within that sent many seekers away from him sorrowful. To those who could capture, pin down, and solve these deeper issues of inner healing and pastoral identity with any formulation, be it theological or psychological, Wise stood opposed. To them he remained as illusive as a butterfly. It was this central thrust which often brought charges of "anti-intellectualism," a charge which, to anyone who can read, is patent nonsense.

I contend that Wise so believed in the primacy of experience (as all good Methodists should!) that he would feel that whatever risks might be involved in the development of the specialized ministry of pastoral counseling were worth it. Set against the backdrop of his doubts as to whether the Church had the will or the capacity to understand the meaning of his fundamental insights, I believe Wise felt that the AAPC represented the best chance to nurture and develop the healing ministry of the Church. He realized the tremendous potential for good that could evolve from trained, supported, and organized pastoral therapists who in their individual ways had discovered the power of the Spirit to heal them in their "inward parts." If risks existed in the formation of the AAPC and the certification of specialist pastoral therapists, far greater risks, in his opinion, would come without a certifying agency which would also support, promote, and guide the development of pastoral psychotherapy on behalf of the Church.

Wise's Contribution to the AAPC

According to Van Wagner's (1986) fascinating chronicle of the early years of the AAPC, the initial meeting of what was later to evolve into the AAPC was sponsored primarily by the American Foundation of Religion and Psychiatry in 1963 in New York. (p.33) Those invited to attend were the directors of pastoral counseling centers and pastoral counselors with other types of practices but not seminary professors. (Ibid.) Howard J. Clinebell, Jr., invited because he happened to be both a pastoral counseling center director and a professor of pastoral counseling, was concerned at this omission. He personally attempted to recruit Carroll Wise, Paul Johnson, Seward Hiltner, and Wayne Oates for the organizational meeting scheduled for St. Louis, in 1964. (Ibid.p.53) Of these, Wise and Johnson accepted immediately; Hiltner declined with considerable resistance; and Oates refused but with milder opposition. (Ibid.)

From the St. Louis meeting forward, Wise became an active participant in the development of AAPC. His first role was that of reporter and apologist. He reported on the St. Louis meeting for Pastoral Psychology (1964), discussing the issues dealt: the need for AAPC as a standard-setting organization for specialist pastoral counselors, the deep concern for the Church and the role of the specialized minister of counseling in relation to parish ministers. In this last emphasis, he tried to answer one of Hiltner's major critiques, though certainly not to Hiltner's satisfaction. Also he noted the democratic spirit of the meeting and an awareness of the need to develop relationships with the National Council of Churches, the denominations, the Council for Clinical Training, and other professional mental health organizations. Finally, he enthusiastically urged all pastoral counselors to get on board. Following the 1965 annual meeting, he wrote a similar report which appeared in the Christian Century. (1965) In these two instances he lent his considerable authority and prestige to the new organization, becoming one of its most vocal and well-known apologists.

In 1965, Wise took a step to formal leadership when he was elected First Vice President. Van Wagner states:

Certainly his [Wise's] election to this office strengthened the national credibility of the young organization. Wise was well known throughout the country among clinical pastoral educators and pastoral counselors. (Van Wagner 1986, p.135)

Wise's addition to leadership was a significant step for the AAPC. In addition to his achievements as a writer and teacher, he also had been the chair of the Methodist Committee on Pastoral Counseling, was known for his published support of the AAPC discussed above, and had served on the AAPC Board of Directors as a Member-at-Large during the year preceding his election. Because he was respected and known, he brought strong leadership potential to the organization.

While many interesting side roads beckon us, the writer refrains from reciting details regarding Wise's term of office in AAPC. Suffice it to say that, in his service as Vice President and later President (1967-1969), he emerged as a strong and at times, controversial leader. He was efficient and aggressive, ready to take his committee chairs to task for their laggardly ways or ineptitude. According to Van Wagner's

172

account and my memories, Wise ruffled feathers, but also led with an obvious genuine concern for AAPC and the issues which confronted it. But, in addition to his forcefulness as a leader, he insisted upon the maintenance of the democratic process in matters of governance. To the date of this writing, the AAPC has continued to maintain high standards in dealing with minority opinions, a tradition which was carefully nurtured by early leadership such as Wise's.

Among the significant achievements of Wise's administration were the following:

1. Organization of the first fund-raising effort and procurement of a matching grant from the Stone Foundation. (Van Wagner 1986, p.197)

2. Revision of the Constitution penned largely by Carroll Wise, in consultation with [Frederick] Kuether, [Otis] Maxfield, and Leila Foster, chairperson of the Legislative committee. (Ibid., p.208)

3. Supervision of regionalization, as established in the new Constitution in a pioneering effort. (Ibid.)

4. Initiation of discussions with ACPE leading to joint national conferences and continuing dialogue with other professional organizations. (Ibid.)

5. Achievement of agreement with ACPE for the joint publication of The Journal of Pastoral Care. (Ibid., p.243)

6. Initiatives toward reconciliation with the Association of Theological Schools over the issue of the accreditation of training centers for pastoral counseling. (Ibid., pp.246-47)

To keep these achievements in perspective one must realize, of course, that although Wise did not do all these things by himself, he provided leadership of and support for those who were the prime movers in these areas of concern. Further, his leadership fostered a stimulating environment, which enhanced the development of the growing association. Those familiar with the present structure and function of AAPC will appreciate the lasting importance of these contributions.

At his retirement from active leadership in AAPC, Carroll Wise, though small physically, left large shoes to fill. He had been an articulate spokesman for the specialized ministry of pastoral counseling and therapy, had overseen and guided the new Association of specialist pastoral therapists through some of its most critical years and thorniest issues, and had given the developing profession the benefit of his prestige. In all these things he offered his energy and intelligence, often in sacrificial ways.

A Final Appraisal

While Carroll Wise's achievements and contributions to the specialized ministry of pastoral psychotherapy as apologist, administrator, and member of AAPC reflect an enduring legacy to the field, to the mind of this writer, his most profound gift was his deep insight into the nature and meaning of the healing process as it becomes manifest in the depth encounter called pastoral psychotherapy. His push toward excellence and equality with other psychotherapeutic disciplines has endued his students, including this writer, with a willingness to live deeply into the tension of what it means to be a pastoral psychotherapist. His insistence upon the ultimate reconciliation of conflict as a mysterious gift mediated by a healing relationship and the validity of that process as ministry continue to undergird us.

It is difficult to know where we are as a specialty within the profession of ministry at this writing. In terms of the acceptance and understanding of this ministry by the Church, theological education and our peer mental health groups are further down the road than we were in 1970 when he left office. However, questions remain about the role of the pastoral counselor and therapist, and about these issues we should be concerned appropriately. But it is helpful to remain cognizant of the fact that, at the level of pastoral identity he was addressing in his life, the conflicts and tensions will never be resolved by our best intellectual efforts. Carroll would counsel us to live into and trust our experience at this deep level and fight the good fight. Perhaps that is what we must do to be faithful servants of the process which has benefitted so many and has offered new hope to the Church and the world. A deep source of healing is alive in the Christian Community.

This was, in its depth and breadth, Carroll Wise's mission.

PASTORAL COUNSELING CENTERS AND THE WISE MODEL

Allen R. Gilmore

Over the years (1959-1962, 1963-1967) the rooms at the seminary in which seminars were held varied in size; the seats varied widely in comfort. Yet, the format was always the same. Students grouped themselves around a large table with professors who declared themselves learners also, thereby becoming colleagues. The faculty led seminars on various subjects for the graduate students taking the course for credit. Carroll Wise and an array of professionals co-led the sessions: Carl Christensen, M.D. taught diagnosis and disposition; Alfred Flarsheim, M.D. taught the process of individual psychotherapy; Bernard Greene, M.D. worked with us on the processes of marital therapies.

Several things happened simultaneously as in any human interaction: didactic material was transmitted; the "human document" was a central focus of discussion; forays were made into integrating material from human experience, church history, systematic and historical theology, biblical studies, Christian education; even church administration was integrated with the didactic material of the course. Attempts were made also to understand the relationships between the methodology of the psychiatrist and that of the psychologists/researchers who taught us at The Graduate School at Northwestern University.

The discussions were indescribably invigorating. Sometimes debates led to brilliant insights or to novel formulations of problems which were under discussion. Occasionally, there was a cacophony of sound and fury that was not very illuminating, but left us all stimulated and exhausted. It did not matter because there was always another kind of teaching and learning taking place regardless of content. The learning had to do with the interdisciplinary collegiality that was the driving force of the seminars. The ambience was as important for the training of pastoral counselors as the course content itself. In truth, that ambience became the basis for a model of the modern pastoral counseling center. Significant elements of the ambience were: a sense of mission, a collegiality characterized by mutual respect for persons and their field, professionalism and discipline, a desire to learn, a willingness to become a participant in and a bearer of "oral tradition," and a sense of awe and compassion.

Dr. Wise did not articulate a specific model for a pastoral counseling center in these classes or in his writings. He did, however, become himself the leader of a model and eventually had a hand in developing centers in several locations. We need to think of "centers" in the broadest sense here. That is how Wise thought of them. A "center," for him, was any location where the ministry of pastoral psychotherapy was carried on by professionally trained pastoral therapists. He himself was personally involved with the development of centers that were parish based, associated with hospitals, related to a seminary, and some which were denominationally or ecumenically sponsored. Regardless of setting, all were characterized by the same elements of ambience cited above as characteristic of the graduate seminars he led. We consider each in turn.

Mission

Wise clearly believed that professional pastoral psychotherapy involved a sense of mission. The pastoral counseling center was to be rooted in a sense of mission characterized by an understanding of the church's historic ministry of healing or "the cure of souls." The mission was to bring healing to persons and to become the incarnate reminder to the institutional church that it must foster such a ministry if the church were to maintain its relevance and vitality.

He saw the ministry of pastoral psychotherapy as rooted in Word and Sacrament. As a student of Tillich, he had a great sense of awe at the power of symbols. The pastoral counseling center was to understand its mission of healing to individuals and institutions as the counselors themselves become the embodiment of God's healing love. Consequently, mission always involved a sense of pastoral identity on the part of the pastoral psychotherapist. Pastoral counselors have their professional identity rooted in the sense of awe that comes from standing in relationship to the "Ground of our Being." It is from this grounding that the dialogue with the behavioral sciences can take place as the pastoral therapist seeks truth about human development and healing. Wise often stated that we needed to spend less energy talking about the love of God and more energy "being the love of God to persons."

Sometimes Wise would speak of the pastoral counseling "movement." This movement had as its mission the healing of persons and the informing of the church about the ministry of healing. Some critics within the institutional church mistakenly believed him to be uninformed theologically or theologically disinterested. They saw him as only interested in the psychologizing of religion when he was actually a great student of the psychology of religious experience. He believed, therefore, that the pastoral therapist also had a mission to other professionals in the behavioral sciences with whom they were to be in regular dialogue. He taught much to the psychiatrists and psychologists with whom he worked. He sometimes taught the theologians and biblical scholars who were his colleagues.

It is important for those in pastoral counseling centers today to remember the double aspect of Wise's concern about the mission of pastoral counselors in a "center" setting. One thrust was inward. The focus was on what the institution could do to foster and promote the ministry of healing. On such institutional support depended the

176

survival of the center. Yet the other thrust was equally important and often forgotten. Pastoral counseling centers existed, in Wise's view, to be a constant reminder to the institutional church that true worship reaches beyond liturgy and into the brokenness of human beings as they deal with the pain and joy of human existence.

Wise devoted his life to training clergy to be sensitive to their own humanity and to be sensitive to the feelings and pain of those to whom they ministered. Pastoral counseling centers are ideal places to provide clinical pastoral education for religious workers. They are also places where dialogue with clergy and committed lay persons can provide an impetus for the religious institutions always to look beyond themselves and narrow sectarianism to the widest range of human need. Wise, a United Methodist, believed with John Wesley that the "world was his parish." The denominationally connected centers he associated with always reached beyond a narrow parochial interest to serve the widest possible community. In this way, pastoral counselors in centers practice evangelism in its broadest sense.

Collegiality

From the beginning of his career as an educator, Wise fostered close relationships with professionals from allied professions. He spoke of collegial relationships with psychiatrists at Worcester State Hospital in Massachusetts, especially Flandars Dunbar, M.D. At Garrett the relationship included an informal structure as well as relationships forged in mutual teaching. The formal "structure" was a multi-disciplined discussion group founded by Wise and dubbed the "headshrinker's group." It included himself and various seminary staff who taught theology, church history, Christian education, and biblical studies. Other members taught psychology at Northwestern University or were practicing psychotherapists from Evanston. One of these relationships became personal as Wise and Christensen, became fast friends and collaborators in many teaching projects. (See Christensen in this volume.)

It was clear from Wise's attitude about such collaboration that he believed that the pastoral counselor must not work in isolation. Interdisciplinary collegiality promoted intellectual growth. He believed that the insights of religious faith interfaced with the behavioral sciences enhanced the search for truth. He also believed that the behavioral sciences needed to be informed by the insights of religious faith in order to avoid becoming mechanistic and dehumanized.

Wise's style of relating to his professional colleagues was interesting and instructive. There was clearly great mutual respect between himself and the persons with whom he worked. The key word here is "respect," as contrasted with "awe." Many of us have been in what were allegedly collegial relationships which turned out in fact to be hierarchical. Ordinarily, the pecking order would show the psychiatrist and other M.D.'s at the top with rankings down through psychologists, social workers, pastoral counselors, and "others." One could be in a room and some seminar type settings where there were interdisciplinary conferences and be struck by the fact that pastoral counselors often felt like second class citizens. Wise simply refused to think of himself as a second class citizen, but he was very respectful of the professional colleagues from other disciplines. His attitude seemed to have a profound effect on the people with whom he associated. They clearly respected him as both a scholar and a person.

One of the instructive features of this style of relating to professional colleagues from other disciplines, and the key to its development, was clearly a lack of either arrogance or excessive piety on the part of Wise himself. He was not defensive about himself, his faith, or his discipline. He was never pedantic with his colleagues and most certainly was never apologetic. It would be too much to describe him as "one of the guys," but among his colleagues there was a great feeling of camaraderie when they gathered.

Again, this was powerful modeling for the development of a pastoral counseling center. As students, we were treated as colleagues. We were all seen as pilgrims in the search for truth. This demanded respect from each of us for what the other person knew and a belief that each person in his or her own human journey had come to understanding and insight which could be valuable for us all as we continued our journey.

I do not want to leave the impression that this was an egalitarian system. It clearly was not. However, the air of mutual respect overcame anyone's tendencies to presume to positions of eminence on the basis of office, tenure, background, and training that might have been awe inspiring in other settings. It was always clear who were the professors and more experienced therapists and who were the students and less experienced therapists. This recognition in no way detracted from the mutual learning experience.

Wise was a strong believer, therefore, in pastoral counselors needing to have collegiality with persons from other disciplines. These included the traditional disciplines of the church but also all of the disciplines in the behavioral sciences. I stress all because Wise was not afraid to examine the writings of persons in the behavioral sciences who seemed sometimes very far removed from the interest of a pastoral psychotherapist. He was open to new ideas and looked for ways to relate those insights to the work in which he was engaged.

In his view, therefore, all pastoral counseling centers need to make sure that they are in serious dialogue with other persons in the helping professions. These would include academicians as well as practitioners. This creative mixture is often misunderstood as an attempt to make sure that the pastoral counselor does not work in isolation. That is a

178

relatively superficial understanding of Wise's concern. It is true that such collegial relationships would prevent the pastoral counselor from becoming intellectually myopic. On the other hand, it also provided the pastoral counselor with a wonderful opportunity to engage persons in the behavioral sciences with concerns about issues such as meaning, reverence for life, the nature of the healing relationship, and other issues which were difficult to pin down in a scientific sense.

In other words, the dialogue was genuine dialogue. Pastoral counselors were not simply supposed to be recipients of the wisdom and expertise of colleagues from other disciplines. We were also expected to contribute to these colleagues our understandings of the nature and purpose of our task, namely the fostering of healing and growth.

Professionalism and Discipline

Wise was a pioneer in the Clinical Pastoral Education Movement. As such, he attempted to move the training of the pastoral counselor away from a strict academic routine into a clinical setting. He hoped that in such a setting pastoral would move from rigid positions characterized by intellectualization of their faiths to pastors becoming more compassionate and concerned as they experienced their own feelings. He once summed up this struggle to me by stating, "When I was at Boston University School of Theology, they kept wanting to talk about Personalism. On the other hand, I wanted to talk about persons."

He was committed to the proposition that if persons could move toward self-understanding, they would be better equipped to carry on the kind of interpersonal relationships which were productive. Specifically, he believed that pastors could utilize themselves more effectively in healing ministries if they began to trust their own intuitions and to value serendipitous cathartic experiences as part of their relationships with persons who came to them for help.

By the late fifties, when Wise was teaching graduate level courses at Garrett and Northwestern University, this model for the training of pastors in Clinical Pastoral Education was well accepted. In fact, it had become a mandatory part of the curriculum in most major denominations across the country. This led to another dilemma.

Many pastors were attracted to the pastoral counseling movement because it gave them more freedom of expression than what they had experienced as rigid constraint within their own denominational training. However, this sometimes led to pastoral counselors acting out of intuition and sometimes acting out their feelings as opposed to approaching the counseling ministry in any disciplined fashion. That was unthinkable for Wise. It led to fuzzy thought and sloppy work. He subscribed to the theory that a trained pastoral counselor was a professional who could think in an organized, systematic way, and was sufficiently well grounded in his or her own personal dynamics so as to be able to utilize a blend of insight and theory in order to effect change. The idea of pastoral counselors intuiting their way through counseling sessions, for him, would be tantamount to loose cannons on the deck of a ship.

This means that a pastoral counseling center should be characterized by professionalism. That is, pastoral psychotherapists must have a solid sense of the office of the pastor being utilized in a counseling setting. This means that pastoral psychotherapists should be those therapists who are able to explore issues such as meaning and value as well as those of psychopathology. It follows, therefore, that the pastoral counselor must be as thoroughly trained as any other practitioner, i.e., must be a well trained professional.

In order to become a professional, Wise believed that a great deal of discipline was involved. First, there was a discipline of knowing one's subject. That required academic preparation, which took a great deal of time and care. Wise had no respect for pastoral counselors who were simply the products of the last book they had read or workshop they had attended. He believed in years of rigorous interdisciplinary training. Second, he believed that in order to be an effective pastoral counselor, one had to know himself or herself very well. Consequently, he required of all doctoral students an experience of individual personal psychotherapy. This became the bane of existence for a number of students who attempted to approach the personal psychotherapy rubric as though it were a training analysis. Wise was quite happy to let peer group pressure, both from his interdisciplinary colleagues and from other students, work its magic on any student who approached personal psychotherapy in this way. He believed strongly that we who are pastoral therapists are all "wounded healers." We all very much need personal psychotherapy not as a training tool but to be able to blend intellectual formulation and intuition in a way unencumbered by psychopathology in order to affect the healing process. There were no substitutes; there were no short cuts.

The implications for a pastoral counseling center are clear. If we hold ourselves up to the general public as persons who are professionals, we must be thoroughly trained professionals. We must have a body of knowledge which we understand, an interdisciplinary grasp of the field of human behavior, and a sense of self that is not incumbered with psychopathology to the extent that we might harm those who come to us for healing.

It was with these things in mind that he was one of the founders of The American Association of Pastoral Counselors whose standards for training instantly became the most rigorous of any of the helping professions and remains so today. He insisted that the AAPC be different from other professional associations in that it would certify to the general public the competency of persons who were members of the organization.

180

A Desire to Learn

Professionalism based on discipline is closely related and dependent upon a strong desire to learn. The continuing "student posture" of the pastoral counselor is not always evident in many of the pastoral counseling centers which have sprung up around the country. The Wise model would make a pastoral counseling center a great center of learning and intellectual activity.

This posture is most easily achieved in a setting where training is being done as well as clinical practice being carried out. Wise would have been most comfortable with such a model. This is seen by his support of the tiers of membership reflected in AAPC, i.e., pastoral counselor-in-training, member, fellow, diplomate, professional affiliate. He fully expected that a person would want to become a member of AAPC and proceed through the ranks of Fellow to Diplomate, which ranks are characterized by the person's increasing ability to teach others the craft and discipline of pastoral psychotherapy. He would have been very concerned about any center solely concerned with treatment rather than with maintaining a quality service and training program.

The establishment and maintenance of a training modality immediately makes the practitioner think in disciplined ways in order to communicate with those who are trying to learn the craft. It does not matter whether the center has one practitioner or dozens of practitioners. The model is the same. Clinical practice and the offering of an educational program go hand in hand with the model of a pastoral counseling center that Wise lived out.

Unfortunately, many centers have not been able to achieve this balance between practice and education. The desire to practice the art of pastoral psychotherapy must always include the desire to learn from other colleagues. To become a more creative learner, one must also be a teacher. Centers borne of an activistic desire to help those in need, without the twin goals of treatment and education, begin with a shaky foundation. Individuals often are hired as clinical staff who do not have the training and background to teach clergy, and other students in the area, the craft of pastoral psychotherapy. An over-emphasis on clinical practice and a dependency on fees for such clinical practice leave little room for genuine intellectual growth. Wise, indeed, has much to teach us in this area.

Oral Tradition

We spoke above of Wise's characterization of the pastoral counseling discipline as a "movement." This term was not chosen lightly by him and others who used to do it. He and they had a profound sense of a tradition of healing ministries going back to biblical times. They saw

181

themselves to be a part of that tradition. Like many histories, it was at times a history of disagreement and schism. It also was characterized by great moments of warring factions coming together to form organizations which have lasted to today. Most notable, are the Association for Clinical Pastoral Education (ACPE) and the American Association of Pastoral Counselors (AAPC). I was privileged to listen to Wise reminisce about experiences with Anton Boisen, the father of the pastoral counseling movement in the United States, and stories about his relationships with and disagreements with some of the other leaders in the movement. He had great respect for those who were also working to establish the profession, especially those with whom he sometimes disagreed. We often had long and invigorating discussions about the work and opinions of people like Boisen, Seward Hiltner, Reuel Howe, Ernest Bruder, Wayne Oates, Richard Young, Frederick Kuether, John Billinsky, and Howard Clinebell.

That oral tradition was important for Wise because he saw the pastoral counseling center as being in the church, but not of the church. For him, the pastoral psychotherapist was part of a large ecumenical (although, at that time, largely Protestant) movement that interfaced with the church and the world. This model is extremely instructive for a pastoral counseling center.

It is clear that most centers see themselves as living in a tension between the world of health care providers and the world of the church. It is not so clear that many also see themselves as carrying on the Judeo-Christian tradition of a healing ministry. We have a witness to others who practice the healing arts. We also have a witness to those in the church who may see its ministry in a narrower sense. Wise believed that by living in such a creative tension, we would become more productive and faithful to our calling.

This is an extremely important concept, and one which speaks to the issues raised by the structures of many pastoral counseling centers today. Some centers have been tied closely to a single denomination or a group of congregations. They have little trouble helping staff to identify themselves as pastoral psychotherapists. The theological and organizational concerns of these institutional bodies permeate the structure and fabric of those centers. If problems do arise from such close ties, they arise when the sponsoring institutions become involved heavily in the day-to-day operations and erode the professional quality of service through an emphasis on doctrine or insistence on adherence to a particular organizational structure. In such cases, funding by the institutional supporters often depends on how well the center meets these goals rather than the goal of quality service rendered.

On the other hand, centers have been established which have very loose or little connection to faith organizations. They resemble group private practices, but lines of accountability often are blurred or non-existent. Within such centers, the emphasis is on pastoral psychotherapist, and the pastoral identity of the staff is weakened.

Traditionally, Wise would insist the pastoral psychotherapist must practice ministry in organizations which live within the tension of being in the faith group, but not of it. When such tension is dealt with creatively, the center enriches the institution by providing a vital compassionate service to those seeking help. Simultaneously, the center receives support, strength, and creative criticism from a faith organization which sees pastoral psychotherapy as a central function of ministry.

A Sense of Awe and Compassion

Those who came to know Wise well understood him to be a person who, while contending very vigorously for things in which he believed, was also a person of deep faith and extraordinary compassion. He marvelled at the complexity of human beings and the ways in which God would speak in and through the lives of persons. Despite the demands which he placed on students at both the M.Div. and other graduate levels, he always was compassionate and very interested in the personal dilemmas which befell any of his students. As he grew older, and prior to the birth of his own grandchildren, his sense of awe was seen most easily as he began to develop the hobby of photographing infants and young children. This man, whom many found to be a formidable adversary or a rigorous intellectual critic, could display a sense of awe in the presence of an infant that was very moving.

In terms of a model of a pastoral counseling center, Wise would have us understand that professional persons need to make sure that they avoid any sense of haughtiness and superiority. Our practices and teaching methods always must be characterized by a sense of understanding our dependence on the healing power of God and a concern for human beings that leads us to do our work well. This sense also enables us to minister to persons from all strata of society.

Wise employed a black CPE supervisor, Merrell Bettner, to teach in the Garrett program before there was any consciousness raised about race in the training and practice of pastoral counselors. Moreover, he admitted qualified women to the doctoral level program before there was much of a push to do so. His sympathies and sensitivities were ever inclusive.

The implications for a pastoral counseling center in these areas is clear. It needs to be a multi-disciplined organization, and an inclusive one as well. It needs to concern itself with a full range of human experiences in every stage of life from birth through death. The "Wise model" of a pastoral counseling center has a staff which is not only well trained but which also has a sense of dependence upon the "Ground of our Being" if we are to facilitate healing and growth processes. A sense of compassion is central. Because of such compassion, a center provides services for persons regardless of their backgrounds or ability to pay.

Summary

Carroll A. Wise left us no explicit model for a pastoral counseling center. In his writings and his method of teaching, however, he left us an implicit model, which includes the elements listed above. Clearly, Wise believed that a pastoral counseling center was essentially a religious institution. For him, the therapeutic and religious struggles were inextricably bound up with each other.

> The chief struggle in either religious or therapeutic processes is the modification of that narcissism or self-centeredness which demands that life in the universe, including others, revolves around us. The task is to learn to use self-concern and self-esteem to make those decisions which enhance rather than destroy the self. When we move out of our self-centeredness, we see that what enhances our own life also enhances the lives of others and that decisions which hurt others also hurt us. Our welfare is inextricably bound to that of others. (Wise, 1983, p.298)

He also notes that:

> The healing that takes place in pastoral therapy does not replace the ancient experience of worship. Therapy is essentially the process of discovering the self in relationship to the self, to others and to God. Worship is essentially the discovery of the presence of God, and the self-disclosure, renewal and commitment which takes place through that discovery. (Ibid., p.299)

We speak here of a pastoral counseling center model which includes the religious in both the broadest and narrowest sense. Wise calls us to a model that is identified closely with the worship life of the Judeo-Christian tradition. For him, apart from this tradition, there can be no pastoral counseling center.

THE LIVING HUMAN EXPERIENCE ACROSS CULTURES

John E. Hinkle, Jr.

The "living human experience" has been identified in this festschrift as a phrase which expresses the central thematic interest of Carroll Wise. This same phrase, the living human experience, provides an appropriate departure point for the explication of Carroll's interest in the diversity of the human experience across a variety of cultures, and the significance he attached to such diversity. In the following pages I will attempt to show that Carroll was keenly aware of the need for cross cultural understandings of the experience of humanness as a clue to the meaning of transcendence, both proximate and ultimate.

This chapter also contends that Carroll viewed the understandings derived from the multicultural variability of living human experiences as having the capacity to present a challenge to monoculturally based (traditional) parochial and para-parochial pastoral skills. I argue here that Carroll viewed the multicultural variability of the living human experience as capable of providing a broader range of data for use in the critique of monocultural theoretical perspectives of humanness, as well as enabling a critique of pastoral skills, traditionally conceived. Additionally, his position reflected a view that broadening the data base of human experience through cultural variability with its consequent critique of monoculturally based theory in turn provides an avenue for the development of a more adequate understanding of both humanness and transcendence. Consequently, it is argued here that Carroll was able to envision the significant contribution cross-cultural understandings could make to psychological and theological understandings of theory and practice of pastoral care, pastoral counseling, and pastoral psychotherapy.

Carroll stated his position in these matters more often in theological than in psychological terms. He spoke of the transcendent dimensions of human experience, by which he meant, in part, the universally human.[1] But he was also quick to point to resources in the discipline of culture and personality studies as the broader frame of reference for personality theory. On more than one occasion he said, "The future of personality theory lies with the discipline of culture and personality studies." (Hinkle, Class Notes, 1962.) This comment, taken in its historical context, is the more remarkable because other writers of that period were not so sanguine about prospects for contributions to theory from culture and personality studies.

Wise on Culture and Personality

A major reason that the field of culture and personality studies was not highly respected in scientific circles during the early years of Carroll's tenure at Garrett was due in large measure to the presence and ascendancy of an increasingly narrow and rigidified logical positivism in the social and behavioral sciences. As a consequence of this rigidified logical positivism, theory and methodology in the field of culture and personality studies had fallen into disrepute in the social science community, as had the more comprehensive personality theories and the derivative clinical methods being utilized by clinical pastoral counselors and other mental health professionals. Theories of personality in these disciplines had been built up over several decades through work based largely on the results of clinical, as contrasted with empirical, observation. Hence Carroll's view about the importance of studies in the field of culture and personality, and the potential importance of such studies to personality theory and pastoral psychotherapy, was not widely shared at the time.

Currently, however, culture and personality studies are re-emerging in the form of studies of culture and the self. (Marcella, Devos, Hsu, 1985) The outlines of cultural conceptions of selfhood are being traced with more enthusiasm by researchers. (Geertz, 1977) The ethnocentricity and egocentricity of "Western Scientific" conceptions of the self as individualistic are more and more suspect. Alternatives are being offered. (Sullivan, 1984) Psychology is more and more perceived by its friendly critics as needing to redefine itself as an interpretive and hermeneutical discipline. (Sullivan, 1984; Schafer, 1975; Spence, 1987) The symbolic cultural dimensions of the pastoral role are increasingly being seen as central. (Holmes, 1978) Wise's view that studies of the relationship between culture and personality hold promise for the development of both theory and practice appears as both accurate and visionary.

Carroll was of the opinion that clergypersons had a unique contribution to make to culture and personality studies in terms of both theoretical and practical concerns. As early as 1942, he wrote,

> The clergyman [sic] has a unique contribution to make to the problems of personality and of culture, but this contribution may be made only through the development of the methods of the clergyman [sic] to the place where they are adequate for present day needs. Of course the problem is deeper than methods. The clergyman [sic] must have a living faith to express through his [sic] methods. (Wise, 1942, p. 257)

The unique contribution is to be made through the development of methods consistent with clergy identity, adequate to present day needs, and expressive of "a living faith." The language of this quote illustrates Carroll's concerns for the interface between faith and function, theory and practice, and personality and culture.

Given the twin concerns of theory and methodology for culture and personality studies on the one hand, and the implications of these studies for the pastoral role on the other, it is important to remember

186

that Wise himself would have approached these issues, where he could, through the phenomenology of his own experience. He would proceed, not in the role of scientific observer (a power relationship), but in the role of dialogical participant (mutuality). His sensitivity in these matters was based on a particular understanding of humanness and a particular view of interpersonal relationships.

Alice Graham McNair is a black female who was a Master of Divinity student at Garrett during Carroll's tenure. Her experience of him is instructive in this regard. She shared the following at the Memorial Dinner for him in Downingtown, Pa., on the occasion of the Annual Conference of the American Association of Pastoral Counselors, April 1986:

I want to share with you how I experienced Carroll by the following incident. In a course on creativity, Carroll asked us to do a study on cultural symbols. Well, I didn't know prior to this class much about cultural symbols and Carroll attempted to teach us all. When I said to him that I had some difficulty identifying a cultural symbol, he said, "What about Langston Hughes' character Jesse B. Sempler, as a symbol?" Now the Jesse character was Langston Hughes, as a black writer, kind of an alter ego, and this character would speak about the black condition.

Well, first of all, Carroll Wise was not supposed to know anything about Langston Hughes, much less the character Jesse as symbol. That for me was a very validating experience--to have this man talk to me about this character out of my own experience. And for the first time I understood why I had been an academic under-achiever. Because nobody had ever talked to me . . . and that's the thing I remember about Carroll . . . and the thing I take into my own work with students and clients.

Carroll had a profound respect for human beings, a tremendous curiosity about who people were. With him, there was not the experience of being labeled. I never felt with Carroll that I was a woman, though I was, or black, though I was. I was a human being and that was the important thing about our interaction. He did not deny the realities of a culture, but he did not confine me to that-- that authentic experience of humanity is what I value about my experience with Carroll which was consistent throughout my M. Div. work, and throughout my Ph. D. work in every encounter I had with him. I am sometimes not as good as I would like to be in expressing that kind of authenticity, but I do strive to be that kind of authentic person with human beings because it meant so much to me. (McNair, 1986)

As Alice clearly indicates, Carroll was in relationship with those from cultures other than his own as one human being to another, in relationships of mutuality and authenticity. He was interested in Alice both as a human being, and as a cultural person. Carroll bothered to do his homework. He became familiar with literature from that culture; he knew something of its heroes and other symbols. But, as Alice notes, his relationship to her as a person from that culture was first and foremost as one human being to another. Cultural symbols were employed in the interest of facilitating the human dimension of their relationship.

Wise was clear about the way in which cultural symbols could facilitate human relationships. He was also clear about the way in which cultural symbols could be used defensively and destructively.

Theory Expressed Theologically: Utilitarian Religion vs. Genuine Insight

As Hessert points out elsewhere in this volume, Wise was clear about the necessity for utilizing cultural forms in daily functioning. And he was keenly aware of the potential idolatry of utilizing cultural forms as a way of defending against the potential for human growth in the encounter with those "realities" which transcend cultural forms. In this connection Wise writes of "utilitarian religion" in contrast with "genuine insight". He wrote, "Much of our utilitarian brand of religion seeks to help people by protecting them from the necessity of a profound change through giving easy answers to external situations." (Wise, 1951, p. 148) Insight, on the other hand, is understood as ..."the emotional apprehension of reality . . ." and, ". . . insight results in the possibility of conscious, intellectual formulation of what has already taken place on the deeper dynamic levels of personality . . ." (Wise, 1951, p. 119) in a non-defensive manner.

Penetration of personal and cultural issues and images to the point of achieving transparency about, as well as both emotional and cognitive apprehension of, the point of their interface with the Ultimate in a manner which transforms, is for Wise the primary, dominant, everpresent, and overriding concern of pastoral care and counseling relationships. In order for this self/other/God transparency (apprehension or insight) to occur, a relationship of trust, acceptance, and sensitive communication must be established. These are the conditions for this experience of insight (or in Hessert's terms "faith") to occur.

Here, at the level of theory, Wise's concern about the transcultural experience of the Ultimate, and the formulation of that experience in non-defensive language, may be seen. In addition to the openness of his theory to the metacultural and transcultural aspects of human experience, Carroll's methodology reveals the same openness to cross cultural varieties of human experience. He sought to encounter the culturally other as dialogical partner rather than as detached observer, through and in the cultural frame. A further word about method is in

188

order at this point.

Methodology: Empathy and Objectivity

Wise was clear about method in pastoral care. The method was interpersonal/incarnational communication; communication of the inner meaning of the Gospel to persons at the point of their need for healing or growth through relationship. (Wise, 1966, pp. 67-8) He understood this communication to be deeply personal and profoundly symbolic, in other words, transpersonal, cultural, and transcultural. In that respect he followed Tillich's understanding of the symbolic, (Tillich, 1964) that is, a symbol has the capacity of opening up deeper levels of both intrapsychic (personal) and interpersonal (communal) meaning in the exchange.

Wise defined pastoral care and counseling as both 1) presence, and 2) communication with the parishioner or client in a way that allows and facilitates a deeper and deeper apprehension of the realities of self and other. Because of that apprehension insight (for Hessert, faith) can occur. By communicating in this manner, the pastoral caregiver is pointing beyond herself or himself to the Incarnate One, Jesus Christ, who was and is the communication from God through the Holy Spirit. Pastoral care, thereby, is participation in this dimension of communication, through cultural symbols to the point of transcending cultural symbols in order to return to such symbols with a new vision (hermeneutic) and a new Spirit.

Wise and Freud: Methods and Models

While Wise was appreciative of psychoanalytic psychology and psychotherapy, the model for his method, as indicated above, is Jesus Christ. In contrast, Freud's model was "the observing ego or little scientist." (LeVine, 1973, p. 221-24) That model for the exploration of the human psyche was a research model, the detached observer and the observed! How strange that it should become a "treatment" method with so little modification! I raise the question: is the Wise model also intended to provide a way to explore the human psyche, but from the perspective of Enlightenment Mysticism rather than Enlightenment Rationalism? Could this tension between the mystical and the rational (the right brain and the left) explain the continuing emphasis that Wise placed on the empirical and transcultural, along with the intrapsychic and interpersonal method in his development of research and training? I am persuaded that Carroll was pointing to the transcendent by means of the transpersonal and transcultural.

Goal: Relationship in Terms of The Living Human Experience

In referring to his own background, Wise has been quoted as saying that his theological colleagues were interested in studying "personalism," while he was interested in studying persons. (Moss, 1976b; Thompson,

189

this volume) Wise seems to have meant by this quip that he was more interested in learning how to relate to persons as "human beings" in a manner that was expressive of (perhaps even facilitative of) basic humanness, rather than as objects of rational analysis. The analytic approach provides distance, and grows out of a paradigm of technical rationality, i.e., Freud's model of the little scientist, the detached observer. (LeVine, 1973) Wise does not feel that relating to others in primarily a left brain analytic mode communicates or even allows for a full humanness. At the same time he insisted that students master the left brain theoretical and empirical research procedures appropriate to their disciplines, whether those disciplines were academic or professional.

While Wise appreciated what the intellectual disciplines could contribute to understanding the human experience, he was vigorously opposed to the use of such theory for the control and/or manipulation of others, as well as self (and/or God). Intellectual analysis was not to be a substitute for a manner of relating which involved the affective as well as the cognitive aspects of experience. Rather than seeing the affective and cognitive processes as dichotomous, it is more helpful to view them as dialogical, or interpenetrating.

Wise considered the "emotional apprehension of reality" as an event in which the affective and the cognitive are experienced as integrated within the self. That experience involves both the affective connotations as well as the conceptual denotations in one intrapsychic and interpersonal gestalt. Such an experience is spiritual. It results in a sense of personal wholeness and communal connectedness (an I-Thou experience). This is why Hessert can refer to it as "faith" or "faithing," while Wise calls it insight.

Cross Cultural Participation

In the light of his appreciation for the development of theory which could represent the living human experience adequately, it was a natural step for Wise to pursue new knowledge about the humanness of human beings through a knowledge of other cultural experiences and interpretations of that humanness. While others carried out the task of empirical research in the model of technical rationality, he preferred to immerse himself in the task of understanding others through ever deeper levels of participation (interpersonal communication). The experience of Alice, cited above, is both example and testimony to the results of his approach. Additionally, he utilized his role as faculty advisor to recommend cultural studies in the social sciences to students. My own experience as a student advisee was that of being directed by Wise to engage in cross-cultural studies through the discipline of culture and personality research methods and results.

At the level of knowledge accumulation and theory building Carroll was interested in taking account of the ultimate, as well as the proximate, basis for meaning in human experience. As Hessert's piece in this volume shows, the theological underpinnings for Carroll's theory of pastoral counseling taps into a level of human experience that is transcultural, even though the symbolic and thematic content would be culturally relevant, that is, culturally conditioned. He showed interest in knowledge and theory building, as well as in the making of meaning, at both personal and cultural levels.

Carroll's Method and Cross Cultural Method

Beyond this, however, the argument here is that Carroll's method of relating to others is consistent with his interest in cross cultural research. If, as Clinebell indicates, referencing Dunne's work, the great adventure of our time is, ". . . the passing over into another culture, and then coming back to one's own culture a transformed person," (Augsburger, 1986, p.6) then Wise's method of empathy and objectivity is of more than casual interest in cross cultural studies. Both his method and theory open the possibility of escaping from cultural encapsulation through the utilization of cross cultural research. Indeed, the necessity of first crossing over (empathy) and then coming back (reflection), in Wise's view of pastoral care and counseling relationships, is paralleled by Dunne's method for culture bridging. Dunne also describes "crossing over" and "coming back" as movements in crossing cultural boundaries. (Dunne, 1972. p. 53)

To explicate Wise more fully, the pastor is to enter into the experience of the other to the extent that deep levels of human communication can occur, and then is to move back to the individuated and autonomous self for reflection and preparation for further communication.

In the empathy aspect of the movement, the goal is to understand the world as the other sees and experiences it, i. e., to see the world from the other's point of view.

In the stage of reflection, theory may be utilized to formulate the human experience in ever more adequate ways based on the experiences of each new encounter.

But, while the similarity of Wise's methodology with that suggested by Dunne seems evident, the crossing over by empathic relationships indicated by Wise assumes that such empathy is indeed possible between those persons who are relating. The "catch" is that such an assumption cannot usually be made when the parties involved are from contrasting cultures. It is difficult enough for each of us within our own cultural matrix.

Cultural Encapsulation and the Limits of Empathy

David Augsburger writes, "One who knows but one culture knows no culture." (1986, p. 18) The meaning of this remark is that just as a fish would not experience the existence of water until it comes out into the air, so individuals cannot know their own culture until they have experienced an alternative culture. This statement may be applied to Carroll, even though, as a monocultural person, he appears to have been able to work with persons in a way that suggests a high degree of cultural awareness.

For example, his ability to transcend cultural differences was rather clearly in evidence in the account Alice gives of her experience of Carroll. She and Carroll do, however, share a common language, including many of the cultural assumptions that the shared language entails, i. e., they share a compatible, if not an identical, world view. But in situations where the cultural frame of a common language is absent, or is significantly different, the method will work only after the culture is learned. In fact, language learning may be a significant aspect of the "passing over" into another culture.

Wise as an Enlightened Monoculturalist

Carroll may be properly viewed as an enlightened monoculturalist rather than as a multicultural person. Nevertheless, the central characteristic of his method allows for an openness to the learning of another culture, namely the notion that "passing over, and then coming back" (Dunne, 1972, p. 53) is essential to human communication. This notion is qualified in that Carroll apparently had in mind the transcending of ego boundaries more than of cultural boundaries, though he was mindful of the latter as well.

While one may view Carroll's work with mental patients early on in his career as the learning of another culture, or his exposure to the study of European languages during his graduate days as a beginning exposure to other cultures, or his encounter with ethnic differences in terms of direct personal relationships with students, clients, and parishioners from ethnic groups other than his own, there were, nevertheless, clear limits to Carroll's actual "in depth" experience of a culture other than his own. Even though he had become a participant in the process of "going over and then coming back," his encounter with contrast cultures was limited, as were the cultural understandings out of which he worked.

Critique

A review of Carroll's writings suggests rather clearly that he was operating within the monocultural frame of Western Civilization. Further, he worked within a notion of personhood that is distinctively Western, which may be characterized as individualistic. Alternative views of the self, i.e., non-Western views, are nowhere discussed in his writings. Views of bi-cultural self understandings, which could take into account bi-culturality of functioning, are not only absent, but perhaps would even be in conflict with his view of integrated, autonomous selfhood or personhood. Hence, his lack of cross cultural experience limits the universality of his views of the living human experience. His view would be identified more accurately as "the living human experience of the self understood in an individualistic Western frame." The discussion will turn to some examples of these alternative views of the self in a moment. It is important to note at this point, however, that the inadequacies of a monocultural frame for the development of theories of personality are significant, and not to be passed over lightly.

Returning to Augsburger's statement, this author maintains that unless one encounters another culture with sufficient depth and intensity of functioning that one must develop an alternative "self image" or persona for use in that culture, then the extensive and pervasive nature of cultural encapsulation is likely to remain more a vague impression than an enduring basis for new behavior, attitudes, and actions, or more specifically, creative new scholarship. It is in this latter definition of monocultural that the work of Wise, while pointing outward to other cultures and inward to transcultural experiences of ultimate meaning, was and is culturally encapsulated. (This statement is intended to include rather than ignore critiques from within the culture such as gender and ethnic bias, which are addressed at length in other chapters in this volume.)

The thematic area of "conceptions of the self" can serve to illustrate the dilemmas involved in culturally encapsulated work. Definitions of the pathological, as well as normality, will be applied in the context of a discussion of the self concept as a focal theme.

Culture and the Self

A bright Korean student stepped forward following a class session at the seminary in which a group of ministerial students had viewed the film, "Everybody Rides the Carousel," a dramatic rendition of Erikson's theory of psychosocial development. He observed in a cautiously questioning and imminently respectful manner, "It seems that the objective of living in America is the development of a strong personal identity. Is this not correct?"

The stark simplicity, yet profundity, of his statement of the "dominant culture ideal image of personhood" was startling. Anthropoligist Francis L. K. Hsu characterizes this view of ideal personhood with the words "self reliance." And, Hsu goes on to say, a major difference between the view of self reliance held in the United States and the view of self reliance held in other cultural contexts is that the U. S. holds it as a "militant ideal." (Hsu, 1961, p. 217)

Whether one agrees that the notion of self reliance is an accurate description of the good, ideal, or optimal person in the United States, it might be agreed that cultural conceptions of the "good", "ideal", or "optimal" person tend to focus a cluster of values which are functional in a given society. Hence, different kinds of societies tend to have quite different views of the good, the ideal, or the optimal person. For most members of Western Civilization, notions of personal autonomy, self reliance, and individuated integrated selfhood are preferred over other traits in the definition of the ideal person.

These Western notions of personhood, when viewed from the perspective of other cultures, often seem strange, and even unique. For example, given the personal, social, and cultural distance which my Korean immigrant student could maintain from the American view of the ideal person, based on his contrasting cultural background, it was possible for him to observe the "cultural reality" of the American view of personhood. He could identify with accuracy and simplicity a major objective of "life in the U. S. A.," that is, that a major goal of growing up in America is the development of a strong sense of personal identity.

Conceptions of the Self: From the Native's Point of View

Clifford Geertz notes that,

> The concept of person is, in fact, an excellent vehicle by which to examine this whole question of how to go about poking into another people's turn of mind. (Geertz, 1977, p. 483)

He continues,

> The Western conception of the person as a bounded, unique, more or less integrated motivational and cognitive universe, a dynamic center of awareness, emotion, judgement, and action organized into a distinctive whole and set contrastively both against other such wholes and against a social and natural background is, however incorrigible it may seem to us, a rather peculiar idea within the context of the world's cultures. Rather than attempt to place the experience of others within the framework of such a conception, which is what the extolled "empathy" in fact usually comes down to , we must, if we are to achieve understanding, set that conception aside and view their experience within the framework of their own idea of what selfhood is. And for Java, Bali, and Morocco, at least, that idea differs markedly, not only from our own but, no less dramatically and no less instructively, from one to the other. (Ibid., p. 483)

Alpers makes a similar comment in discussing both the Homeric Greeks (as does Jaynes [1976, p.255ff] in a somewhat different way) and the Polynesians. Alpers says of both the Homeric Greeks and the Polynesians,

194

. . . the very notion of the individual as we have conceived it since the Renaissance had never emerged in those societies. (Alpers, 1970, p.14)

Geertz describes at length the "selves" of Java, Bali, and Morocco, characterizing them as quietistic, dramaturgical, and contextual, respectively. Limitations of space preclude a full rendition here, but an example from Bali may indicate the range of differences from our peculiarly Western view of the self. Geertz writes,

. . . there is in Bali a persistent and systematic attempt to stylize all aspects of personal expression to the point where anything idiosyncratic, anything characteristic of the individual merely because he is who he is physically, psychologically, or biographically, is muted in favor of his assigned place in the continuing and, so it is thought, never-changing pageant that is Balinese life. It is dramatis personae, not actors, that endure; indeed, it is dramatis personae, not actors, that in the proper sense really exist. Physically men, women, and children come and go-- mere incidents in a happenstance history of no genuine importance, even to themselves. But the masks they wear, the stage they occupy, the parts they play, and, most important, the spectacle they mount remain and constitute not the facade but the substance of things, not least the self . . . There is no make-believe: of course players perish, but the play doesn't, and it is the latter, the performed rather than the performer, that really matters. (Ibid., p. 486)

In such a culture the fear is

. . . that the public performance to which one's cultural location commits one will be botched and that the personality (as we would call it but the Balinese, of course, not believing in such a thing, would not) of the individual will break through to dissolve his standardized public identity. (Ibid., p.487)

In short, the fear is that a "personality" will break through due to poor role performance, ". . . that the audience (and the actor) loses sight of Hamlet and gains, uncomfortably for all concerned, a picture of bumbling John Smith painfully miscast as the Prince of Denmark." (Ibid., p. 487) But the breakthrough of "personality" in this sense would be "pathological" rather than normal, unhealthy and socially disruptive rather than healthy and socially affirming.

The individualizing transformation of the role into personhood would amount to a psychotic episode for those participants in the drama. In Bali, it is the role and the drama that are the 'real' thing, not the self. In the Western concept, individualism and self reliance are valued so highly that anything which contributes to dependency and loss of individuality will be seen as pathological. From the perspective of

195

"pathology" and "health," what is healthy in Bali is pathological in the Western Caucasian North American view of the self, and what is healthy in Western Caucasian North American view of the self is pathological in Balinese view of the self (if one can even speak in this manner of a view of the self in Bali).

Westerners, with their individualistic view of the self, have such great difficulty in understanding other views of selfhood that they try to re-work those conceptions in Western terms. As Kassam says,

> When a European or an American (U.S.A.) goes to Asia or Africa, he or she brings not an unwillingness to understand or a lack of understanding, but more an inability to understand. Like the explorers who preceded them, such persons are mapping the world on a principle of perpetual extension. The explorer always brings-- automatically--one civilization to scrutinize another. (Kassam, 1987, p. 64)

Cultural Encapsulation

The foregoing discussion can serve to alert the reader to the pervasive nature of the impact of the encapsulated monocultural Western view of the self upon the work of Wise. He was, of course, directing his work toward the enhancement of effectiveness in pastoral ministry in mainline Protestant denominational settings in the U. S. A. So his use of the monocultural frame is understandable. And we have shown that he was an enlightened and culturally sensitive monoculturalist. Nevertheless, it must be said that the multicultural frame of reference, which is largely missing in the work of Wise, provides a more substantive frame for formulating the living human experience, and hence ministry in such a context, than does the monocultural frame which characterizes his work.

The ethnocentric biases of monocultural views of ministry and mission have been the cause of much mischief on the part of the Church and the academy over the centuries. The monocultural frame, even in an "enlightened" form, simply will not do any longer. Whether it was ever adequate is a question. Multicultural perspectives are essential to more adequate conceptualization of the living human experience and ministry to persons in the context of our day and time.

Changing Paradigms: Self and Culture Studies

The dictatorial reign of that philosophy of science known as logical positivism, which held sway in Carroll's day, has largely ended in the social and behavioral sciences. Problems can be pursued whereever they lead with fewer scientific methodological restraints. A hermeneutical, interpretive perspective, with roots in the humanities, is gaining credibility. (Smith in Marsella, 1985; Geertz, 1973; Sullivan, 1984; Gerkin, 1984; Spence, 1987; Schafer, 1975). This broadening of

196

perspective includes interpretive, symbolic, and hermeneutical considerations basic to new advances in personality theory (Smith in Marsella, 1985). A cross-cultural approach is seen once again as essential if personality studies are to advance toward more adequate ways of conceiving "the living human experience." Conceptions of the self as experienced across cultures and through cross cultural studies can provide essential data for winnowing out the bias of monocultural frames.

Cross Cultural and Multicultural Approaches

Donald T. Campbell (in Hsu, 1961) comments on the need for these multicultural approaches at the level of method. He demonstrates the "mutual methodological relevance" of anthropology and psychology by maintaining that cultural anthropology provides an important part of the scientific apparatus of psychology, particularly for personality theory. Campbell notes:

In the absence of the possibility of experimentation with modes of child rearing and personality formation, a science of personality would be all but impossible were it not for the "laboratory" of cross-cultural comparison opened up by the anthropologist. (Campbell in Hsu, 1961, p. 335.) Anthropological evidence has been, and can continue to be, of invaluable service as a crucible in which to put to more rigorous test psychology's tentative theories, enabling one to edit them and select among alternatives in ways in which laboratory experiments and correlational studies within our own culture might never make possible. (Ibid, p.334)

Cross-cultural approaches to the study of the living human experience share a multicultural frame. Multicultural frames can be utilized to study the self-in-culture unit within each cultural frame without a loss of the larger multicultural frame. Comparisons between such units then become possible. Rather than becoming focused on studies of the self which implicitly assume that self-as-this-culture-defines-it is a universal frame, the way is open to the view that self-as-this-culture-defines-it is one of many views of self.

In a multicultural perspective, one culture's definitions of self may be compared with other cultural definitions of self so that the metaphorical basis of selfhood can be studied, for example. Within the context of multicultural frames a researcher can approach ideal conceptions of the self across cultures, viewing conceptions of normalcy and pathology within cultures and across cultures. Such perspectives can enable etic (transcultural) as well as emic (within culture) points of view to be brought to bear on conceptions of the self in Bali, Java, and Morocco, as well as in the U.S. of A.

From Empathy to Interpathy

In a multicultural perspective the empathy and objectivity method of relating to others endorsed by Wise needs to give way to the development of interpathy (Augsburger, 1986). Augsburger writes,

Interpathy is an intentional cognitive envisioning and affective experiencing of another's thoughts and feelings, even though the thoughts rise from another process of knowing, the values grow from another frame of moral reasoning, and the feelings spring from another basis of assumptions. In interpathic caring, the process of "feeling with" and "thinking with" another requires that one enter the other's world of assumptions, beliefs, and values and temporarily take them as one's own. (Augsburger, 1986, p. 29)

Interpathy goes beyond empathy. Interpathy involves passing over into the cosmology and value system of another to the point of gaining a capacity to experience the world from that perspective. Such is the basic requirement of multicultural methodologies.

The multicultural interpathic perspective means that an ethnographic schedule of questions and explorations needs to be integrated into the traditional personal and/or family case history questions of the initial clinical pastoral interview for cross cultural clients or parishoners. If the pastor is to break through his or her monocultural assumptions of cultural similarity, and begin the process of passing over into the cosmology, value system, and ideal conception of self of the culturally other, ethnographic questions which explore that assumptive world are required. The clergyperson, whether as pastor or as clinical pastoral counselor, needs to utilize interpathy in order to be able to achieve genuine dialogue (mutuality in communication, to use Wise's language) across cultural boundaries.

Summary

Wise contributed in major ways to the task of integrating theological and psychological insights into an effective theory and practice of pastoral care and counseling ministries. He did so in what appears to be, largely if not entirely, a monocultural frame. Yet both his theory and method point beyond the monocultural frame, which he never fully transcended, to a utilization of cross-cultural methods for further work. As he states explicitly, the future of personality theory lies with the discipline of culture and personality studies. Interpathy as a replacement for empathy, at the level of method, presents itself as an appropriate revision of Wise for engaging in such efforts.

Like a Moses on a mountain, Wise looked beyond the river of the momocultural frame into the Promised Land of cross-cultural methods in a multicultural frame, and like Moses, he could not cross over. The developments of his day did not permit an extensive exploration of these possibilities. In going beyond Wise, our task requires a move from monocultural to multicultural concerns in the classroom; from interdisciplinary to intercultural consultants in the clinic; from empathy to interpathy in pastoral and psychotherapeutic method; from monocultural to multicultural frames for understanding ministry in parochial and paraparochial settings; and for a mutual dialogical participation in the broader reaches of the living human experience which multicultural perspectives can provide.

PART IV

EMPIRICAL EMPHASIS

QUALITY INFORMATION AND VARIETIES OF APPLICATION

Part I has skectched the impact of Carroll and his ideas. Parts II and III have highlighted issues of pastoral identity and clinical concerns. However, from the perspective of the late 1980s it may well be that, in addition to the professionalization of pastoral psychotherapy as a specialty, his greatest significance comes in the research generated as a result of his influence.

Rich as impressionistic hunches and moving anecdotes are, the responsible professional needs quality information about the needs of hurting people and approaches that mediate healing. In describing "Carroll A. Wise and The Empirical Research Tradition," Richard E. Augspurger describes Carroll's insistence upon "a theoretical framework for discernment." He came to that competence in theory out of his learning from Boisen to identify data that distinguishes "religious experience" from psychiatric behaviors. Although it was more implicit than explicit, Carroll set the stage for "the integration of theory and practice" in empirical inquiry as well as in pastoral psychotherapy. By listing the doctoral dissertations of the Garrett-Evangelical Ph.D. program in Pastoral Psychology and Counseling, Augspurger gathers in one place the topics investigated.

John L. Florell investigated what constitutes pastoral care in the hospital. More importantly, given today's cost-conscious milieu, whether that care is cost-effective. Evidence clearly showed that anxiety level, use of pain medication, length of hospitalization, and other specific factors were related directly to support and support-information interventions. John identifies quality information, or what he calls "naming" and knowing, as the single most crucial factor facilitating patient improvement; and pastoral care made that information sharing process more likely. Through exploring patients' faith and feelings,--particularly the feelings of "doubt, fear, helplessness, and anxiety"--the chaplain helps them identify "the meaning of [their] illness." Florell concludes that "[by] combining information, spiritual support, and strong relational skills, clergy can provide a strong foundation of healing for the hospitalized patients."

In "Measuring Unresolved Grief," by J.Colby Martin and Ronald R. Lee make use of a simple, though sophisticated, questionnaire about bereavement, and through a description of three different case illustrations, the authors illumine the grieving process. Further, they link that with selfobject theory about patterns of investment individuals have with significant others. The report, therefore, combines empirical research, with theoretical speculation, in the service of pastoral care.

At first glance, J. Jeffrey Means' essay entitled "C.A. Wise On Professional Education for Ministry" seems out of place. It belongs more logically in the earlier section on clinical concerns. In perspective, however, it belongs equally, if not more so, in this section on empirical research. Let us explain.

Carroll insisted on holding the pastoral, humanization of ministry in healthy tension with its professionalization. He identified the power of "the emotional dimension" of our lives, especially the "crucial role . . . of self-knowledge and insight in the development of pastors." Because of that realism about the power of emotional factors in effective ministry, Wise fought for a professional education which integrated "a body of knowledge and practical skills with personality dimensions and faith commitments." It was this emphasis on the person of the pastor which led him to press for "professional" education, in contrast to vocational or academic education. Means' citations come primarily from Carroll's writings in the 1940s and 1950s when the clinical orientation and supervision were the primary tools available. It was those convictions which led to sophisticated research, and resulting interventions, from the 1960s on into the present.

Reports of several specific investigations follow. While informative for the researcher, they may be technical for the nonspecialist. However, the nonspecialist can gain a sense of the intricacy and care with which empirical research is conducted. Even more, the nonspecialist is given understandable specifics about the value which can derive from systematic investigation.

Within a process of systemic change, John H. Hinkle, Jr. and Emily Demme Haight chart the course of introducing personality assessment in seminary and denominational contexts. By means of specific illustrations, they elaborate Wise's distinctive contribution to the area of personality evaluation and personnel selection as it has unfolded over the last forty years. The key concern is shifting from an "other-oriented and cognitive" focus to one that understands ministry in terms of "self-reflective and relational" dynamics.

The United Methodist Church, with which Garrett-Evangelical is associated, is a system of clergy appointment with tenure. That context allows for the development of more specific criteria for ministerial selection than for the prediction and selection for ministry in general. (See Ashbrook, 1970) Because of that, "A Professional Model for Ministry" could include both the personal and professional fitness and competencies which were Carroll's concerns.

Under the guidance of the Department of Pastoral Psychology and Counseling, the seminary developed procedures, with criteria, for remedial decisions as to readiness for Clinical Pastoral Education, more specifically, and for preparation for "the practice of effective professional ministry," more generally. The authors lament the failure of the seminary to utilize assessment for "routine and curricular" growth issues, though they do allude to the educational use of The Theological School Inventory and the Learning Styles Inventory in the

Introduction to Ministry groups the first year and the Myers Briggs Type Indicator with the Field Education Groups in the second year. Nevertheless, they detail how a consenusal, theoretical/empirical model for professional ministry was developed and is being implemented in the seminary.

Ronald R. Lee explains (and generalizes) a specific omponent of that model in his report on "Need for Approval Behavior and The MMPI." The material is based upon an analysis of that instrument's obvious/subtle scales. The pattern appears in those who accommodate themselves to the culture of the institutions in which they work. By means of case illustrations from business executives, those struggling with marital failure, and instances of ministerial effectiveness and depression, Ron illumines how research can identify patterns of pain and ways of modifying and, in some instances, eliminating, pain.

In the final essay, Emily S. Haight organizes and interprets the entire research legacy. She identifies eleven categories of inquiry. It is an impressive tradition of research. Topics range from issues of maternal care to death and grief, from the impact of pastoral care on rehabilitation patients to those recovering from surgery, from marital patterns to adolescent development, from attitudes toward anger and sexuality to mystical experiences and life themes. Even more significantly, research turned attention to introducing change into various systems, including the selection of ministerial candidates, a major hospital system, and entry systems for pastoral counseling centers in the black community. Emily sets this work in the context of shifts in epistemology and research from "an objective, quantified, observable, and replicable route to truth" to one "which acknowledges multiple avenues to truth and multiple faculties of knowing."

Quality information--whether resulting from clinical acumen or from systematic control--contributes to our being more faithful stewards of the Gospel as we seek to minister to people at the point of their need. Research, like that reported in this section, holds promise of such "quality" and such faithfulness.

206

C.A. WISE SPEAKS ON PROFESSIONAL EDUCATION FOR MINISTRY

J. Jeffrey Means

With experience as a CPE student, CPE supervisor, minister of counseling in a parish setting, professor in a theological seminary, and pastoral counselor, Carroll Wise brought a breadth of experience to the understanding and conceptualization of professional education for ministry that was profoundly encompassing. The uniqueness of his view manifested itself in his ability and desire to keep a pastoral orientation to people, while at the same time pushing for professionalism within ministry. In other terms, he saw the need to keep alive a healthy tension between the humanization and professionalism of ministry. To err on either side would have been viewed by Carroll as disrespectful of the complexity of ministry. Given the unrest some persons experience when ministry is talked of as a profession, Wise's undaunting emphasis on the human and pastoral dimensions of ministry are both radically conservative as well as refreshing.

This piece lifts up key elements in Carroll Wise's view of the important components of professional education for ministry.

If nothing else, Wise was a realist. This theme grounds how he viewed ministry and the preparation for it. This emphasis on reality took two tacks. In a general sense, Wise had little patience with persons or ideas that were not grounded in reality, at least as he saw it. In a response to a commentary by Seward Hiltner to the question of whether pastoral counseling should be viewed as a specialized and certifiable form of ministry, Wise criticized Hiltner for "missing certain facts of life that are part of reality today." (Wise, 1961)

More specifically, Wise was committed to the belief that to be helpful to people, pastors have to be realistic. He firmly believed that the development of persons requires that they be dealt with in a realistic fashion. He also believed that when a person experienced the reality of himself or herself in the presence of another person who was understanding and accepting, transformation and growth could occur.

For him, this type of realism was made possible by the resources of the Christian faith. He constantly pushed for human strivings to be interpreted in a theological frame. As he stated in Psychiatry and The Bible:

> The Bible, being a record of [humanity's] search for the meaning of human experience, is as contemporary as though it was written yesterday . . . the Christian faith holds that [individuals] and [their] problems cannot be fully understood unless also seen in the light of a creative loving God who is seeking [their] redemption. (1956, p.ix)

In a sermon given at the Hennepin Avenue Methodist Church in Minneapolis, he talked of the Christian faith offering a balance between two truths: "All men [sic] have sinned; you are Sons [sic] of God." (Wise, 1947)

With a firm belief in the Christian faith's ability to address the human condition directly as it really is, it is not surprising that Wise easily embraced the knowledge base about human development and behavior provided by the scientific community. The theories and hypotheses of fields such as psychology, other behavioral sciences, empirical and clinical research, and cross-cultural anthropology were viewed by him not as threats to his religious views, but rather as additional windows through which the truth about human life might be enlightened and understood. In his own words, ". . . a scientific understanding of [human beings] is not necessarily in conflict with a profoundly religious understanding of [humanity]." (Wise, 1950) Yet even here, his realism made itself known by calling him back to another central commitment, a commitment to the practical, a commitment to use knowledge and theory to better understand and ultimately be helpful to persons.

His own clinical training experience impressed upon Wise the importance of focusing on the individual in distress. He saw this focus as clearly harmonious with the major task of the clergyperson--to seek and save lost persons; and of religious educators--to keep persons from becoming lost in the first place. (Wise, 1943) To be helpful to persons, future pastors must be guided in learning how to relate religion to the emotional life of persons, for it is at this level that religious formulations and symbols take on positive or negative meaning in one's relationship to self, others, and God. (Ibid.)

While Wise's own experience of clinical training allowed him to see its unique value as a part of seminary education, he did not stop there. His contribution to professional education for ministry in general was his unswerving devotion to pushing seminary faculties to become aware of the vital role the emotional dimension of persons plays in their own ability to learn and in their ability to be truly helpful to others. In the process, however, he never lost sight of the pastoral focus of ministry.

The realism of Wise also pushed him to lift up the crucial role played by self-knowledge and insight in the development of pastors. While he considered it necessary, he did not consider it sufficient for a pastor to have a knowledge and practice base informed by Christian faith and commitments. It was also necessary that emphasis be placed on an understanding of the person and personality of the pastor himself or herself. There are two reasons for this.

First, Wise strongly believed that as "Sons [sic] of God" the deeper we understand ourselves the deeper we understand and gain insight into the nature of God and into the ethical and religious structures of life.

(Wise, 1949) This was a further ramification of his firm belief that religious and scientific views of persons were not opposed to each other. These views represent different entry points and methodologies for gaining insight into the nature of persons, and different languages for expressing the insight gained. In this sense, Wise supported the view that the more we come to know about human beings, the more we will come to know about God. Insight into others and ourselves becomes a methodology for doing pastoral theology.

Second, heavily influenced by Anton Boisen, Wise was committed to the direct "study of the human document." This was no dispassionate study. It grew from a profound respect for what persons can teach us about themselves and ourselves, and about how we can be most helpful to them at the point of their need. All we are required to do is listen.

In an interview with Wise in 1979, he underscored the importance of understanding both the individual to whom the pastor sought to minister and the pastor understanding himself or herself.

At Worcester, we stressed two things, and I got this from Boisen. One was understanding the patient on two levels. Understanding, for example, what it meant to be a schizophrenic. You could get some of that out of books, but you had to understand the individual. That was Boisen's emphasis on learning to read the human document. The other thing was how do you relate to the patient. The student always began with how the patient related to him . . . "The patient won't talk to me. What can I do?" "Well, what's happening to you, then?" Get the student to thinking about why the patient wasn't talking in terms of what he was doing to stop the patient, block the patient, or what might he do to loosen up the patient, to give the patient confidence so he would talk, instead of blaming the patient. This introduced a whole new approach in theological education. (Means, 1980)

Abstracted knowledge, theory, and theology take on flesh and blood in the form of real live human beings. A life situation calling for pastoral intervention and care that can be objectively dissected into its constituent parts in the classroom must be dealt with in an integrated and subjective fashion at the funeral site, hospital room, pastor's office, or parishioner's home. Since pastors will ultimately deal with people in these practical settings, it only makes sense that the training of pastors use such practical opportunities.

One of the realities such a need for practical education introduces into the current topic is the fact that seminaries must depend upon outside settings to provide these opportunities. This reality is a result of the traditionally major focus seminaries place on the academic/classical fields. Continuing from the interview with Wise,

It was and still is hard to get seminaries to sense the fact that being a pastor is more than just an intellectual process . . . (Ibid.)

He went on to state that an intellectual focus can even be used by some students as a defense against their own emotional life. "You can get ideas into their heads, but they can't use their feelings, they have no access to their intuitive powers, their sensitivity . . ." (Ibid.)

This traditional, and at times fiercely fought, battle between the academic/classical and the practical fields within seminary faculties is also compounded by how seminaries must relate to the judicatory and funding structures that support their work. Wise was not the first person, and will not be the last, to point out the often competing and conflicting roles and emphases these three components of seminary life bring to the preparation of persons for ministry.

The inherent and unresolvable nature of these realities suggest that seminaries must locate and develop sites outside their own contexts (e.g., field education placements, CPE programs, etc.) in which students are pushed to focus on the practical, pastoral, and personal implementation of the knowledge they have gained in seminary course work. Thus, reality suggests that professional education for ministry requires a multi-context and multi-method approach to education in which each element is willing to hold the others in respectful tension with itself, for as one falters, all falter.

Also central to Wise's thought was the importance he placed on relationship. He viewed all of life as undergirded by a relational frame. Theory and practice, faith and realism, faith and science, illness and health, pastor and parishioner are related one to another. We have already seen how this aspect of his thought influenced the debate between various elements of theological education.

At the level of interaction between pastor and parishioner, the emphasis on relationship takes on profound implications. In one of his most often quoted sentences, from his classic book, The Meaning of Pastoral Care, Wise defines pastoral care as the "art of communicating the inner meaning of the Gospel to persons at the point of their need." (Wise, 1966, p.9) This implies that the person of the pastor becomes the relational link between Gospel and parishioner.

We already have stressed the importance Wise placed on understanding the person served, a pastor's understanding of himself or herself, and the ability of the Gospel to speak to the human condition. However, it is the nature of the relationships a pastor establishes with his or her people that determines whether that interaction will be care-giving and healing, or hurtful and devisive. In talking of the counselor role pastors are often called upon to play, Wise states, "It is not what the counselor does to or for the counselee that is important, the important thing is what happens between them." (Wise, 1951) As pastor and parishioner interact, the parishioner communicates the "inner condition of his or her soul," and the pastor seeks to communicate the "inner meaning of the Gospel" in ways that the two can meet in meaningful, healing, and transforming ways.

In a sermon entitled, "To Preach . . . To Heal," (n.d.) delivered in the chapel at the seminary, Wise lifted up this thought in the following way,

> The crucial fact of life is this: we are hurt by other persons, we are made sick through our relationships with other persons. We are also cured through other persons. The healing process is a process of relationships. It is not a product of our beliefs, nor our theological positions, nor of any method or technique . . .

> To what extent are we healing persons? To what extent does our relationship with others bring to them something which reduces their anxiety and increases their faith; which removes some of their isolation and increases their sense of belonging or of community; which accepts them in spite of their deep sense of unacceptability; which does not ask them to prove themselves, but just to be themselves before God?

From Wise's perspective, the basic objective of professional education for ministry is to foster the development of persons who can be healing and therapeutic in their pastoral interactions with others. The material reviewed to this point suggests some of the characteristics of such "healing persons."

More specifically, Wise believed that such persons must have at least three basic attributes. First, it is necessary for one to be an acceptor--a person who can accept others as they realistically are in the present. Second, one must be able to listen to and understand the soul speaking in another person as it expresses itself in language, symptom, or behavior, in direct or symbolic ways. And last, one must be able to interpret human strivings in the light of the Gospel message so as to bring meaning and hope to people often caught in a state of confusion and despair.

For one to be healing and therapeutic in his or her interactions with others, those interactions must be guided, as much as possible, by the pastor's conscious awareness of and sensitivity to himself or herself, the person in need, and the particular situation. This requires that a pastor be sufficiently free of unhealthy mental and emotional processes that may unconsciously effect interactions in unhelpful ways. This was a topic of great concern to Wise, and he could speak quite despairingly of the neurotic needs or character problems some ministers had that would lead them to "possess their church rather than see it as a flock of God to be shepherded." (Wise, 1958)

Wise clearly viewed awareness of one's own motives, frustrations, and unhealthy reactions as a mark of emotional maturity. He also saw such maturity as necessary for effective ministry, regardless of its form or setting. (Wise, 1943, p.162) It was not uncommon, therefore, for him to consider a ministerial student's personal psychotherapy to be a necessary ingredient of his or her professional education experience. From his perspective, this was merely another manifestation of his belief that seminary education needs to focus on the whole person--the emotional as well as the intellectual and spiritual dimensions.

But neither was relative freedom from unhealthy personality dynamics and structures sufficient. Wise also believed that professional education for ministry must devise ways to help ministerial students become free of the illnesses inherent in the cultural structures in which they work and live. People are not only hurt and made ill through their interactions with others, but also through interactions with institutions and social structures.

Based on his view that health pertains basically to one's relationship to the world and others, Wise saw religion as having a responsibility to develop cultural patterns that foster health. Thus, churches must constantly assess the extent to which their activities carry potential for health or illness. (Wise, 1941)

Wise considered the goal of life to be the "fulfillment of the person, the realization of and by each person of the potentials given in creation and enhanced by experience with the self and others as these are influenced by ultimate values and meanings." (Wise, 1977) Cultural, social, and institutional structures which hinder this goal do harm to individuals. Pastors who are sensitive to how such structures can foster self-deception and keep people from discovering themselves as they really are can also be instrumental in finding the fulcrum points and leverage necessary to play transforming roles in their own interactions with such structures.

Yet how does one become a pastor who is healing and transforming? The answer to this question would seem to be the central task and dilemma of professional education for ministry.

In addition to one's having a vital and creative Christian faith experience, it is commonly accepted that preparation for ministry is preceded by a "Call to ministry." In seeking to understand this complex phenomenon, Wise was quick to point out the need psychology and theology have for one another. In this respect, he largely was responsible for encouraging the use of psychological assessment work in clergy candidate selection processes and seminary programs aimed at preparing persons for professional ministry. He considered it a pointless and incorrect effort to study "Call" in isolation from the whole person. In defining exactly what a "Call" is, he states that it is

. . . not a matter of fact, but a theological interpretation of a complex constellation of processes and experiences in the life of the person. As a theological interpretation it attempts to state how a person and certain experiences he [or she] has had are related to God. (Wise, 1958, p.11)

He goes on to suggest that one of the most common fallacies committed by religious people is that of assuming theological interpretations as matters of fact. Those persons or groups that function as gatekeepers to ordained ministry, in various faith groups, are confronted with the difficult task of assessing the validity of one's Call to ministry. This task is fraught with snares and pitfalls, some of which can be avoided by keeping in mind Wise's admonition not to separate "Call" from the "person who is called." Psychology can and does make a helpful and significant contribution in such assessments by providing an alternative perspective from which the constellation of life events leading up to one's sense of Call can be evaluated.

Once one has experienced a personal sense of Call, and that experience has been affirmed by others who know the particular person and his or her work, the task if formal preparation for ministry begins. But what exactly is "professional education" for ministry? Based upon what has been reviewed so far, professional education for ministry can be defined as a multi-method, multi-contextual form of education which facilitates the integration of a body of knowledge and practical skills with the personality dimensions and faith commitments of students-in-training toward the end of effective ministry to others. The particular emphasis placed upon the integration of personality material into constructive role behaviors, as guided by faith commitments, makes education for ministry unique among the professions.

The value of Wise's work for providing much of the material needed for viewing professional education for ministry this way can be seen by taking a quick glance back in history. In 1966, Charles Feilding conducted a study of theological education for the Association of Theological Schools. There was general unrest within American academic institutions at that time, and the relevancy of educational programs was being questioned. Within this social climate, Feilding collected sufficent data to state that "Ministry today is generally discontinuous with the preparation for it." (Feilding, 1966, p.15) After turning attention to the roles and duties ministerial students must perform upon graduation, Feilding concluded that "Knowledge, professional skill, a full humanity, and Christian commitment are essential to the work of the minister." (Ibid., p.50)

The material reviewed in this paper, most of which predates Feilding's work by at least a decade, makes clear that Carroll Wise was a pioneer in the effort to connect ministerial education with the actual work of pastoral ministry. In the process, his work provided a theoretical and theological base from which to argue for a professional, rather than an academic or vocational, emphasis in ministerial education.

213

In terms of the definition of professional education for ministry given above, Wise's thought has made its greatest impact at two points. The first is the importance he placed on paying attention to the personality/emotional dimensions of students-in-training. The second is the emphasis on finding ways to facilitate the learning and integration of the knowledge and skills necessary for effective functioning in ministry.

There is little doubt that the strong clinical training background of Wise, as well as his close relationship with Boisen, contributed heavily to his emphasizing these factors. It was this same base of experience that led him to emphasize the crucial role supervision can play as a primary methodology in professional education for ministry.

The central role played by supervision comes from the fact that the main emphasis in supervision is the integration of theory and practice, as demonstrated in and through the person of the student. There is little doubt, that the Clinical Pastoral Education field has developed and finely tuned the science and art of clinical supervision. When Wise moved into the seminary context in 1948, he began attempts to bring his knowledge and expertise of supervision to bear on the area of "field work" in seminary education.

This was a task worthy of his effort, for as he stated in an article addressing this subject, "Field work supervision seems to be somewhat in the category of an unsolved problem in theological education." (Wise, 1954) This particular article is central because of the clear distinctions Wise makes between the type of supervision that seeks to instruct the student in the proper approach to a problem and that which addresses the student's own resources for dealing with the problem at hand. Clearly, his bias is in the direction of teaching a method of approaching problems, rather than a specific approach to a specific problem. In his own words, "What a student really needs is a method by which to approach his [or her] problem and study it." (Ibid., p.191)

Expanding on this thought, Wise lifts up the importance of helping students to understand the processes creating the problem or situation, to visualize oneself in the role of pastor in the situation, to bring to bear theoretical considerations that might apply and be valid, and to visualize various roles that are uniquely pastoral in approaching the situation. (Ibid., pp.191-192) In summary, he states,

Clinical training has a definite contribution to make to field work supervision at the point of enabling the student to know how to approach and study a situation, to discover resources within his [or her] command, and to bring those resources to bear effectively on a given situation. This involves the emotional and professional maturity of the student. (Ibid.)

214

A further importance of supervision, as Wise envisions it, has to do with the issue of the relevancy of theoretical studies to the actual work of ministry. Rather than attempting to "tell" students what relevancy exists, Wise favors a supervisory approach which helps students discover for themselves the relation of theological formulations to life processes, to discover the practicality of the theoretical, and to discover that basic theological formations are an outgrowth and formulation of dynamic life experiences. (Ibid., p.193) More specifically, students need direct experience of realizing that no matter what they do, they are guided by some theory. They are responsible for the presuppositions the theory entails, its criticism, evaluation, and reformulation. Supervised pastoral work is not synonymous with experience. Rather it represents a method for helping students to discover what they are learning and the meaning of the experience they are having.

The preceding paper has identified some of the contributions Carroll Wise made to the current conceptualization of professional education for ministry. It has pointed out the fact that in many respects he was a man ahead of his time. He was also a person who sought to introduce radically new and transforming ideas into the halls of seminary academe. As frustrating and personally demoralizing as that was at times, his own stubbornness, and a faith based upon experience, kept him true to his goal--the professionalization and humanization of pastoral ministry.

CARROLL A. WISE AND THE EMPIRICAL RESEARCH TRADITION

Richard E. Augspurger

Those who knew him well, knew Carroll A. Wise to be a master of understatement. His incredibly quiet but firm emphasis upon solid empirical and theoretical research, integrated with sound clinical principles, is yet another poignant example of his mastery of understatement. The Appendix of this chapter has a chronological list of Garrett/Northwestern doctoral dissertations (57 Ph.D.s and 2 S.T.D.s) completed in the Department of Pastoral Psychology from 1952-87 which illustrate that integration.

Not once during the seven years I was affiliated with Garrett Seminary did I hear Carroll explicitly emphasize research. Carroll would say instead, "Read Anton Boisen's book, The Exploration of the Inner World: A Study of Mental Disorder and Religious Experience." In this book, and indeed in many of Boisen's writings, one learns of his deep and unending search for data--data to distinguish "religious experience" from psychiatric illness, data about pastoral care concerns and religious behaviors of parishioners. In fact, one of Boisen's first jobs upon completion of his undergraduate degree was to do sociological research as it pertained to church and religious behavior.

Even Carroll's definition of pastoral care implicitly points to the need for research: ". . .the art of communicating the inner meaning of the Gospel to persons at the point of their need." (Wise,1966) Three phrases in his definition point to the need for further exploration and research: 1) "art of communicating;" 2) "the inner meaning of the Gospel;" and 3) "to persons at the point of their need." Research in this instance means looking for and searching for possible alternatives in approach. Carroll believed that providing pastoral care was an art form which was forever changing, depending upon language intonations, body language, and choice of words.

Searching for the "inner meaning of the Gospel" to share with persons was, of course, done in the context of the needs of the person(s)--A word of hope! A phrase of forgiveness! Sacramental cleansing through communion! A statement of prophetic confrontation!

Discerning and determining the "needs" can also be an art form. One needs a theoretical framework for discernment, whether it be Oglesby's (1980) "broken relationships," Menninger's (1963) five level's of "dysfunctionality," Pruyser's (1976) "theological diagnostics," the nine choices of the Enneanagram (Bessing, 1984), or DSM III-R (American Psychiatric Association, 1987). Regardless of the theoretical scheme utilized, it needs to result in feedback to pastoral counselors and clients which makes sense to them. Perhaps each one of the described research efforts continues a life time and is a part of God's creation which is dynamic and ongoing.

Personally, Carroll was quite interested in research about living human documents and their use of symbolic language, much like his mentor, Anton Boisen. One of Carroll's favorite aspects of supervision was to "brainstorm" all possible meanings of a given word used by a client, which had been recorded on audio tape and played in supervision. In Carroll's seminar on Religion and Health (Fall 1973), he was also interested in historical research to discern other "pastors of the soul" who were attuned to listening with the "third ear," persons like George Fox and John Bunyan.

Even though Carroll may have understated the importance of research, his actions explicitly supported thorough investigation. He cleverly gathered together some of the most sensitive, creative, and talented secular psychotherapists, pastoral psychotherapists, and research methodologists at Garrett Seminary and Northwestern University, e.g., Alfred Flarsheim, Bernard Green, Peter Giovaccini, Carl Christensen, Donald Campbell, Thomas Cook, Kenneth Howard, Francis Hsu, Morris Taggart, Ronald Lee, and John Hinkle.

Word of mouth around Garrett was that nine out of ten dissertations through the Department of Pastoral Psychology, "The old Garrett Program" as it had affectionately become known, had to be empirical, that is, statistically based. Research methodology and statistics were the "language requirements" of the joint program.

Northwestern University was rich with highly skilled researchers and methodologists in the social sciences. They were interested in "field research" and "unobtrusive measures" even before those two principles became popular. In fact, the publication of Experimental and Quasi-Experimental Design for Research, by Donald T. Campbell and J.C. Stanley (1966) introduced many new concepts into field research. The publication of Campbell's second book on design with his Northwestern colleague, Thomas D. Cook (1979), Quasi-Experimentation: Design and Analysis Issues for Field Settings, helped many quasi-experimental (field setting) concepts become common parlance in research. Campbell later became President of the American Psychological Association.

Garrett faculty provided the theological and pastoral theoretical material in the Ph.D. program, while Northwestern faculty provided the research methodology and statistical knowledge for each student. Lutheran General Hospital and Kendall College provided the "clinical component" or access to "living human documents" (with additional didactic input and supervision) to provide comprehensive balance to the program. Each student would learn the art of pastoral psychotherapy and provide the blood, sweat and tears to integrate the theological, psychological, and methodological material and to "measure" something of significance to add to the body of literature in the field. My own dissertation included designing an 8-item questionnaire which "measured

218

healthy resolution of grief" following the death of a spouse.

I shall not forget the day phenomenologist Ken Howard said in his Northwestern University class on Psychological Measurement (Fall, 1973), "You can measure anything you want, it just depends upon how much time and energy you want to put into the process." That was all the encouragement I needed to design and confirm the reliability on the grief resolution scale which I first learned in Don Campbell's course on measurement (Social Attitude Measurement, Spring, 1973). Each student was to select a topic and generate extensive questionnaire statements on a topic. We were then to go through the necessary steps to reduce the number of questions which did not distinguish between persons-- grieving and non-grieving for my population--on their respective questionnaires. Checking the reliability meant finding at least one hundred persons, bereaved and not bereaved, to complete the original 44-item questionnaire. Statistical procedures (Pearson Product Moment Correlations) were then used to establish the internal validity of the questionnaire to discern which eight items discriminated the most between grieving and non-grieving persons. The non-discriminating items were then dropped to prepare the final 8-item questionnaire.

One of the fun rumors around Garrett was that Northwestern professors enjoyed being on dissertation committees of Garrett students because they were doing research on a wide variety of areas in field settings which were of interest to them. So, depending upon the student's area of research interest, he or she would select one or two Northwestern faculty members to sit on the dissertation committee, along with the Biblical, Historical, Theological, and Pastoral Psychology faculty members from Garrett.

Carroll A. Wise's Other Contributions To Research

It is probably from Carroll himself that I learned intuitively the correlation between doing research and doing psychotherapy. That is, one formulates hunches (hypotheses) about an idea or person or family, and then searches for data which either confirms or disconfirms that original hunch. Each time a hunch was confirmed or disconfirmed it subsequently pointed toward a confirmation of, or a change in, the pastoral psychotherapeutic plan with that person, couple or family. The gentle and quiet, but firm, insistence upon the integration of theory and practice was a "hidden genius" of the entire program.

Another indication of Carroll's explicit use of research was when he was "on loan" from Garrett as a consultant to Lutheran General Hospital. His thoroughness and research emphasis became evident in the extensive "needs assessment" that was conducted to determine the "need" for an outpatient pastoral counseling center to be affiliated with the hospital. He was the first mentor to that center, which is now known as The Pastoral Psychotherapy Institute.

The name, "Pastoral Psychotherapy Institute" is an explicit reminder of one of Carroll's prime interests--that of providing pastoral psychotherapy. He preferred the term "pastoral psychotherapy" to "pastoral care and pastoral counseling" later in his mission (Wise, 1983) because he strongly believed in "depth work" and wanted to distinguish himself and his training efforts from current pop theories and theorists abundantly available in the marketplace. He also placed greater emphasis, as he grew older, upon training "specialists in pastoral psychotherapy" with less emphasis upon general training for ministry-- more emphasis upon Ph.D.'s rather than M.Div.'s.

Carroll did not adopt the use of the term pastoral psychotherapy to be chic or "with-it" among the healing professions. That would have been one of the most remote notions from his mind. He selected these terms because he was in the business of educating graduate level pastors, seminarians, and churches. Pastoral psychotherapy is a serious (and not superficial) endeavor, undertaken to work at integrating the best that both theology and psychology have to offer living human documents.

One of Carroll's doctoral students, John Florell, became the first editor of the Abstracts of Research in Pastoral Care and Counseling in 1972. The Abstracts research summary volume has been published annually, and has been edited by a staff member of the Virginia Institute of Pastoral Care (Address is % Editor, P.O. Box 5184, Richmond, Virginia 23220). I was the second editor of the Abstracts and recently completed a four year term as Chairperson of the Research Committee of The American Association of Pastoral Counselors. A disproportionate number of Garrett Ph.D. graduates have been chairperson of the AAPC Research Committee over the 20+ years of the life of the Association.

Another principle relating to research began to be emphasized by some of Carroll's graduates who later became faculty members in the department at Garrett. Morris Taggart, Ronald Lee, and John Hinkle began thinking of research as a means of introducing change into various systems. Again, this point was implicit for it was not stated explicitly by these bright and active researchers.

Carroll's emphasis upon research was more implicit than explicit, but solidly in support of sound (theoretical) and clinical integration. Carroll knew there needed to be rigorous theoretical work done for the field of pastoral psychotherapy to become more widely respected as a profession.

CHRONOLOGICAL LIST OF GARRETT/NORTHWESTERN DOCTORAL DISSERTATION TITLES (AND AUTHOR'S NAME) IN PASTORAL PSYCHOLOGY, 1952-1987

YEAR	AUTHOR	DISSERTATION TITLE
1952	Einar A. Nilsen	The Idea of God and Personality Integration with Special Emphasis Upon Self-Evaluation as a deciding Integrating Factor - An Historical-Clinical - Experimental Approach.
1959	Homer L. Jernigan	A Summary of the Meaning of Faith: A Theological and Psychological Study.
1962	Morris Taggart	A Study of Attitude Change in a Group of Theological Students.
1965	Ronald R. Lee	Theological Belief as a Dimension of Personality.
1966	Leila M. Foster	Theological Implications of Ego Identity.
	James D. McHolland	A Summary of the Influence of Pastoral Care on the Attitudes of Patients in the Rehabilitation Unit of a General Hospital.
	Donald S. Williamson	Selective Inhibition of Aggression by Church Members in a Local Church Setting.
1967	Allen R. Gilmore	Some Theological and Personality Correlates of a Mode of Conflict Resolution.
	Richard G. Bruehl	Perceptions of the Pastoral Role by Staff and Patients in a General Hospital and Pastor's Stereotypes of Medical Personnel's Attitudes Toward the Pastoral Role.
1968	Gary L. Phillips	The Contribution of Eric Erikson and Anna Freud to the Pastor's Work with the Adolescent.

1969	Robert R. Blake	Attitudes Toward Death as a Function of Developmental Stages.
	Richard M. Boyer	Sudden Human Change.
1970	Theodore F. Cole	An Investigation of Alienation as Expressed in Three Revolutionary Theologies: Black, Secular and Indian.
1970	John E. Hinkle	A Study of Attitudes Toward Anger and the Expression or Inhibition of Anger in a Religious and a Non-Religious Population.
	Donald C. Houts	The Use of Ego Identity Measures in Evaluating a Seminary Curriculum.
	George E. Pestrue	The Effect of N Achievement, Self-Esteem and Instructions on the Performance of a Simple Addition Task by Hospitalized Physically-Ill Patients.
1971	John L. Florell	Crisis Intervention in Orthopedic Surgery.
	Bruce M. Hartung	Requests of Hospitalized Patients for a Religious Ministry.
	Bruce F. Mase	Changes in Self-Actualization as a Result of Two Types of Residential Group Experience.
1972	Douglas A. Dahlquist	Sexual Attitudes in the Baptist General Conference.
	Philip C. Greer	Field Dependence and the Practice of Ministry.
	Robert L. Smith	The Relative Proneness to Shame or Guilt as an Indicator of Defensive Style.
	Roy W. Trueblood	Attitude Changes Among First Year Theological Students.
	James R. Zullo	T-Group Laboratory Learning and Adolescent Ego Development.

1973	Henry S. Davis	The Role of a Crisis Intervention Treatment in the Patient's Recovery From Elective Surgery.
	Herbert L. Landes	Treatment of Anxiety in the Families of Children Undergoing Tonsillectomy.
1974	David M. Moss III	A Clinical Application of Giovaccini's Model of Marital Interaction.
1976	Paul A. Donnovan	Birth Order and Catholic Priests.
	Theodore A. Stoneberg	Pastoral Therapy Intervention With the Family of the Lingering Patient.
1977	Richard E. Augspurger	Grief Resolution Among Recent Spouse Bereaved Individuals.
	James F. Bach	Hospital Nurse Morale.
	Ellery H. Duke	Meaning in Life and Acceptance of Death in Terminally Ill Patients.
	John A. Ortmeyer	Anxiety and Repression Coping Styles, and Treatment Approaches in the Integration of Elective Orthopedic Surgical Stress.
1978	Homer U. Ashby	An MMPI Scale for Narcissistic Personality Disorder.
	Gerald J. DeSobe	Marriage Communication Labs: Perceptual Change and Marital Satisfaction.
	Heliodora Gonsalvez	The Theology and Psychology of Glossolalia.
	Clinton D. McNair	The Effects of Pastoral Counseling on the Patient's Adjustment to Hemodialysis.
1979	Charles E. Alcorn	Self/Partner Perception of Couples: At the Engaged and Six Month Married Period.
	Richard E. Guest	Resource-Limited Intervention in a Macro-System.

	Steven C. Nahrwold	A Comparative Case Study of Four Different Organizational Models of Pastoral Counseling Centers.
1980	John C. Carr	The MMPI, Ministerial Personality and the Practice of Ministry.
	Emily S. Demme Haight	Psychological Criteria for the Selection of Ministerial Candidates.
	John J. Means	An Investigation of an Assessment Model for the Evaluation of the Capacity of Seminary Students to Utilize Clinical Pastoral Education as a Professional Learning Experience.
1981	John K. Best	Reducing Length of Hospital Stay and Facilitating the Recovery Process of Orthopedic Surgical Patients Through Crisis Intervention and Pastoral Care.
	Lucille S. Dayton	The Relationship Between Ego Development of Mothers and Their Emotional, Social and Cognitive Support of Their Children.
	Robert C. Fite	A Psychological Study of Persons Reporting Mystical Experiences.
	John C. Martin	Dimensions of the Grief Experience in Recently Bereaved Spouses.
1982	Michael F. Conroy	Dimensions of Moral Character.
1983	Michael P. Comer	Psychometric Characteristics of a Ministerial Assessment Battery.
	Alice M. Graham McNair	Exploratory Study of Pastoral Care Intervention with Hysterectomy Patients.
1984	Vergel L. Lattimore	Pastoral Care Strategies of Black Pastors.
	Robert K. Myers	The Relationship Between Dreams and Dreamers in Modern Psychological Literature.
1985	David A. Hogue	The Measurement of Job Satisfaction for Clergy.

Pamela J. Holliman	A Study of Psychological Assessment Procedures as Adjunctive to Personnel Selection Processes in a Religious Organization.
Joan Scanlon	Life Themes in the Wives of Roman Catholic Deacons.
Benoni R. Silva-Netto	Culture, Personality, and Mental Health: An Ethnographic Study of Five Filipino Immigrant Families.
1986 Arthur L. Pressley	A Study in the Use of Consumer Marketing Theory to Develop Entry Systems for Pastoral Counseling Centers.
1987 Ruth W. Hennessey	Personal Bereavement and its Effects on the Choice of Religious Vocation.
James David Pierce	A Multidimensional Scaling of the Cognitive Dimensions Used by Seminary Students in Their Perception of Biblical Material.

CONTRIBUTIONS OF CARROLL A. WISE
TO PERSONALITY ASSESSMENT
IN SEMINARY AND DENOMINATIONAL CONTEXTS

John E. Hinkle, Jr. and Emily Demme Haight

A major feature of The Legacy of Carroll Wise was the initial implementation, and subsequent elaboration, of personality assessment for use in seminary admissions decisions, selection for field placement in Clinical Pastoral Education, and approval for pastoral ministry in judicatory contexts. These evaluations took the form of pastoral and clinical psychological assessments through the Department of Pastoral Psychology and Counseling.

Carroll's contributions were of particular significance in the assessment of "fitness for preparation for ministry" in the Seminary. Concepts and procedures developed at the seminary were later extended to include evaluative consultation regarding "personal and professional fitness for ordained ministry" for denominational selection committees.

The following highlights of the development and institutionalization of these procedures include a description of two distinct but complementary models for the identification of criteria for use in pastoral assessment; the consensual model and the theoretical/empirical model.

Assessment At Garrett Theological Seminary

In a personal interview with J. Jeffrey Means on September 15th, 1979, Wise said, "One of our problems in the beginning of the CPE (Clinical Pastoral Education) movement in the '30's was that seminaries tried to select students for CPE. What they did was to send us problem students we couldn't train. There was nobody on the seminary faculties that had the slightest idea of what kind of person we needed or was trainable. We simply had to make our own selection."

The conversation continued. Means: "Within your work (as a faculty member) at Garrett, did you do any work in terms of helping to select or screen students who wanted to go for CPE?" Wise: "Sure. . . We weeded some people out. We told a number of students, 'No clinical training until after you get therapy. You couldn't take it.' We didn't want a burdened down student taking CPE. This was the kind of thing I had to face at Worcester in the '30's . . . students coming in for training and going psychotic in the program after 2 or 3 weeks because the seminaries sent us unstable students to cure (rather than to train)."

Means:

"Can you put into words, then, what you see as the seminary's responsibility in that selection process?" Wise: "Yes, in a way I can. One would be to send only those students into CPE who would profit from it. Garrett was giving academic credit, you see. O. K., is that student going to get enough out of it to be worth [justify on educational grounds] the giving of academic credit [for the learnings]?"

Later in the interview the topic broadens to counseling in terms of vocational decisions. Means: "What would you say was the overall role of that work [counseling and evaluation] in the seminary?" Wise: "Dealing with the personality problems of the students." Means: "For what purpose?" Wise: "Trying to help them become better persons and then go on from there to make their decision about vocational choice. Sometimes the vocational choice was what brought them in. They were in seminary, but they didn't want to be there, and they didn't know it. They were there because somebody else wanted them there. It's a lack of real personal identity on the part of the student. He [or she] doesn't know who [they are]. [They've] got problems to resolve. [Their] identity is diffused in several different ways. If I were going to put this under one heading, it would simply be to promote the growth of the student by focusing on whatever is the specific nature of the immaturities he [or she] is displaying . . . academic failure, behavior problems, or what not."

Finally, at another point in the interview, Means asks, "Do you feel that CPE settings were better equipped to deal with relational issues than a seminary?" Wise: "At Worcester, we stressed two things, and I got this from Boisen. One was understanding the patient on two levels. Understanding, for example, what it means to be schizophrenic. You could get some of that out of books, but you had to understand the individual as well. That was Boisen's emphasis on learning to read the human document. The other thing was, how do you relate to the patient. The student always began with how the patient related to him [or her]...i.e., 'The patient won't talk to me. What can I do?' So I would ask, 'Well, what's happening in you then?' I would get the student to thinking about why the patient was not talking in terms of what the student was doing to block the patient from communicating, or what might the student do to loosen the patient up, to give the patient confidence so that he [or she] could talk....instead of blaming the patient. This introduced a whole new approach in theological education." (Means, 1980, pp. 198ff)

Commentary

The foregoing material is notable on several counts. It is "vintage" Wise. In the interview he addresses the issue of screening for CPE in the seminaries as well as in CPE centers. He notes that two major issues of such selection for CPE are, first, a coalesced (rather than a diffuse) sense of personal identity, and, second, a clear and autonomously motivated vocational decision. Further, Wise emphasizes an understanding of ministry as both self reflective and relational in contrast to an approach that is simply and only other-oriented and cognitive.

In the discussion which follows, the institutional influence of Wise and the adequacy of the foundation he provided are seen in terms of his participation in the development of an assessment committee called the Personal and Professional Qualifications Committee comprised of members of the Garrett Faculty. The document that describes the work of this committee, and other documents developed during Garrett's history of work with selection and screening issues, will be referenced. Other developments, which flow from the framework of evaluation and screening for fitness for preparation for professional ministry, will be elaborated. It will be seen that this early committee was mixing two related, but potentially distinct, kinds of criteria.

Criteria related to "fitness for ministry" are both continuous with, but distinct from, criteria based on "fitness for preparation for professional ministry." "Fitness for preparation" criteria lean more toward the learning, developing, exploratory, growth processes that are appropriate to an educational environment and a "student" role. "Fitness for professional ministry" criteria contain more of an emphasis on mature and effective intrapsychic and interpersonal functioning. Both sets of criteria are appropriate to the socially defined roles in which they are set, that of "student" on the one hand and "functional professional" on the other. The discussion returns to this point following a presentation of historical materials.

The Consensual Model Of Criteria Development
Defining Personal And Professional Qualifications For Preparation

As a member of the Garrett Faculty, Wise was involved deeply in the effort to define personal and professional standards for the development of effectiveness in parish ministry. While his own activities in these matters cannot be separated from the activity of the faculty as a whole, his influence was distinctive. As a member of the Committee on Personal and Professional Qualifications, he was part of the process which led to the first faculty legislation regarding personal and professional, i. e., non-academic qualifications for ministerial service.

The first document on criteria goes back to March 15, 1957, when the Faculty established "The Committee on Personal and Professional Qualifications." However, selection and screening concerns had been around Garrett long before the development of the '57 criteria and procedures document.

Carl Christensen's comments indicate that assessment concerns arose in the early 50's. He writes,

Our [Garrett's] program for the diagnostic evaluation of students in the early '50s was more effective than our attempt to work with local clergy. Frequently, students, hesitant or resistive to suggestions made by members of the department of pastoral counseling, responded positively to a psychiatric evaluation. Many, with problems, were helped at Garrett. Others came into therapy with me or were referrred elsewhere in the community . . . In time, a fair percentage of Garrett students were receiving some form of psychotherapy. (Christensen, 1972, p. 90)

These observations by Christensen point out that prior to the procedures of (1) evaluating students in terms of fitness for preparation for ministry through the PPQ Committee procedures, (2) carrying out the selection/screening interviews for CPE, (3) providing counseling and evaluation about vocational choice, and (4) providing evaluation of personal and professional qualifications for ministry, Wise and the department, in liaison with psychiatric back-up, were providing diagnostic services regarding the possible need for psychotherapeutic intervention for students. The extent of these services varied from quarter to quarter and year to year. Nevertheless, what began in the early '50s and, in one form or another, have continued to the present.

Growth In Assessment Competency

Out of these activities, Wise, and the department he was building, began to develop expertise in personality assessment and personnel evaluation. An institutional need was being met. As noted above, assessments were conducted (1) at the time of application for, and placement in, professional training in Clinical Pastoral Education; (2) at the time of application for admission to the seminary; (3) on the basis of self and/or other referral; and, (4) in co-operation with the processes of the Committee on Personal and Professional Qualifications for Ministry (PPQ). Since this committee became a standing committee of the Faculty, more needs to be said about it.

The PPQ Committee was concerned with ". . . the physical, mental and emotional health of the individual student and the adjustment the student makes to his [or her] own well-being, to the total Garrett community, and to his [or her] own professional purpose." That concern continued throughout the student's career at Garrett, though special attention was given to the first year of residence, and to these concerns at the point of admission to candidacy for the degree. Note was taken of the growth the student had made in such qualities of Christian personality as would give promise of Christian leadership.

The PPQ Committee document notes two basic obligations. The first is a concern for the indivdiual student, and, second responsibility to the church for the education of persons suited to and properly prepared for

230

its ministry (suitability = fitness, Webster). (Meine, 1954) The document sets forth the committee's task, namely: "the committee shall define standards for the determination of personal and professional qualifications for the ministers of the church and the evaluation of students in these terms." It later says that in evaluating students ". . . it is necessary that standards be determined for the personal and the professional qualifications for the ministries of the church today."

The document continues, "Both in the student's seminary life and field service within the program of the church, there should be evidence of growth towards responsible Christian leadership in the following areas." Among the ten areas listed are: responsbile management of personal financial affairs, wholesome relationships with fellow students and increasing sensitivity to their rights and needs, co-operative relationships with those of other age and authority groups, acceptance of opportunitites for spiritual development and private and corporate worship, constructive reaction to criticism and hospitality to new truth, expression of Christian love in relationships with those who may disagree with and oppose the student's views, Christian attitudes towards sex and the family, self-understanding involving a realization of one's own motivations, abilities, and limitations, and ability to relate oneself helpfully to persons of varied background and personality types.

Further, the PPQ Committee, whether on its own initiative or upon request, could give consideration to personality factors in the student's development. Its recommendations were to be presented to the faculty committee on candidacy at the time of the student's application for admission to candidacy for the degree. The committee was mandated to review the cases of all students whose oral examination in one or more of the three content areas (Scripture and History, Theology and Ethics, and Theory and Practice of Ministry) of the curriculum was found to be unsatisfactory, and, further, the PPQ committee was to make a recommendation about re-examination to the committee on candidacy.

The PPQ Committee document is an historic benchmark in that it illustrates vividly the commitment within the Faculty to review and assess personal and professional qualifications of students for the ministry as early as 1957. Clearly, fitness for ministry and fitness for preparation for professional ministry are not new issues, either for the Department of Pastoral Psychology, or for the Faculty. With this background, it is not surprising that Garrett has achieved national recognition as a leader in the area of assessment? (Weidman, 1976, p. 4)

Assessment In The Midst Of Student Revolt

During the student revolt of the late '60s, the regular processes of the seminary were disrupted. Many policies could not be implemented. (Norwood, 1978, pp. 196-225) The attention to issues of "fitness for

231

ministry and for preparation for professional ministry" suffered from forces moving in the student community and in the wider society.

At the beginning of the '70s, a particularly painful student case arose which ended in the courts. While Garrett won the legal case, the depth of pain for faculty and trustees alike, who sought to minister redemptively to the student, was exacerbated by the "broken and immobilized structures" through which such matters had been dealt in prior years.

Consequently, in the Fall of 1972, the Faculty set about to establish procedural due process and substantive due process through which matters of fitness for preparation for professional ministry could be assessed, redressed, and remediated. (Hinkle, 1979, p. 9)

By April 1973, a year and a half later, a document setting forth procedural due process was in place. Difficult as the decisions concerning procedural due process were, the effort to reach agreement on substantive due process, that is, the criteria by which assessments would be made, was even more painstaking. The process of developing consensus about criteria involved a much wider constituency and took much longer. It began on December 18, 1974, when President Northfelt appointed a Task Force on Fitness Criteria. This Task Force, consisting of GETS Faculty and Students, worked in collaboration with the Boards of Ordained Ministry of the North Central Jurisdiction of the United Methodist Church, to develop standards for Fitness for Professional Ministry, and with its own GETS constitutent community to develop standards for Fitness for Preparation for Professional Ministry.

Since the North Central Jurisdictional Committee on the Ministry of the United Methodist Church had been at work on ordination criteria for some years, the document setting forth their criteria for ordination was available by May of 1975. (Board of Ordained Ministry Handbook, 1985 pp. 22-24) The seminary document, entitled, "Criteria for the Evaluation of Student Tenure in the Special Students Needs Committee Process," was given final approval by the Faculty on November 15, 1976. (A copy may be obtained by writing the Dean, Garrett-Evangelical Theological Seminary.) In spite of these remarkable institutional achievements in an area of such sensitivity and difficulty, the regular curricular use of psychological assessment (as a means for operationalizing and measuring fitness criteria in the personal and professional development of the student) remains a remedial rather than a developmental/educational procedure.

Assessment Of Growth Processes

For the senior author, the issues of personal and professional development for ministry are inextricably linked to the processes I have come to know and utilize in working with the growth and formation of persons in my responsibility as a Professor of Pastoral Psychology and

232

Counseling. As such, I am deeply aware of both the vitality and the vicissitudes of the "spontaneous maturational processes" (Winnicott) that unfold in and through the human person.

When I (Hinkle) speak of psychological assessment, I refer to the assessment of those growth processes the intrapsychic structures, and the interpersonal styles which have resulted from the fulfillment or frustration of those processes in a given individual person. Hence, psychological assessment, to me, refers not so much to a particular instrument or procedure, as it does to a way of looking at an individual in a particular frame of reference in order to ascertain where growth and development may be enhanced.

Theologically speaking, those "spontaneous maturational processes" are an aspect of the work of the Creative and Healing Spirit of God, hence psychological assessment is, in our view, a psychological way of asking the theological question, "How is God at work in this individual's life and development?"

Pedagogically speaking, clinical procedures designed to facilitate the growth and development of the person are frequently, even regularly, useful in class work as well as in the clinic. For example, a knowledge of the various "character types and related traits" helps in knowing how to communicate more effectively with a particular student. Notwithstanding the obvious fact that a seminary is not a mental health clinic, and that students are not clients and instructors are not therapists, it is clear to us as professors that developmental understandings of the human person are useful in the educational contexts provided by theological seminaries. In contrast to this perspective, however, seminary faculties generally invoke psychological principles primarily in terms of remeidal work. They fail to see the value those same principles can have when applied to the normal developmental processes throughout the regular curriculum. Garrett-Evangelical is typical in this failing.

Based on data gathered in November 1982, at a Consultation held by the Division of Ordained Ministry of the Board of Higher Education and Ministry of the United Methodist Church, and attended by those who conduct the pastoral clinical psychological assessment procedures in the seminaries of the United Methodist Church, it appeared that, 12 of the 13 UM Seminaries were utilizing psychological assessment in some form. (Hinkle, 1982) Most used it primarily as a remedial tool, and then typically only when strong indicators were present that personality problems of some significance were in evidence, as judged by various observers. In addition, six of the thirteen seminaries utilized clinical psychological assessment as an on-going aspect of the personal and professional development (formation) of the ministerial student. In two of these six seminaries, the results of a clinical psychological process (including learning and leadership styles assessment) was seen as foundational to the fuller development of the student within prescribed curricular structures.

In at least one instance, assessment was utilized to assist in field placement, including Clinical Pastoral Education when taken for academic credit. In another setting, the opposite appeared to the be case, i.e., results from field placements were utilized to determine when and whether clinical psychological assessment was needed by the student. Again, however, this assessment was seen as diagnostic and remedial rather than as routine and curricular.

When clinical psychological assessment is understood as the evaluation of personality functioning in its normal patterns, as well as in exaggerated forms labeled psychopathological, it seems obvious that routine evaluation of personality functioning, with formal feedback sessions to the student, should be a regular feature of every seminary curriculum. If such assessments are appropriate when major features of personality functioning are in disarray, then the logic seems inescapable that the assessment of minor (within the normal range) features of personality functioning equally could and would be helpful to the student in the processes of self development and the seminary processes of personal and professional formation. A study of this kind of process at Garrett-Evangelical resulted in the finding that students placed highest value on this aspect of the seminary assessment program in the years 1979-81. (Justes, 1981) Such a procedure does meet acknowledged student needs.

The senior author now wishes to return to the issue of criteria for ministry. The crucial question is, "What is the meaning of 'professional' when that term is applied to calling, vocation, and the 'set-apartness' of ordained ministry?" In a certain sense, the term professional is itself antithetical to what is meant by ministry, i.e., authentic human presence in relationship to those who are in need.

A Professional Model For Ministry

Jackson Carroll argues for a reconceptualized version of a professional model for ordained ministry. He writes,

> Besides being the dominant cultural and social form for the delivery of important services in our society, the professional model of ministry has considerable merit functionally for the church's mission in the midst of complexity and rapid change. I have tried to spell that out in terms of professionals whose fundamental competence lies in their capacity to function in a variety of clergy roles as reflective practitioners; who function interdependently with lay Christians as they carry out their ministries in and through the church; and who model the union of expertise and authenticity, competence and calling, in their being and doing as professional persons. (Carroll, 1985, p. 44.)

234

This model provides a frame for a further analysis of psychological role requirements appropriate to considerations of potential for effectiveness in full time professional ordained ministry. The professional role model structures expectations of fitness for ministry. Dimensions of fitness provide a set of concepts of personal and professional capacities for the fulfillment of those expectations which lead to the achievement of effectivenss in ministry.

Personal And Professional Fitness And Competencies

Research studies have shown repeatedly that effectiveness in ministry involves both personal and professional competencies. For example, ministers do not lose their positions because they fail to have specific skills, such as preaching or administration. A recent study of "clergy firings" determined that most clergy are "forced out" because they have poor interpersonal skills or they are contentious and authoritarian. (Leas, 1985, p. 12) Further, a Needs Assessment for Continuing Education Study for United Methodist Clergy revealed that the greatest number of pastors expressed a need for better methods of relating to others. (Yeager, 1985, p. 26) Out of a total of 3249 respondents, 2107 ranked this first in their own priorities for continuing education.

The need for intrapsychic and interpersonal competence in clergy could be documented in many ways. Likewise, the need for functional competencies that can be identified in the many roles of ministry must be met by ordained clergy. Rather than debating these matters further we will focus on psychological concepts and assessment models currently in use in a theological educational setting which makes the assumption that such issues are largely settled, and that what is needed now are the most useful theoretical and procedural models we can devise in the selection and preparation of clergy persons. The combination of both identity issues and role competencies, along with situational analysis, would seem to provide the most effective dimensions for criteria development.

Selection And De-Selection

While much of the material in this chapter has to do with 'de-selection', a word about selection is in order. Many of the gifts and graces of the individual who will be ultimately effective in ministry can be, as Pamela Holliman notes, "...nurtured, guided, and developed. They do not, however, primarily result from instruction or training. They are, instead, aspects of the development of the individual as a person." (Holliman, 1985, p. 73-74) Or as Urban T. Holmes explains,

The personal qualities of an individual, e. g., [one's] imagination, creativity, empathy, stability, spiritual depth, humility and sensibility, are hard enough to measure and report. It is next to impossible to conceive how they may be taught where they do not exist. Such persons cannot be "created;" they have to be found . .

. If a person does not possess at least latent qualities such as we believe are both desirable and necessary for the effective priest, then [one] should never be sent to seminary. (Holmes, 1978, p. 183)

In the context of this model of personal fitness for professional ministry the following categories of criteria are set forth.

Fitness Criteria And Beyond

Reference was made earlier to the fact that the old PPQ Committee at Garrett was mistaken in extrapolating from criteria appropriate to the professional role of clergy directly to the role of student. Criteria applied to a student in seminary differ from those that apply in the church. The following sketch distinguishes between the role of student and the role of professional. The issues involved in full functioning in the professional role of minister take us beyond fitness criteria without leaving them entirely behind. The following formulation distinguishes these sets of criteria at the same time it suggests an interface between them.

Fitness for preparation for the practice of effective professional ministry initially means that an individual possesses the fitness or potential (capacity) to develop competencies (skills needed in ministry) to the point of readiness to begin the practice of effective professional ministry. (Hinkle, 1979, p. 1)

By ministry is meant ordained parish ministry, though many forms of ministry are valid. The term professional includes ordained ministry, distinguises professional from lay or general ministries, and avoids a narrowly denominational focus.

The term effective points toward quality of ministry as viewed by various constituencies, and avoids the negative connotations of an overemphasis on the professional to the detriment of essential hummanness in the role, that is, avoids professional-ism. Further, the phrase effectiveness in ministry relates to performance, and points to procedures for termination of ministerial tenure on grounds of ineffectiveness.[1] Finally, effectiveness indicates our interest in lifting up an "ideal" of ministry, that is, how ministry can or should be, so that we are not left content with a phenomenology of ministry as necessarily "normative."

The term readiness points to that cluster of criteria identified by the Association for Theological Schools' "Readiness for Ministry Project" as relevant to entry to actual professional practice. (Schuller, 1980)

The term competencies refers to the develop of competence in those skills esstential to the effective practice of professional ministry. Theological education is seen as competency-based education. For example, at Garrett-Evangelical the stated goal of seminary education in

236

the Master of Divinity Degree Program is to equip men and women with those competencies necessary for the performance of ministry in a pluralistic and rapidly changing world. The seminary offers a "competency based" curriculum. Meaurement of competencies is standard practice in considerations of both course grades and advancement.

The term fitness, as noted earlier, refers to the presence of the potential or capacity in the student to develop competencies to the point of readiness for effective professional ministry. The fitness criteria identified in the Student Special Needs Document represent one seminary's effort to reach consensus about the identification, definition, explication, and utilization of such criteria. The final criterion of "effectiveness in professional ministry," in the case of the seminary student, translates into "effectiveness in learning the skills necessary to the development of effectiveness in performance of ministry."

The "consensus model" for criteria development has been set forth above. The further refinement of consensus based criteria through the procedures of a theoretical/empirical model, which will be presented in what follows, represents both recent and current steps toward the further development of criterion referenced concepts and operations.

The Theoretical/Empirical Model
The Context: Assessment And Counseling Services at GETS

As the foregoing discussion has sought to make clear, counseling and assessment have been a function of the Department of Pastoral Psychology and Counseling since it was founded in 1948. Leiffer comments:

> Not only were Carroll's offerings a significant addition to the curriculum, he also contributed greatly to our students through his personal counseling. As time went on and the need for such counseling increased, others joined him in the teaching and counseling work at Garrett: Ruth Wick ('53-'57),. . . John Vayhinger ('58-'64), and Morris Taggert ('64-'70). Ronald R. Lee came in 1971, and John Hinkle in 1973. (Leiffer, 1985, p. 110)

The Assessment and Counseling Service had its foundation in the use of clinical interview methods, which evaluated a person's progress toward personal and professional readiness for preparation for professional ministry. The assessment process was expanded, subsequently, to include the resources of psychological testing and to involved all students, not just those applying for CPE for academic credit. Test data were considered in light of how best to counsel students on how to further their growth processes toward readiness for ministry.

By the end of the 1960's, blanket testing of all students upon admission was discontinued. The Assessment and ˙Counseling Services took on a

237

modified focus. Because there were few resources for aiding students needing growth oriented counseling to further their readiness for ministry, and referral to pathologically oriented mental health professionals was no longer considered an appropriate alternative, the Services began providing individual and group pastoral psychotherapy and, on occasion, marital therapy.

During the '70s, the program took on more of the flavor of a student counseling center. The clinical staff was concerned with both professional/educational development and clinical diagnosis of dysfunction as a precursor to offering pastoral counseling services.

By 1979, the appropriateness and feasibility of trying to provide clinical services within the context of an educational institution was re-examined. By this time a variety of excellent pastoral counseling resources had been established in the community, to which students could be refrerred. Further, a revision of the M. Div. curriculum provided the context for a very important rebuilding of the linkages between the assessment services and other educational components. The role of assessment as integral to the overall educational enterprise of the seminary became the staff's primary focus.

Philosophy Of Clinical Pastoral Psychological Assessment At GES/GETS

Throughout the nearly thirty year history of assessment work in the context of this seminary, certain principles have distinguished this type of assessment from other types of clinical assessment in the service of professional development.

1. The focus is always to evaluate a student's progress toward professional and personal readiness for carrying the role of minister (in various settings). Personality strengths and assets are determined from psychological testing and clinical interview, as well as present or potential dysfunction. Therefore, staff learns to read each instrument for signs of strength and goodness of fit with the ministerial role as well as for pathology.

2. Psychological measurement is always adjunctive to, and never sufficient without, a face-to-face interview conducted by a clincially-trained assessment counselor. Numerical results from any instrument must be compared with the person in the room and the context within which the testing was conducted.

3. Assessment within a seminary setting is understood as a three-person two-party contract. The seminary, provides the service as a part of its educational resources, and so has an investment in what will augment its ability to prepare students for ministry. However strong this investment may be, the right of privacy and confidentialy for students is a primary and legal concern for the asssessment staff. This tension is always a relevant feature of the milieu in which pastoral

238

assessment is done.

The Theoretical/Empicical Model Of Criteria Development: A Case Study

The Staff of the Service sought to specify the basis upon which they were making their decisions regarding a student's readiness for Clinical Pastoral Education (CPE). The quest for more specific criteria followed a theoretical/empirical model and involved five steps: 1) sifting through the accumulated experience with the decision-making process, 2) identifying criteria (as concepts), 3) operationalizing the criteria, 4) performing empirical discriminant analysis of decisions made on the basis of those criteria, and 5) determining the philosophical relevance of the criteria.

First, the seven member staff reflected together on their own clinical processes and decision-making criteria. After hours of discussion and detailed self-observation of written reports and staffings of those reports, they drafted a paper which delineated the criteria they had identified. They agreed on three criteria common to all their evaluations:

1. The ability to integrate cognitive and experiential learnings.

2. The ability to form empathic relationships.

3. The ability to accept and carry the role of student chaplain. (Ashby, et. al., 1980)

Having identified these criteria conceptually, the task remained to determine whether or not these were indeed the criteria being applied, and if so, were they being applied consistantly enough to provide a valid representation of the actual decision-making process. Means (1980) undertook an empirical analysis necessary to answer these questions.

Using a criterion sample of 67 students (both male and female) who had been assessed for CPE over a period of a year and a half and placed into accept or reject categories, he performed a discriminant analysis of the psychometric data generated by these students.

The Minnesota Multiphasic Personality Inventory and the Shipley Institute for Living Scale (a reliable approximation of the WAIS) were chosen as the instruments. A team of three psychologists independently specified scales and scale scores relevant to the measurement of each of the three criteria identified by the staff earlier. The variables selected successfully discriminated students into accept or reject categories for two of the three criteria (p.<.05). Only the criterion related to the ability to carry the ministerial role, an attribute more related to past history and professional identification than to psychological dynamics, failed the test of empirical specification.

The fifth step of the theoretical/empirical model involved testing the identified criteria against "reality," that is, do these criteria make intuitive and practical sense as a basis on which to be making decisions about CPE applications? A review of the literature regarding professional preparation for ministry and the learning requirements of CPE showed these criteria relevant. "As a result of this research, the vital role personality assessment can play in professional education for the ministry was affirmed." (Means, 1980, Abstract)

Agreement Between Two Criterion Models

Two distinct models for the development of criteria for assessing a student's progress toward readiness for preparation for professional ministry have been carried out. What is perhaps not surprising to anyone who works with students in formation for ministry is that each of these models identify similar characteristics as essential for effective ministerial practice. Yet for those of us who strive for empirical specificity, the fact that there is such unanimity across these studies appears remarkable. Empathy and the ability to be present interpersonally, plus a solid integration of one's personal and professional identity, seem to be central to the results of a variety of criterian studies, regardless of the method used to generate the criteria.

Psychological assessment, particularly when employed with a trained eye for seeing strength and health, as well as pathology, and an intimate knowledge of the role requirments of professional ministry, can be a valuable tool for any one or any institution concerned with professional preparation for ministry.

Assessment Of Personnel In The United Methodist Church

The consensual and theoretical/empirical approaches to criteria development, as refined at GETS, have been combined with service delivery and evaluation research to provide an extension of the model of pastoral, clinical, and psychological evaluation of clergy candidates for various annual conferences of the United Methodist Church. Principles identified above (in the philosophy section) have been included in the Pastoral Evaluation processes, as outlined in the Guidebook for Interviewing, Psychological Testing, and Pastoral Evaluation published by the Division of Ordained Ministry of that denomination. (Jones, 1980; Hinkle, 1986) The Guidebook includes details of the clinical/empirical procedures utilized in data interpretation, report preparation, clinical interviewing, and norm development. Research archives have been established to provide a collection house for data needed to refine the concepts, procedures, and theory utilized in the program. A Directory of Pastoral Evaluation Specialists has been compiled and is up-dated on a regular basis.

240

Conclusion

The impact of the approach to clinical pastoral assessment which Carroll Wise introduced to the Garrett Community in the early 1950s, as refined and elaborated through the Counseling and Assessment Services over the years, and as implemented through the Division of Ordained Ministry and its Advisory Committee on Psychological Assessment of Clergy Candidates, is being felt in districts and conferences throughout the United Methodist Church, as well as on the seminary campus. His colleagues and former students have been a vital force in implementing these concerns in the Church and Seminary, each of which gave him a place of ministry.

NOTES

1In the United Methodist denomination, ordination and full conference membership bring tenure for the remainder of the member's professional life, unless tenure is terminated at some point through proper exit procedures. Thus, responsibility for, and the obligation of, placing a person in a ministerial position at no less than minimum salary for the duration of their active career.

NEED FOR APPROVAL BEHAVIOR AND THE MMPI:
THE OBVIOUS/SUBTLE SCALES OF THE MMPI
AND MINISTERS

Ronald R. Lee

Garrett-Evangelical Theological Seminary has a thirty year history of testing ministerial students with the MMPI (Minnesota Multiphasic Personality Inventory). This was due primarily to the foresight and initiative of Carroll Wise. Along with John Vayhinger, he developed a major testing program in the late fifties. The tests from this program form a large data pool, inviting future research. John Hinkle, joining the faculty in 1972, introduced the Garrett Pastoral Psychology Department to multi-scaled computer scoring systems which included the Wiener Obvious and Subtle (WOS) scales (Wiener, 1948).

With clinical usage, an MMPI pattern featuring the WOS scales quickly and clearly emerged for Garrett ministerial students. Those with this pattern showed main scale scores around 50, indicating an absence of significant psychopathology. On the WOS scales, however, a low obvious/high subtle pattern emerged. The WOS scales are sub-scales of main scales 2, 3, 4, 6 and 9. On these five main scales, ministerial students scored around 50 ("low") on the obvious scales, but near 70 or above ("high") on the subtle scales (Table 1). What did this pattern mean?

Nearly 40 years ago, Wiener developed his scales to help counselors distinguish a "normal" population. He presupposed that pathologically disturbed persons responded more frankly to items reflecting such pathology. Empirical results supported his position. More disturbed persons generally presented with a high/low WOS pattern, whereas well functioning persons responded with a low/high WOS pattern, or sometimes with a low/low WOS pattern. When Wiener statistically correlated his new sub-scales, a range of -.46 (Hysteria) to .24 (Manic) occurred between obvious and subtle scale scores. These correlations suggested the two groups of scales measured different qualities.

Wiener's article attracted considerable attention among both research and clinical psychologists. Theoretically, the negative correlation between the WOS sub-scales undermined the empirical/external method of scale construction (Duff, 1965; Gynther, 1979). Technically, the WOS sub-scales raised the problem of item response set. The obvious scales contain 89 true items and 57 false, whereas the subtle scales have 28 true items and 82 false (Fricke 1957). Acquiescence in the form of social desirability was attributed to the low/high WOS response pattern (Stone 1965). Under the rule of parsimony, the subtle scales needed replacement by one social desirability scale. However, the item bias of the social desirability scales on the MMPI, including the non-overlapping purified Edward's scale, discouraged replacing the WOS scales of psychometric reasons.   On the Edwards scale, for example, nine items score true, fifteen score false.

TABLE 1. LOW OBVIOUS/HIGH SUBTLE TEST PROFILE

(Main Scales)	HS	D	Hy	Pd	M	Pa	Pt	Sc	Ma	Si
	50	50	50	50	55	50	50	50	50	50

(Obvious Scales)	D-O	Hy-O	Pd-O	Pa-O	L	F	Ma-OK	
	50	50	50	50	50	50	50	60

(Subtle Scales)	D-S	Hy-S	Pd-S	Pa-S	Ma-S
	70	70	70	70	70

- - - - - - - - - - -

To test the extensiveness of the low/high WOS pattern, the author used a sample of 150 MMPIs of Garrett ministerial students from 1982-84. He sorted them into two piles, one for the low/high WOS pattern, and the other for the rest of the profiles.   Seventy-two percent fell into the low/high category.   This surprisingly large percentage raised the question of the specialness of the theological sample.   Did the pattern occur far more frequently among Protestant ministers?   To partially answer this question, the author examined an MMPI sample of 202 persons from a lower middle-class suburban counseling center in Chicago.   This sample also contained a large percentage (49%) with a low/high WOS pattern.   These two samples suggested that the MMPI low/high WOS pattern was broadly based.

The large number of low/high WOS patterns in the seminary and counseling center samples was first interpreted as a sneaky form of dependency.   It was argued that if the low/high WOS pattern was generally present, but the Hysteria Obvious scale score was high, the diagnosis would be hysteria.   How could a hysteric be a hysteric without being obvious (exhibitionistic) about it?   Since Hysteria, by definition, has a dependency component, a low/high Hysteria Obvious/Subtle pattern, it was reasoned, meant a decrease in exhibitionism, but a retaining of the basic dependency.

It was soon observed, however, that these low/high WOS "dependent" theological students preferred doing for themselves and were, in fact, generally very productive persons.   The key to understanding their work effort was the attention, affection and praise from key "others": parents, and parent substitutes, such as, teachers, bishops, and church communities.   This emotional dependency of the low/high WOS person which enables productiveness is in contrast to another, more malignant, helpless dependency which leads to less productivity.   The helpless type of dependency is more measured on the MMPI by the Navran scale (Navran, 1954).   Persons who score high on the Navran scale wish others to take care of them.   In extreme situations; Navran dependents act out their helpless wish by forcing family, church, or state agencies

244

to care for them, or by becoming permanent welfare recipients.

There is a strong negative correlation between those who score high on the Navran dependency scale and those who show the low/high WOS pattern (Sacks, 1972). This supports the notion that the low/high WOS personality is not the helplessly regressed dependent type. In contrast to the high Navran scorer with his/her wish for helpless dependency, the low/high WOS person fears helpless dependency, and welcomes emotional interest from key persons as a way of avoiding it. The need for emotional sustenance is the key to such a person. Support for this idea comes from the fact that those who show the low/high WOS pattern also generally score high on the Harris and Lingoes Need for Affection and Reinforcement scale (3NAR) (Dahlstrom, 1972). This is a subscale of the hysteria scale that measures the trait its name indicates. Clinical experience with low/high WOS dependents suggests that they have a much better prognosis in counseling and psychotherapy than the Navran dependents.

These results are not surprising for students of a mainline Protestant church with bishops appointing pastors rather than congregations "calling" them. Advancing to larger, more important, and more lucrative appointments depends on the pastor gaining the attention, praise, and approval of the church hierarchy. As psychologist Ron Gallimore discovered in testing students from Garrett in the early 1960s, such pastors have a high need-for-approval (personal communication), as scored on the Crowne and Marlowe scale (Crowne, 1964). As long as they are approved and praised, such persons will work long hours in the service of church and ministry.

This work of Crowne and Marlow on need-for-approval expanded the emerging clinical picture of the low/high WOS pattern. The Crowne and Marlow scale was developed from the social desirability studies of Edwards who was concerned with test-taking response sets. Crowne and Marlowe first improved the technical qualities of the social desirable scale by providing better item balance (18 positive, 15 negative). Then they raised questions about motivations behind the social desirability behavior. Three possibilities were:

a. need for success (achievement) in business or school,
b. need for approval, and
c. need for succor.

Need-for-Approval Patterns

While all three descriptions apply to the trait, extensive experimental studies by Crowne and Marlow pointed to need-for-approval as the basic motivation behind social desirability.

The following summarizes the results of their experiments. Those high on the need-for-approval scale are more conforming, cautious, and persuasible than persons from the middle to the low end of the scale. They are more sensitive to the norms of their culture, and are, consequently, more easily socially influenced. In tests they react more favorably to dull or boring tasks, and are more easily verbally conditioned. They display more caution setting goals in a risky situation, are more defended against hostility, and more avoidant of threats to self esteem. In every test-taking situation the high need-for-approval subjects showed a willingness to achieve whatever was asked if it led to approval, but did not manifest a helpless "do-it-for-me" dependence. This personality profile describes the clinical picture of the low/high WOS pattern of ministerial students.

Support for the Crowne and Marlow description of the low/high WOS pattern on the MMPI came from some of their original statistics. Both the Crowne and Marlowe scale and the Edward's scale were correlated with the MMPI Wiener scales. The obvious Wiener scales correlated negatively with the Crowne and Marlow scale and the Edward's Social Desirability scale, while the subtle scales correlated positively with them, the correlations being slightly stronger for the Edward's scale. The strongest correlations were with the Hysteria scale. (Hysteria Obvious Scale -.54 and the Hysteria Subtle scale .71). This lends support to clinical experience that the Hysteria Triad (Hysteria Main, Obvious, and Subtle scales) is the marker scale in the low/high WOS pattern on the MMPI. In practice this means the Hysteria Triad is first screened to see if the need-for-approval pattern is present.

The low/high WOS split on scales 2, 3, 4, 6, and 9, is an ideal pattern. Variations in this pattern, however, enable rich interpretations. Statistical support for these variations comes from the low positive correlations between the subtle scales themselves, suggesting that each scale reflects different, important nuances in the general description of need-for-approval behavior. These pattern variations generally take place in one of the five scale triads (main, obvious, and subtle), while the low/high WOS split remains in the other four, or even three, including the low/high WOS pattern for the hysteria triad.

To the extent that the Manic triad is low, the person will not be as energetic or as successful as high subtle colleagues. On the other hand, if the Manic triad is somewhat elevated, the person will have too much compulsive drive to be content as a team player. If the Manic triad is over 70, an interpretation of a compulsive personality disorder needs strongly to be considered.

Then there is the paranoid obvious/subtle split. Persons with the low/high paranoid obvious/subtle score identify more closely with a group or institution to which they belong. This reflects a less archaic form of Klein's projective identification (Klein, 1982). Low/low paranoid obvious/subtle persons, while partaking of the basic trait of being productive if they receive emotional support and encouragement from their bosses, are able to leave a failing institution more quickly than their low/high paranoid obvious/subtle counterparts.

Turning to the Psychopathic Deviancy scale (Pd), an important variation is a medium/medium or median/high Pd obvious/subtle pattern, when the low/high WOS pattern is present on three of the other four scales. Such persons, while generally conforming out of a need for approval, find indirect ways to resist and thwart immediate superiors if approval is not forthcoming. In the business world, persons with the medium/medium or medium/high Pd patterns rarely rise above the lower rungs of the management ladder despite other positive attributes.

There can be some variations in the Hysteria marker scale. A high/low hysteria obvious/subtle pattern suggests more the need to get attention than approval. Modest, balanced elevations on the Hysteria Obvious and Subtle scales, say 58, suggest a more winsome need-for-approval person than an attention getting hysteric.

In the Wiener depression scales, a high/high obvious/subtle depression pattern without a high on the main scale is rare. When it occurs, it suggests a need-for-approval person who is depressed. Stating this another way, the prognosis is better when there is a high/high pattern on the depression obvious/subtle scales and the low/high pattern is present on the other four Wiener sets of sub-scales.

The low/high WOS pattern also suggests a person in need of healthy selfobjects. As Heinz Kohut (Kohut, 1984) defines the term, a selfobject is anything a self experiences as being in that self's service, that is, as a part of, or extension of, that self. Persons experience as selfobjects those responding to them with genuine joyfulness, strength, and calmness. Healthy adults seek an empathic selfobject matrix. According to Kohut, this need for a healthy form of narcissism is a natural part of every person's development and continuing adaptive functioning.

In contrast to the person who needs a healthy selfobject matrix, some seek archaic selfobjects. In this primitive, grandiose form of narcissism, a person seeking complete control over the selfobject, expects a perfect mirror of himself/herself. This form of narcissism is not picked up by the low/high WOS pattern, but by the Narcissistic Personality Disorder scale (NPD) (Ashby, 1978). The criterion group for the NPD scale consisted of patients in intensive psychotherapy who formed a selfobject transference. Diagnosis was based on the type of transference, not symptoms.

Among Corporate Executives

The WOS pattern found among ministers is also heavily present among corporate executives. Psychotherapy with seventeen vice presidents of a large financial institution and diagnostic use of the MMPI also indicated a high percentage with the low/high WOS pattern. These

247

clients presented themselves as ambitious, upwardly mobile, achievement-oriented executives. Except for three older "passed over" vice presidents, pressured by their management to seek counseling, the rest came for psychotherapy self referred. They sought it as an ally in the ruthlessly competitive executive world. This main group of fourteen executives were well-educated (MBAs), articulate, and in their mid thirties. Five were women. They had been carefully selected from the best Ivy League and Midwestern universities, and given twelve months in the institution's education program to incorporate them into the organization's culture. Here was a sample of the institution's elite, the "creme de la creme."

The fourteen young executives fell into one of two groups. The first consisted of three mildly anxious, obsessional personalities who were able to play the corporate game with vim and vigor, yet despite good achievements, had an internal sense of doubt and low self esteem. These clients reflected the well known 2/7 or 7/2 patterns on the high point codes of the MMPI (Gilberstadt, 1965). Because of their lack of self confidence, these anxious/obsessional personalities were told by management they had little chance of further promotions. The MMPIs of the other eleven executives (65%) revealed the low/high WOS pattern.

Finding the low/high WOS pattern among business executives raises interesting hypotheses. It suggests many productive executives are held loyal to a corporation by their need for emotional sustenance. They stay in a corporation and work well if they are financially rewarded, but more importantly, if encouraged by upper management approval. Such a highly productive, high need-for-approval person differs from the image of a high-powered, autonomous, independent-thinking executive. The low/high WOS pattern suggests that those successful at lower and middle management levels in a large bureaucratic organization, conform to the corporate culture, execute the wishes of higher management, and in general, behave as corporate team players.

The young, truly autonomous executive does not last in bureaucratic structures of large corporations unless the corporate culture is able to make special niches for him/her (Peters and Waterman, 1982). As the norm of corporate life the image of a thriving, achievement-oriented executive is accurate enough, but the image of autonomy is mainly a myth. Perhaps this image of executive autonomy is projected in corporate circles by young executives to defend against the shame of having so little share in real corporate decision making.

The low/high WOS pattern depicts the organization person of lower and middle level management. Because of a high need-for-approval, praise, support, and reward, they accommodate to the corporate culture. But the personality dynamics that make such a person excellent at the middle level work against functioning well in upper management. Most high need-for-approval executives are weeded out before reaching the

248

top. Should one succeed in reaching the top, he/she finds it more lonely and stressful in the power role than other personality types. Successful upper management persons are more naturally power-oriented, and less focused on need-for-approval. This means that some power-oriented persons chafe while surviving the mid-management levels, where low/high WOS colleagues are more adaptive, numerous, and thriving on the management/approval process.

The eleven executives in the low/high WOS pattern went through intensive psychotherapy for a number of years, with all having reasonable to excellent outcomes. Length of therapy ranged from 100 to 300 sessions. Their clinical histories confirm their high need-for-approval. As an example, there is Ms X, a 37 year old Vice President with the low/high WOS profile. Her progress within the financial institution was fast, mainly because she had managers who gave considerable attention and support to her professional advancement. Responding to this attention, she worked long, productive hours and received outstanding evaluations. When her manager needed an extra project completed or help in meeting a lending decision deadline, she willingly worked nights or weekends.

A transfer to another division and a new manager brought a great deal of stress. The new manager, older, less flexible than previous managers, reluctantly accepted women in the executive world. He minutely controlled the actions of his lending officers, especially the women officers. He took a fatherly attitude towards his female executives, encouraging them to feel infantile and helpless. He liked being asked constantly for his opinions. Ms X sensed her new manager's basic hostility. Without the former managerial encouragement and support, her productivity fell off. Based on Ms X's resistance to her new manager's attempt at infantalizing her and her consequential decline in work productivity, the manager gave her a poor annual evaluation, a sign that she was on her way out of the organization.

Feeling rejected instead of supported, Ms X did two things. First, she sought the help of psychotherapy. Second, she unobtrusively scheduled lunches with her former managers, indicating unofficially she was looking for a transfer. After a few months she was offered a transfer by a manager and friend of one of these former managers. She gratefully accepted this offer. The new manager, more flexible than her last one, gave her a free hand and quickly won her loyalty. Her productivity and effectiveness rapidly rose to her former level. Contrary to a belief that executives should be interchangeable without losing their effectiveness or productivity, Ms X showed that she, like the other high need-for-approval clients, very much depended on the affection and reinforcement of her managers. These cases support the high need-for-approval interpretation of the low/high WOS MMPI profile.

In Failed Marriages

A strong need-for-approval largely determines what a low/high WOS person expects from a marriage partner, and how he/she goes about terminating a failed marriage. In a marital dyad the low/high WOS person is usually prepared to accommodate a spouse by being agreeable and adaptive. The low/high WOS person will even accept abuse if it leads to eventual appreciation, approval, and praise. If, however, accepting the abuse leads to being disrespected, the low/high WOS person will stop allowing the abuse. A low/high WOS person can be mistaken as a masochist, absorbing anything dished out. This is not so. Low/high WOS types do not enjoy abuse, they seek approval. A certain recipe for marital failure, therefore, is where a high need-for-approval person has tried to please and satisfy a spouse, only to discover that there is no way to gain the spouse's approval. Rarely openly admitted, once the high need-for-approval person discovers the impossibility of gaining approval, he/she begins emotionally detaching from the relationship.

Revealing this emotional break to the world is another matter, and may take years. It generally involves waiting until the low/high WOS person has the approval of family and friends, and sometimes also involves emotional distancing from important social and religious reference groups or communities. For the high need-for-approval person, terminating a relationship can be a long, cumbersome, drawn-out process. Two tactics commonly used to gain approval for terminating a marriage are either getting sympathy from a protracted period of personal suffering, or from maneuvering the spouse into displaying hostile or unsociable behavior in public to be perceived as "bad" by family and friends.

Among Clergy

The dynamics described in the corporate and marital situations also apply to the low/high WOS pattern in ministry. The author has followed the career of several former low/high WOS students for more than a decade after church appointments. Brief summaries of the vicissitudes of two are presented, with some details changed to aid in disguising their identities. In the first, support by the District Superintendent was crucial.

Newly married, pastor A was appointed to a church in a small, midwestern rural community. His three years there were happy. The congregation responded to his caring with approval of his ministry, his wife became pregnant, and his District Superintendent praised his success in winning the confidence of his people. Pastor A then gained a promotion to a larger church in another district.

The congregation of his new church fractionalized easily. His wife, now pregnant a second time, made new demands on his time. Pastor

A's busy District Superintendent, weighed down by the problems of several large churches, had little time or energy for giving support. Within a year, pastor A was heavily depressed, drained by the multitudes of demands on his time and energy. This low/high WOS person was unable to gain the emotionally recharging approval he experienced in his former church. Eventually, he went through a major illness.

After the pastor survived in that church for another year, his Superintendent was appointed elsewhere. Fortunately, pastor A's former Superintendent was transferred to his district as the new Superintendent. Recognizing pastor A's depressed state, the Superintendent immediately gave him strong encouragement and support, officially visiting the parish twice in the next six months. The pastor's ability to function improved noticeably. The congregation rallied and became more unified. Less depressed, the pastor gave more time to his wife and children. This pastor became one of the most effective in his Conference.

The next case demonstrates the WOS strategy in a divorce. Pastor B wanted to be a minister before entering college. In the Christian Fellowship at college he met his future wife, fell madly in love, and acted in ways to gain her approval. While doing this he neglected his studies. Nevertheless, he achieved grades sufficient to graduate. Secretly, B's future wife had visions of affluence which conflicted with her role as a minster's wife. She kept hoping to deflect him from going into ministry. When her disapproval had little effect on B's ministerial plans, she changed her strategy. Rather than lose him to another woman, she pretended interest in being a minister's wife, married B, and accompanied him to seminary.

Mrs. B was unhappy working to support her husband and living in seminary housing. On one occasion, she dreamed someone was shredding books. In another dream a person missed an important function. Increasingly she became more overtly miserable, giving many excuses for her unhappiness. In constantly trying to make Mrs. B happy, B's studies suffered. Eventually, however, he managed to graduate. Soon after his church appointment, he realized his wife would never be happy in parish work. She, in fact, showed little interest in the church, including worship. More importantly, Pastor B felt it was impossible to satisfy her. His choices were to divorce her or leave the ministry. He decided for a divorce, but shared this with noone for fear of being denied an appointment. He became patient, waiting for a chance to divorce his wife with the approval of church and extended family.

Pastor B served his congregation as best he could for two years. During this time Mrs. B became increasingly depressed, but refused pastor B's efforts to have her seek professional treatment. The District Superintendent and congregation, very supportive, placed minimum demands on pastor B. Knowing that the Superintendent and congregation felt his wife's depression seriously hampered his ministry, Pastor B obtained a "leave of absence" from his Conference, and found secular work. Within six months, Mrs. B recovered from her depression. When Pastor B applied to return to active ministry, his wife threatened to leave him. He persisted with his plans; she separated from him. Pastor B then went through a difficult divorce and eventually returned to ministry.

Summary

A picture of ministers with a low/high WOS MMPI pattern, using converging correlational, experimental and clinical evidence, is as follows:

1. Do not have serious psychopathology.
2. Need above average approval, praise and appreciation.
3. Approval fosters good productivity.
4. Are cautious decision makers and goal setters in the absence of approval.
5. Are sensitive to the norms of church and the broader culture.
6. Reflect a major work ethic profile.
7. Are highly persuasible by a high status person.
8. Hate helpless dependency.
9. Persist in dull tasks if these are a source of approval.
10. Avoid hostility.
11. Use high status persons (Bishop, District Superintendent, boss, manager, supervisor) as a source of selfobject gratification.
12. Will rapidly "burn-out" without approval.
13. Respond well to psychotherapy if self referred.
14. Spouse approval is key to their successful marriage.
15. Divorce involves the careful attempt to gain the approval of church, family and friends, even if it means maneuvering the spouse into the "bad" role.

Measuring Unresolved Grief

J. Colby Martin and Ronald R. Lee

Understanding grief has long been a concern of religious professionals working with the bereaved. The Pastoral Psychology Department at Garrett-Evangelical Theological Seminary (G-ETS), with its traditional interest in grief, and encouraged by Carroll Wise, conducted research into grieving which has pragmatic value for the parish pastor. This article makes available results of that research.

While a person may grieve over the loss of anything valued, where there is investment of self or an emotional attachment, this material focuses on the loss of a spouse. The concerned and conscientious pastor may want to identify bereaved people having difficulty resolving their grief. How to do this is neither clear nor easy.

There is no shortage of "conventional wisdom" about grieving, but much of it is contradictory and not supported by research data. Accordingly, questions arise about identifying persons having difficulty resolving grief. How can a pastor know how much attachment to the lost loved one remains? Does time alone provide the necessary healing? Why is grief so difficult and painful to resolve? When should a pastor make a more concerted effort to help a grieving person? Which grieving persons respond to the pastoral care ministry of a church and/or a pastor? Who should the pastor refer to a pastoral counseling specialist? These are practical questions pastors ask as they work with the bereaved. This article provides a simple tool for measuring unresolved grief. It is hoped that pastors will find it, and the research information that comes with it, useful in day to day ministry.

A first step in identifying persons who are having difficulty grieving is to measure accurately a person's need for grieving. In an attempt to do this, the authors developed a brief, eleven item Bereavement Questionnaire (BQ). The following are the items:

1. I feel good.
2. I have completely recovered from my bereavement.
3. Without ...... I feel life is not worth living.
4. My life is now normal after the loss of ......
5. I feel angry that ...... has died.
6. My grieving keeps me awake at night.
7. I am strongly motivated to initiate new relationships now that ...... has died.
8. I am so upset about the loss of ...... that I can't eat.
9. I now seldom think about ......
10. I look at a photograph of ...... all the time.
11. I am now able to think of ...... without shedding tears.

Pastors are invited to use this simple, quick test in their work with grieving persons to estimate the need for further grieving. A copy of the BQ with written directions is in Appendix A. Research with the scale suggests that it may, in fact, be a better measure of grief than the subjective judgment of a person with clinical training. It is our experience that items on the BQ facilitate discussion of a person's behavior after the BQ has been administered.

Administering and scoring the BQ is remarkably simple. Because it is brief, most people are willing to complete the BQ for their pastor or professional helper. It can be easily introduced by explaining that it is a brief questionnaire that will help assess grief needs. It is desirable to spend time talking with the person, developing rapport, and lowering anxiety about completing the BQ. Depending on circumstances, a pastor may wish to read the instructions to the bereaved person or let them read the instructions for themselves.

After the person has completed the BQ, it is preferable to wait until later to score it. However, a pastor may want to ask the person to guess his or her score. This may stimulate discussion of grief experiences. Pastors may do as the authors, and ask where people would rate themselves on a one to ten scale in recovering from grief. One equals complete recovery, ten means intense grief without recovery.

Scoring the BQ is straightforward. Item one, for "warming up," is not scored. Items two through eleven are scored zero through four. Zero corresponds to no grief; four to a strong grief reaction. Items 2, 4, 7, 9, and 11 are scored negatively, meaning that A = 0, a = 1, ? = 2, d = 3, and D = 4. Items 3, 5, 6, 8, and 10 are scored positively so that A = 4, a = 3, ? = 2, d = 1 and D = 0. These numbers, recorded to the right of each item, are then summed. The total score ranges from zero to 40. Scores from zero to ten indicate mild grief, eleven to 20 moderate grief, 21 to 30 strong grief, and 31 to 40 intense grief.

In measuring the psychometric properties of the BQ, the reliability (internal consistency) of the BQ was estimated at .82, with the Kuder-Richardson Formula 20 on a sample of 79 bereaved persons who responded to it at the request of their pastor. Validity was estimated by three measures. In the first of these, BQ scores were correlated (Pearson Product Moment) with the clinical judgment of one of the authors doing a grief interview. After each interview, and before scoring the test, the interviewer rated the griever's unresolved grief on a one to ten scale, with one representing no unresolved grief and ten representing very intense, unresolved grief. The statistics were: r = .79, p = .001, N = 36. For the second measure, each bereaved person was asked to rate their unresolved grief on the same one to ten scale. The statistics were: r = .74, p = .001, N = 36. A third measure was obtained from a pilot project of a completely different sample (N = 21) where two graduate students in pastoral psychology made clinical judgments on unresolved grief by listening to audio tapes of interviews with bereaved people. A correlation of .56 was obtained. This significant but lower validity estimate may be because the other validity studies had the advantage of "best evidence" afforded by visual cues in their personal interviews and from a clearer understanding of the grief construct.

In the research sample of the 36 who lost a spouse by death, scores on the BQ ranged from four to the maximum of 40. The mean score was 20.02, taken, on average, eight months after the death of a spouse. The results suggest that those with low scores either were not deeply attached to their spouse at the time of death, or had rapidly moved through the grieving process.

In the same sample, the authors also found that BQ scores were not related significantly to the length of time since a spouse's death. Grieving subjects were interviewed between four and eleven months post-bereavement, enough time to expect that if "time heals all wounds," the ameliorative effect would have begun to show. In fact, the correlations between time post-bereavement, the BQ ($r = -.125$), the clinicians' ratings ($r = .017$), and self rating ($r = .016$) were insignificant.

There are at least two possible explanations for those results: 1. while some people lessen their need for grieving over time, others do not, or actually get worse, giving a "wash" or balancing out effect on the mean score over time; and 2. resolving grief takes much longer and is much more difficult than has been assumed previously to be the case.

The population involved in this 36 person study ranged in age from 37 to 71, with the majority in their fifties and sixties. Many of these middle-aged people had greater difficulty grieving than a younger person, such as Mrs. U described below, who readily and naturally struggled through an uncomfortable grieving process. Younger people seem more able successfully to grieve than persons in late middle age, who have "settled in" to life and grown accustomed to "the way things are." This suggests that pastors need to give special attention to grievers in their late middle age.

In addition to assessing the validity of the BQ as a psychometric instrument the research on the 36 subjects also yielded a major finding on the relationship between grief and narcissism. Freud (1917) indicated that the death of a loved one produced a narcissistic wound that complicated and intensified the difficulty of resolving grief. Freud's observation is supported by the strong correlation between narcissism and grief ($r=.48$, $p=.01$). For the purpose of this research, narcissism was measured by the NPD (Narcissistic Personality Disorder) MMPI scale (Ashby, 1978). The importance of this finding is that the death of a loved one is experienced as if it was the loss of a part of the self.

Narcissism is used here technically from a Self psychology perspective, and particularly the views of Heinz Kohut. Those with narcissistic attachments form what Kohut calls "selfobjects." A narcissistic selfobject (NSO) functions as a person's energizing source by praising and encouraging ("mirroring") or through being idealized (Kohut, 1971; 1977), or in experiencing twinship (Kohut, 1984). Narcissism in the more archaic form of a primitive selfobject (PSO) serves more as a source of security and soothing than energizing (Tolpin, 1971; Winnicott, 1951). On the other hand, mature selfobjects (MSO) operate as a matrix of supporting friends so there are multiple sources of energization and less vulnerability because there is more' than one person on whom to depend (Kohut, 1984).

A Case Of Mature Selfobject

Mrs. U, a 26 year old widow, is an example of a person who had formed MSOs and whose need for grieving steadily and naturally declined during the first twelve months after the death of her husband, She sought grief counseling three weeks after her husband of eleven months was killed in a car accident, and was referred by a friend who had been through a helpful therapeutic experience. Her MMPI (Minnesota Multiphasic Personality Inventory) showed the low/high Wiener pattern reflective of a hard-working, adaptive, high need-for-approval person (See chapter, "Need for Approval Behavior and the MMPI: the Obvious/Subtle Scales of the MMPI in Ministers"), and the absence of any serious psychopathology. After the beginning session, she scored 29 on the Bereavement Questionnaire.

The grief counseling lasted 27 sessions, weekly for the first three months and then less frequently until the anniversary of the death twelve months later. Mrs. U's dreams for the first three months reflected the wish that her husband was alive. In one, she was walking past the spare bedroom door when her husband "whistled and yelled to come in." On another occasion she jokingly said to her girlfriend, "Don't kill that spider, it might be . . ." (husband deceased). After six counseling sessions, two months post-death, Mrs. U scored 20 on the Bereavement Questionnaire. She was able to visit her husband's grave and cry.

At the nine month mark, Mrs. U was on the way to recovery. She was able to wear her wedding ring again, this time on her right hand. She was losing weight, had washed her husband's towel (which she resisted doing until now because it still had some of his smell and skin on it), and bought new bedroom furniture. She had boxed many of her former husband's old things, stored them in the basement, and been out on her first date. Importantly, she reduced her score to 16 on the BQ. At the first anniversary of her former husband's death she visited the cemetery, cried a little, but was not otherwise upset. She then made arrangements to place a headstone on it.

256

Two years after terminating counseling, Mrs. U set the date for a wedding. She agreed to take the BQ again and scored 2. This score, her readiness to remarry, and her general ability to function, clearly indicated she had no further need to grieve her former husband who had functioned as part of a MSO matrix. Unfortunately, not all bereaved people are as successful as Mrs. U in resolving their need to grieve.

A Case Of Narcissistic Selfobject

Mrs. O is an example of a person who is both middle-aged and who had related to her husband as an NSO. Accordingly, she experienced the loss of her husband as a profound narcissistic wound. A 49 year old widow, Mrs. O sought grief counseling three months after her husband died of kidney failure. Her grieving was very painful, was getting worse, and she had suicidal thoughts. "There is nothing to live for," she said. She scored 40 on the BQ, the highest possible.

On the MMPI, Mrs. O's profile suggested she was a counter-phobic, counter-dependent, somewhat compulsive, person who had a strong need for approval. Without it, she was tempted to act out impulsively. Although the test indicated that she was at risk for suicide, the risk was not considered serious while in an empathic treatment relationship. It seemed more a ploy to obtain soothing for the self, deeply wounded by losing her husband.

By choice, Mrs. O bore no children, but had a good relationship with her husband's daughter from his first marriage. Until the last six months of Mr. O's illness, her marriage had been stimulating intellectually, fulfilling in a tender way, and deeply intimate. She had lived primarily for her husband, the president of a company, and a shrewd businessman. She herself held a minor administrative position at a large corporation.

Early in the counseling, Mrs. O expressed hostility towards religion. She was Roman Catholic, but had been severely reprimanded by her priest. Before marrying a Protestant who had separated from his wife, she lived with him for several years. For this, her priest and family condemned her as an "adulterous woman." Following a confrontation with this priest, she left her rosary beads in the church's holy and water and never returned. She felt shamed by the priest conducting the funeral service when he dwelt on her husband's alcoholism. The priest also pointedly asked whether her husband was a financially paying member of the Catholic Church. Finally, he insulted her by indicating that she should think more about God than her husband. Angrily, she told the grief counselor that she "could not go to bed with God." After this session she had a "rebellious" dream in which she had sex with her husband. For these reasons the church and religion could not provide the support for her that many are able to derive from these institutions.

As the sessions continued, Mrs. O expressed increasingly negative feelings about her family of origin. These had been buried underneath her happy marriage. The husband had served as a defensive part of her nuclear self, protecting her against the painful associations of the past, but now, she had to face the world without her husband's protection against these phobias. For example, one day she ventured to a public lecture after work, but left when she saw a couple embracing. She was jealous and envious, needing an idealized man to feel energized, alive.

As Mrs. O neared the second anniversary of her husband's death, she began to feel calm and at peace. She had expunged all expectations of any meaningful long-term relationship with Mr. E, an out-of-town business man whom she had met by chance and with whom she had a brief romantic relationship. Her only problem was a twinge of jealousy when watching couples attentive to each other, but she was less phobic in public. She spent more time with women friends and developed one new friendship with a younger woman in her book class. A BQ test at this time scored 16. After 100 sessions at twice a week (total now 160), it was mutually decided to reduce the sessions to once a week.

Mrs. O continued to make good progress until she realized that she had been deceived in another romantic involvement with a man she had met while on vacation. It wounded her to learn that he was married and that she had little hope of any long term meaningful relationship with him. Her wounding led to a temporary regression in the therapy and less effectiveness at work. The main focus of rage was her husband who, by not drinking himself to death, would have prevented the whole painful mess. A BQ test taken at this time scored 26, reflecting the setback. Eventually, Mrs. O recovered from this wounding and, after 200 hours of treatment, had a good prognosis.

A Case Of Primitive Selfobject

Ms. Q is an example of a person who formed a PSO with a significant "Other," and whose grieving over the loss of that person manifested itself in very disturbed mental functioning.

We deviate here from our loss of spouse model because persons who need a PSO and who lose a spouse are scarce. Their marriages generally end in divorce. This 36 year-old person had been in intensive psychotherapy for six years at the time of the death of her father, who was the key stabilizing person in her life. She was diagnosed as a Borderline Personality Disorder which manifested itself in alcoholism, destructive acting-out and brief periods of hallucinations. During these hallucinations she saw black bugs crawling all over the place. In the critical seventh year of treatment she suffered the loss of five key family members: father, mother, paternal grandmother, uncle, and aunt. It was the loss of her father, her primary transitional object, that triggered off a major hallucinatory episode which was controlled by psychotropic medication.

Soon after the death of her father, Ms Q scored 39 on the BQ and 13 months post-bereavement, scored 32. There was little doubt that if she had not been in a therapeutic relationship and under medication, she would have become far more disturbed and probably have needed extensive hospitalization. Instead, she took two weeks' sick leave and then was able to function adequately at work when she returned. Her dreams gave evidence of the archaic selfobject role of her father and of her own archaic grandiosity. In one dream she saw herself responsible for his death because of her sexual feelings. She was able eventually to verbalize this primitive selfobject relationship with him when she said, "When my father died, I lost my identity." The primitive selfobject relationship with the therapist was reflected by her hallucinations when he took a two week vacation, and by her fears that he would die because of her powerful destructive feelings. All this occurred despite the fact she had access to two other therapeutic professionals.

Implications

As these cases illustrate, when grieving, those whose relationship to a spouse was one of a number of special sharing MSOs, the support of the other matrix members helps facilitate the grieving process. Persons with MSOs, such as Mrs. U, recover reasonably quickly and well after the loss of a spouse. It is much different if the deceased functioned as a NSO or a PSO. In the case of Mrs. O, there was mainly an NSO relationship with her husband where she depended on idealizing him for energization. This is why she was so vulnerable when he died, and why she was frantic to find another source of energization through idealization. Idealizing the therapist was a temporary but expensive solution. Gradually, in therapy, she resolved her need for this idealizing NSO as shown by the steadily development of an MSO matrix. In the case of Ms. Q, there was no evidence of idealization despite the critical stabilizing role her father and her therapist played in her life. The primitive nature of the selfobject relationship was seen from the extreme disturbance in her behavior and thought processes when the PSO was absent.

From this self psychology theory, and the results using the BQ, it is obvious that those who needed spouses to serve as primitive or narcissistic selfobject relationships will have difficulty resolving their grief if the spouse dies before they do. This is because NSOs and PSOs are integrated into the core self of the person who needs them. Hence, the death of a spouse when he or she was a NSO or PSO means a narcissistic wound of major proportions. The loss is experienced as if a large part of the self has been torn away. Such a deep wound evokes feelings of shame and rage, and reawakens an early struggle to gain mastery over one's sources of gratification. It is for this reason

259

that grief is experienced so painfully, and that rebuilding and restoring the wounded self is such a difficult and arduous task.

The data also noted a strong relationship between social isolation and higher grief scores. This relationship held up when the question of employment outside the home was added. Persons who were employed outside their homes had significantly lower grief scores. This raises the question of whether it is involvement with other people which facilitates grieving or having some kind of activity in which to invest one's self that helps. When subjects were judged only on the basis of whether or not they were involved in some kind of activity (whether that activity involved social contact or not), there was only a weak relationship to indicate that the activities were useful in promoting resolution of grief.

This suggests that activities alone have very little, if any, value in helping resolve grief. This is because only selfobjects can bring satisfying relief. Nearly all among the 36 grief subjects commented that "keeping busy" helped them cope by keeping the loss from their minds. However, keeping busy as a means of coping is much different than being involved in relationships with other persons to help in the resolution of grief. For example, one man was still actively involved in working in the extensive flower gardens that he and his wife had enjoyed doing for years. But he now spoke of it as a burden and lamented, "What's the use?" This man was socially isolated, and had high grief measures (all three measures were up).

Another woman took up employment in her husband's business and, as she remarked, it helped her keep his memory alive. She too had high grief scores. In her case, activity and social involvement through work (which was minimal because it was not regular employment) actually were used to prevent grief work and defend against the loss, in short, not to facilitate resolution. Accordingly, it is more important to understand the purpose of activities (social or otherwise) rather than simply noting the presence or absence of them. The underlying issue for those who work with the bereaved is that activities as such do not nourish people; interpersonal relationships of depth and acceptance do.

In summary, there is one extrapolation from our studies of immediate benefit to pastors. Persons who score over 15 on the BQ twelve and one half months after the death of their spouse probably need special attention from their pastor. They are probably not making a normal adjustment to the loss of their spouse because of excessive unresolved grief. Hence, the first anniversary of the death of a spouse is an ideal time for a pastoral follow-up. The anniversary itself may stir the pangs of grief. In those who have gone through a reasonably successful grieving, however, this anniversary yearning will be but a brief, temporary reversal of an otherwise diminishing emotional attachment to the dead spouse. To avoid this temporary elevation due to an anniversary reaction, it is important that the BQ be administered a couple of weeks after the first anniversary of the spouse's death.

For those persons with low BQ scores soon after the death of a spouse, or with originally high scores which steadily decline to an extrapolated score of less than sixteen after twelve months, pastors can feel confident that their ministry, the support of the church, the matrix of MSOs, and the internal resources of the grieving person have been sufficient to promote healthy grief. These persons will find activities and social relationships that provide a sense of satisfaction and meaning.

This research also suggests that a significant number of bereaved persons, generally but not invariably middle-aged or older will not follow the above "normal" pattern of grieving. It is for this group of people that the concerned and conscientious pastor can be the key to effective ministry. If after a year, the bereaved person's score is over fifteen, the pastor should make counseling available on a regular basis. Such a recommendation assumes the pastor feels comfortable providing the grief counseling and has time available. If, after a dozen or more counseling sessions a BQ retest shows there is no tangible decrease in the BQ score, and if the pastor and the bereaved person feel that insufficient progress is being made, the pastor should refer to a pastoral counseling specialist. Where such specialists are not readily available, the pastor needs to refer to a professional psychotherapist experienced with the bereaved.

Appendix A
Bereavement Questionnaire (5/87)

These questions presume you have lost a spouse through death. To personalize the statements, a blank allows you to mentally insert your spouse's name. You have five choices. You indicate your choice by circling the appropriate symbol:

A You strongly agree with the statement.
a You agree somewhat with the statement.
? You neither agree or disagree with the statement.
d You disagree somewhat with the statement.
D You strongly disagree with the statement.

There is no time limit, but please answer all questions in the order in which they occur. There are no right or wrong answers. Please give your own leanings on each question whether you feel strongly about it or not. Erase completely any answer you wish to change. Please try not to mark answers with a "?." Your opinions will be kept confidential. Using the back of this sheet, you may make explanations or raise objections to any statement, but number the items to which you refer.

Your name ....Your age....Today's date......
Spouse's death date ....Was spouse's death sudden? (Yes/No)

1.	I feel good.	A a ? d D
2.	I have completely recovered from my bereavement.	A a ? d D
3.	Without ..... I feel life is not worth living.	A a ? d D
4.	My life is now normal after the loss of	A a ? d D
5.	I feel angry that ..... has died.	A a ? d D
6.	My bereaving keeps me awake at night.	A a ? d D
7.	I am strongly motivated to initiate new relationships now that ..... has died.	A a ? d D
8.	I am so upset about the loss of ..... that I can't eat.	A a ? d D
9.	I now seldom think about	A a ? d D
10.	I look at a photograph of ..... all the time.	A a ? d D
11.	I am now able to think of ..... without shedding tears.	A a ? d D

Score ....

EFFECTIVE PASTORAL CARE IN THE HOSPITAL

John L. Florell

Carroll Wise had a keen interest in pastoral services to patients in a hospital setting. He believed ministers needed to learn practical, effective ways to deliver their services that other professionals would recognize. Though Carroll saw that clinical pastoral education often accomplished, through supervised experiences, effective pastoral care, there was no consistent model to which to point. What factors produced effective hospital ministering?

Research in the area of pastoral care was anecdotal, single or group case reports, made by the person providing the care or training. Though these efforts were helpful, they were not empirically based, and so did little to convince people beyond our own field that we were being of aid in ministering to hospitalized patients. Wise hoped that as part of the doctoral work residents of local hospitals would contribute to empirical information about effective pastoral care in the general hospital setting.

When I began my residency at Evanston Hospital in the late 1960's, I consulted with Dr. Wise about putting together his concept of practical methodology with the holistic emphasis that I had been exposed to at the Menninger Foundation. Specifically, I wanted to research how crisis intervention techniques, using traditional pastoral approaches, would affect the healing process of patients. I wanted to see if there was an effect that could be measured about pastoral care's impact on healing and possibly specific elements of giving care that were more effective than others.

Carroll suggested I start by doing a pilot study of a restricted group of hospital patients, those who were going to have elective surgery. This was further refined to focus just on orthopedic surgery. I interviewed approximately 45 patients over a three month period trying to get their opinions about how they were being treated in the hospital, their reactions to surgery, staff, religious, family support, and the emotional impacts of their healing.

To my surprise I found patients' personal needs being met best by aides who would talk to them as they cleaned their rooms. The aides would pass on helpful information about how the hospital operated and what patients should expect from professional staff, dietary, administration, and even their physicians. Though aides did not provide this kind of information consistently, nearly a quarter of the patients interviewed mentioned helpful information gained from aides. Another quarter of the patients said their hospital stay was helped by religious support, usually from their local clergy person. When clergy showed a personal interest in the patient by visiting and having prayer the hospitalized person seemed helped.

From this pilot study, extensive literature research, and using accepted research methodology, a project was designed to study the effectiveness of two different treatments against a control group. Patients were assigned randomly to one of three groups called control, support, and support-information. The control group got regular hospital treatment; the support group got visits from clergy trained to give supportive relational visits that focused on emotional and religious questions; and the support-information group received special information about the hospital rituals, staff, and administration, as well as the emotional and religious support of the relational method.

Over 150 patients participated in the study along with 10 physicians. These orthopedic patients were studied before, during, and after hospitalization on more than 43 different variables concerned with healing. Statistical analysis showed no significant difference among the three experimental groups pre-surgically. However, post-surgically, patients in both treatment groups left the hospital from one to two days sooner than the control group members, which received only regular treatment.

Another significant finding was that patients' transitory (not characterological) anxiety in the treatment groups was higher before surgery and lower after surgery than control group transitory anxiety. Though their anxiety scores rose before surgery, control group patients' scores were far below the raises in the treatment groups. It seems that helping patients face their fears of surgery initially raised their anxiety, but helped them adapt to recover and lower their anxiety post-surgically. Patients who received the support and information treatment were significantly less anxious than the support group. This indicated that the anxiety of the treatment groups pre-surgically was helpful because it was related directly to the realistic threat of surgery.

Research has indicated that levels of patient anxiety can influence the patient's perception of pain. The study's correlation of the use of pain medication and the transitory anxiety scores of patients seemed to support this evidence. Pastoral visits that may help lower transitory anxiety by providing support and information actually could lower the use of pain killing drugs. In the study, this was exactly the impact of the support and support-information group on patients' use of pain medication post-surgically. Both groups of patients used significantly less pain medication than the control group.

The calls each patient made to the nursing station were noted on a prepared check list. The control group patients made many more requests for service from staff than either treatment group. Good pastoral care lowered the demands patients made on the regular staff and their physicians.

264

In addition, aspects of pastoral care appear to affect the physiological responses of the patients. These responses were seen in the lower respiration and pulse rate of the treatment groups over the control group, and indicate the treatment groups were less anxious and had less physical tension. This indicates that pastoral care techniques can be used to aid patient's physical recovery.

Obviously, pastoral care cannot guarantee healing or even a better adjustment to hospitalization. However, it seems to help make patients more realistic about their attitudes and help them relax in a difficult situation. In the study, patients rated their perceptions of pain, stress, and satisfaction with their hospitalization and operation. These perceptions were then compared to their physicians' ratings on the same variables. The treatment groups' ratings were very similar to their physicians' ratings, where the control groups' ratings were not.

The treatment group patients also were more satisfied with their treatment than were the control group patients. An important part of the attitude treatment patients had was related to their feeling less pain, recovering more quickly and being released earlier than the control group patients. The positive attitude these patients had could provide a positive base of patients' attitudes toward hospitals. The interface between clergy helping patients face the crisis of hospitalization and hospitals trying to deliver health care has tremendous potential.

This research project did more than show empirically that pastoral care can have an impact on healing. It isolated elements that go into providing effective pastoral care. These elements certainly do not represent all of the ways to minister effectively to patients in a hospital setting. Nevertheless, they do appear effective with hospitalized surgery patients in a general hospital setting. Other factors such as a patient's personality, susceptibility to anxiety, and cooperativeness significantly influenced patient healing rate, attitude about hospitalization, and assessment of chaplain performance.

Three main factors came out of research conducted in six Midwestern hospitals. In order of their effectiveness these can be generally described as informational, spiritual, and relational. Each factor was rated for its effectiveness by patients, chaplains, non-reactive measures of physiology, lines of nursing notes, use of pain mediation, anxiety measures, and length of stay after surgery.

The most important element in these ratings appeared to be information. The essence of information was the Chaplain's ability to tell patients about the hospital, procedures, staff, and how the hospital operated. The chaplain often served as a clearing house to introduce the patient to the staff and to give helpful guidance as to who to ask for help. The chaplain helped patients rehearse their surgery and recovery by focusing on what the patient expected of himself or herself and the staff, and what the staff expected of the patient. The pattern of the hospital was interpreted by the Chaplain to patients to give them a feel of what was going on around them.

The activity of information was like a metaphorical naming process that gave patients some sense of order in the confusion created by hospitalization and surgery. This concept of being able to name the elements of hospitalization is similar to God's inviting humanity to incorporate the animals, friendly and dangerous, into their life through naming them (Genesis 2:19-20). The act of naming enables people to reach into the confusion of life and bring together that which belongs together. The reassurance of knowing what was happening gave patients a sense of realistic understanding, which helped them recover more quickly than their uninformed counterparts.

I believe the implication for effective pastoral care that is raised by this informational element is the necessity of local clergy knowing the hospital and staff where his or her parishioners are receiving care. This does not mean a minister has to know everything about the health care delivery system. It does imply establishing a working relationship with physicians, nursing personnel, social workers, and administrative staff. Though pastors do not have to have all the information about how a hospital operates, they can serve as a vital link in enabling the patient and family to obtain the information essential for rapid recovery.

Often the hospital where parishioners are treated has a full-time chaplain or chaplaincy staff that can inform the local pastor of many of the elements that go into the information aspect of pastoral care. If such resources are not available, the clergy, as an expression of their ministry, may work with hospital administrators and staff who wish to enhance the health care delivery to their patients and the clergy's ministry to their parishioners.

Hospitals are usually supportive of the second element of pastoral care which is summarized under the term "spiritual." Patients expect pastoral care-givers to provide for their spiritual needs. This usually takes the form of discussing faith or religious issues, particularly in relation to the patient's reason for being in the hospital. Other common expectations include reading from the Bible, conducting prayer, and/or providing the sacraments.

My research identified a number of other elements that contribute to patient healing. The most effective was dealing with patients' feelings. It is through the language of feeling that the patient shares the meaning of illness. There also appears to be a hierarchy of emotions that clergy and patients find helpful. Feelings such as doubt, fear, helplessness, and anxiety, which were the top four emotions, become the means through which the patient struggles with such spiritual issues

266

as: "Who am I now that my body failed me?" "What about my role-value-relationship to my family, my job?" "Why, God?" "Where are you, God, in my illness?"

Other feelings include grief, sadness, depression, and loneliness. Many of these reflect the patient's loss of control and feelings of isolation. Sharing of these emotions with a clergy person helps empower patients and has therapeutic benefit. There is a confessional or sustaining quality that helps the patients purge themselves of feeling that could cause them to work against their own healing. Often clergy are a symbol of a person to trust during a time of crisis. Providing pastoral care during hospitalization when a person is allowed to express their emotions will significantly contribute to the patient's healthful environment.

Another part of the healing environment is the encouragement the patient receives from a clergy person. Encouragement is based on the reality of the sickness or medical procedure while holding up the hope and faith of God's healing power. As patients share their positive and negative thoughts and feelings about their faith and how those relate to their health crisis, patients often experience a renewed relationship with God.

Though the patient still may be ambivalent in relationship to God, this is often one of the best opportunities for prayer the religious professional may have. Prayer invokes God's presence in the midst of struggle. Both laity and clergy find that this can be a powerful moment to aid the patient's emotional and spiritual health. Often patients speak about these moments in deep religious terms, such as "sensing the presence of God," "knowing Jesus is my Savior," or "experiencing something Holy." The religious professional's reaffirmation can give the patient an even stronger sense of security.

This sense of security can be enhanced further by the use of scriptures. I make a strong distinction between using scripture to deny a real threat and using scripture to support a patient facing the crisis of surgery. Too often clergy believe they should deny illness as a reality lest they align themselves with evil. Denying the illness or surgery usually does a disservice to the patient. A clergy person can give reassurance of God's love and support without promising miraculous, painless cures.

The more relaxed and in control a patient feels after surgery, the more likely the patient will enjoy a quick recovery. Biblical readings that appear most effective to the healing process denote God's support through the process of suffering.

In similar manner, the sacraments can become a tangible reminder of God's loving presence. For those whose faith community reflect a sacramental tradition, the receiving of holy communion or the

267

sacrament of the sick is supportive. For parents, baptism or a dedication service can become an enacted expression of faith at the time of miscarriage or infant death. The purpose is not to conceal the reality of death, but to denote the reality of God's presence in death.

Certainly, scripture, Bible reading, and the sacraments are traditional means of grace in the Christian tradition. The clergy is not limited as he or she seeks to minister. Significant readings from a variety of books, music both secular and sacred, poetry, tangible expressions of hope and peace which have particular value for the patient or family, relaxation tapes, each can denote God's support and fellowship through the process of suffering.

The clergy person does not come as an isolated individual. He or she comes as one who becomes God's spokesperson, a representative of the fellowship of faith. Clergy often forget that they bring the power of prayers and support of their whole congregation. The hospitalized patient often likes to talk about their local church as a way of identifying with the support and nurture they feel from the church. Talking about church affiliation can evoke positive feelings that aid in the patient's health.

While a means of support, these discussions also can uncover negative concepts or false ideas. An effective pastoral care method deals with these superstitions and misunderstandings. A number of people in my study saw their thoughts were affecting them. A restoring of broken fellowship can aid in the patient's health.

Conveying information, honoring spiritual struggles, celebrating at-oneness with God, and restoring and enriching a sense of belonging are tangible ways clergy can contribute as a member of the health care team.

The final factor was the relational element of pastoral care. Put simply, this is the ministry of presence. Our research showed the optimal number of visits for hospitalized patients by their clergy equaled the length of stay in days minus two (7 days stay - 2 = 5 visits). Patients reported less positive results from either more or fewer visits. It should be noted that most patients preferred not to be visited the day after surgery, probably because of the effects of the surgery and anesthetic.

Simply talking to patients about general topics or listening to subjects of interest to the patients make up most of a relational ministry. This gives the clergy person and the patient an opportunity to socialize on a surface level. Many patients do not wish to go further than this, particularly early in the hospitalization or just before checking out.

Listening to patients is important in establishing rapport and focusing on where each patient is. A majority of patients (78%), no matter what group they were in, found talking about their upcoming surgery an important element of the pastoral visit. Even though patients may not voice emotions in an open way, talking about surgery can be a release for tension and anxiety.

A moderate number of patients (28%) also found that talking about previous hospitalizations helpful in adjusting to their current hospital visit. Research has shown that people build on previous experiences as a way of adapting to current crises. If people have had a good experience, they tend to anticipate good experiences in their new situation. However, having had a bad experience will cause people to anticipate further negative experiences. Often this can alert the pastor that the patient he or she is seeing will need more support in their hospitalization than a person who has had good experiences.

The important element that ties together the relational factor is the ministry of presence. Clergy do not demand anything from patients. They represent the faith community, and bring to bear spiritual resources which transcend the physical limitations of medicine. By combining information, spiritual support, and strong relational skills, clergy can provide a strong foundation of healing for the hospitalized patients.

THE RESEARCH LEGACY OF CARROLL A. WISE

Emily S. Haight

> The task of the teacher is not to pour ideas into the mind of the student, but to awaken in him [or her] the latent processes that lead to insight and understanding. (Wise, 1966, p.126)

Carroll Wise often trained his students through holding them in the tension created by unresolved or opposing viewpoints and challenging the student to determine creatively his or her own position, therapeutic style, or theological conviction. The clearest example of this was the Ph.D. program which he created between Garrett Theological Seminary and Northwestern University. Doctoral students constantly were exposed to opposing views of human nature, theories of mental illness and its treatment, and methods of research for determining truth. Out of this crossfire, his students developed the strength to think analytically and discerningly, to become sensitive therapists with their own unique skills and personalities intact, and to inquire into the depths of pain and joy. For this gift, his students have praised him by using their training in widely varying ministries.

Dr. Wise served as a communication bridge between professionals who previously had little opportunity or language with which to share their "truth:" psychiatrists and clergy, theology professors and psychologists, behavioral empiricists and analytic practitioners. He wrote of the dialog needed between the rigors of science and the intuitive knowledge of religion.

> The pastor with a strong religious identity will find much in the field of science which he [or she] can accept and use without sacrificing [one's] religious orientation. On the other hand, there is a difference between using ideas and methods from science and replacing religious orientation with the faith of science. . .The question for the pastoral therapist is, To what extent can the model of behavioral therapy be used by those who operate from a Christian understanding of the nature of [humanity] and of the healing experience? A second question is whether the faith and methods of science are able to give a completely adequate account of the nature of [humanity]. . . (Wise, 1983, pp.29-30)

Although Dr. Wise would never have acceded to the worldview of the laboratory empiricist, he was adamant that his students be informed and skilled members of the dialog he worked so hard to initiate. To insure this, he brought to the faculty persons with research skill and expertise. Students were required to recognize quickly the "junk and the bunk" that passed for empirical research and to respect the well-constructed and well-analysed study. By looking at the research of his graduate students, one can see this tension illustrated repeatedly in the

271

topics chosen, the settings in which research took place, the methods used, and the results reported. (See Augspurger in the volume for a complete listing of the dissertations.)

Each project explored a particular human need encountered by pastors, chaplains, or therapists. Each dissertation used scientific methods to determine better ways to minister to the human heart. When there was a choice between the sterile certainty of a laboratory setting in which to test a narrow, abstract concept and a field study in the actual place of ministry, the choice was for the "living human document." Then one worked rigorously to overcome the problems of field research, the ever-present alternative hypotheses that haunt the quasi-experimental methods, the need to create appropriate measuring instruments, and the institutional roadblocks. The results satisfied the exacting standards of research design and statistical analysis and still retained the human relevance and "pastoral" quality so often missing in psychological lab studies. Each study, like Carroll Wise himself, provided a communication bridge between the "faith of science" and the faith beyond science.

Research Contributions to Pastoral Care and Counseling

Of the sixty doctoral dissertations completed by 1988, only five percent were studies of a theoretical or historical nature with no experimental or statistical method involved. Eleven categories of topics are evident:

1. Pastoral Care to Hospitalized or Ill Patients
2. Ministry to those Dying or Bereaved
3. Moral or Religious Traits of Persons or Groups
4. Description and Selection of Clergy
5. Seminary Curriculum and Pastoral Training
6. Marital Assessment and Treatment
7. Organizing and Administering Pastoral Counseling Centers
8. Ministry to and by Women
9. Ministry to and by Cultural and Ethnic Groups
10. Ministry to Adolescents
11. The Integration of Theology and Psychology

A brief summary of the research in each of these areas provides the flavor of the breadth and contribution to pastoral care and counseling made by these studies.

PASTORAL CARE TO HOSPITALIZED OR ILL PATIENTS

Twelve of the sixty studies were conducted in a hospital setting or with patients who have been diagnosed with particular on-going illnesses. In two of the studies, the focus is upon the perceived role of the hospital chaplain. Richard Bruehl (1967) investigated the attitudes held by pastors about medical personnel and those of medical personnel as to the place of pastors in the healing process. Bruce

Hartung (1971) analysed the particular kinds of requests and expectations patients had in seeking a religious ministry during their illness.

The effectiveness of pastoral care in making a direct intervention, particularly in the areas of the anxiety experienced by surgery patients, was the subject of five studies. James McHolland (1966) was the first to undertake a study of pastoral care in the hospital setting and found that morale and self-esteem were positively affected by pastoral care. The use of crisis intervention techniques with surgical patients was the focus of the studies by John Florell (1971; see this volume), Henry Davis (1973), John Ortmeyer (1977), and John K. Best (1981). By using unobtrusive measures such as medical records of nurse calls, pulse and respiration rates, length of stay, amount of pain medication used, and number of lines in nursing notes, Florell demonstrated that a crisis intervention treatment resulted in a shorter stay in the hospital, less use of pain medication, less elevated physiological responses to surgery, and less use of nursing staff time in the recovery process. Although anxiety was higher before surgery for the treatment group than for the control group which received no intervention, the post-surgical anxiety was lower, This landmark study was replicated by Davis and then by Best ten years later. Ortmeyer used Florell's measurement and treatment techniques to evaluate whether high or low anxiety and repression traits caused persons to respond differently to the treatment.

Ministry to the hemodialysis patient was studied by Clinton McNair (1978) and to the hysterectomy patient by Alice Graham McNair (1983). The results give insight into the needs of those patient groups and specific methods for aiding healing in such cases. A study by Herbert Rodney Landes (1973) showed that the anxiety of children experiencing tonsillectomy surgery was lowered by the pastoral care and crisis intervention treatment given their mothers.

Ministry to Those Dying or Bereaved

The effect of pastoral care with family members of patients was the focus of the first of four studies on death and bereavement. Theodore Stoneberg (1976) observed the degree of "comfortableness" of terminally ill patients by using the unobtrusive measures devised by Florell to determine whether pastoral care with the patient's family, which focused on anticipatory grief work, had an effect on the dying patient. The length of time the patients lingered was shortened, although the differences between the control and treatment groups was not statistically significant.

In 1977, Richard Augspurger reported the results of the Bereavement Questionnaire which he developed to study the process of grief resolution and identify active and non-active grievers. He demonstrated that when persons are blocked in the grieving process, pastoral visitation facilitates grief resolution. John C. Martin (1981) used the

BQ to study the long-term grieving process of bereaved spouses and their specific needs for accurate diagnosis and informed pastoral intervention.

Ellery Duke (1977) again used the unobtrusive measures of the hospital studies, as well as other attitude and adjustment measures, to investigate the relationship between a person's sense of meaning in life and their acceptance of death as a terminally ill cancer patient. There is strong suggestion that Protestants and Roman Catholics respond differently to the experience of dying and that the type of pastoral care offered affects a patient's acceptance of dying.

Moral or Religious Traits of Persons or Groups

A variety of personality traits which relate to religious or moral functioning were chosen for investigation. In many cases, specific measuring instruments had to be developed to make a quantified, empirical study possible. Often a major task was simply the definition of the trait. These studies gave pastors new insights into the behavior and moral development of their parishioners, and added much to the dialog betwen psychology and religion.

Three studies focused on the role of aggression and conflict resolution among religious and non-religious groups: Donald Williamson (1966), Allen Gilmore (1967), and John Hinkle (1970). Moral and psychological development were of particular interest to three researchers. Robert Blake (1969) related attitudes toward death to life developmental stages. Robert Smith (1972) utilized measures of guilt and shame as indicators of defensive style in personality functioning. Father Michael Conroy (1982) wrote an exhaustive summary of knowledge in the field of moral development. The more mystical aspects of religious life were studied by Heliodora Gonsalvez (1978), who related the occurrence of glossolalia to personality style, Robert Cotton Fite (1981), who examined mystical experiences, and Robert Myers (1984), who summarized the meaning and uses of dreams in Biblical and recent times. Richard Boyer (1969) and Bruce Mase (1971) studied how persons are inspired to change and move toward self-actualization.

Considering the elusiveness and experiential quality of many of these traits, the significant statistical results obtained are remarkable. They open new areas for further investigation.

Description and Selection of Clergy

Two early studies described particular attributes of ministers. Philip Greer (1972) studied the influence of field-dependence on the practice of ministry and Paul Donnovan (1976) related birth order to the experience of Catholic Priests.

An impressive series of studies was conceived in 1976 under the

274

leadership of Dr. Hinkle based on the needs of judicatory boards which evaluated clergy candidates. An initial study by John Carr (1980)related MMPI results of seminarians to later performance in ministry. He relied heavily on the previous work of Homer Ashby (1978) who devised an MMPI scale which indicates the presence of narcissistic personality traits, common among practicing clergy. Emily Haight (1980) used archived clergy candidate MMPI results to determine the particular criteria used by psychological consultants and the boards themselves in selecting candidates. Complex multi-variate statistical analysis revealed that consistent criteria could be identified.

Michael Comer (1983) replicated Haight's results and expanded the data to include other instruments in the testing battery, such as the Adjective Check List, The SHipley Institute for Living Scale, the Strong-Campbell Vocational Interest Blank, and references. Consistent criteria were again recognized by computer analysis. Pamela Holliman (1985) reported on an extensive survey of judicatory boards to learn how they were using psychological measurement in their screening and nurturing processes with candidates. She applied evaluation research techniques to her analysis. David Hogue (1985) derived and validated a Job Satisfaction Scale for Ministers.

This series of studies, largely funded by the United Methodist Board of Higher Education and Ministry, has provided the underpinning for an extensively used system of clergy candidate assessment. A by-product of this research is the development of specific normative data on the MMPI for male, female, and Black clergy candidates.

The effect of personal bereavement on the motivation of people to select a religious vocation was the subject of a recent study by Ruth Hennessey (1987).

Seminary Curriculum and Pastoral Training

Two studies investigated the role of seminary training in producing attitude change. Morris Taggart (1962) found several factors related to whether a student's attitude toward the importance of pastoral psychology and counseling to the work of ministry changed as a result of having a course in that subject. Roy Trueblood (1972) found that interpersonal relations training during orientation week increased students' self-actualization scores soon after, but the effect did not last eight months later.

J. Jeffrey Means (1980) evaluated the assessment process used at Garrett-Evangelical to screen students wishing to take Clinical Pastoral Education for seminary credit. He showed that the criteria applied were consistent with the educational goals of CPE and were measurable through the use of MMPI scales.

Marital Assessment and Treatment

Three students influenced by the teaching of Bernard Greene in marriage dynamics and treatment completed research projects in this field. David Moss (1974) combined the theories of Robert Winch and Peter Giovacchini to build a model of why some marriages endure and others do not. They then tested the model by using personality studies of couples in therapy. Gerald DeSobe (1978) discovered that while marriage communication labs had a positive short-term effect, the effect did not last over time. He concluded that such popular interventions were not a substitute for intensive marital therapy. Charles Alcorn (1979) studied the self- and partner-perceptions of engaged couples, and found that couples with more accurate perceptions of each other had better marital adjustment scores during engagement. However, this did not predict adjustment six months later.

The Organization and Administration of Pastoral Counseling Centers

Three studies related to establishing and maintaining structures for the delivery of pastoral care and counseling services. The advantages and disadvantages of four organizational models used by pastoral counseling centers were delineated by Steven Nahrwold (1979). Consumer marketing strategies were applied to the problem of delivering pastoral counseling services in the Black community in a study by Arthur Pressley (1986). Richard Guest (1979) described and evaluated an administrative intervention in a hospital system to improve the quantity and quality of pastoral care services.

An additional contribution of the Wise legacy to this field is a published volume entitled The Organization and Administration of Pastoral Counseling Centers (Carr, Hinkle, & Moss, 1981) It was the result of a class project in a course on the subject taught by Dr. Hinkle. Dr. Wise wrote the foreward for the book. It is dedicated to him with deep affection.

Ministry to and by Women

Four studies focused on gender-related issues important to the effective pastoral care of women. Lucille Dayton Groh (1981) studied Winnicott's concept of good-enough mothering and the ego development of mothers. Issues of care for self versus care for others, as developed by Carol Gilligan, formed the basis for Joan Scanlon's study of the wives of deacons in the Roman Catholic Church (1985). As part of a larger project, James David Pierce (1987) studied the effects of one's gender and religious faith stance on processes of perceiving and understanding religious symbols and information. Pamela Mylet (in process) used social attitude change theory to study the dynamics of how women priests are accepted into the life of the Episcopal Church.

Ministry to and by Cultural and Ethnic Groups

Three studies involved work with the religious and cultural life of particular groups. Theodore Cole (1970) studied the concept of alienation in Black, secular, and Indian theology. Vergel Lattimore (1984) described and categorized recognizable styles of pastoral care provided by Black clergy. An ethnographic study of three generation Filipino families by Benoni Silva-Netto (1985) provided important insights into the unique needs and resources for ministry and pastoral counseling within that cultural group.

Ministry with Adolescents

Two studies provide assistance to persons in ministry with adolescents. Gary Phillips (1968) reviewed the work of Eric Erikson and Anna Freud as these relate to adolescents. James Zullo (1972) studied the T-Group Laboratory as a method for affecting adolescent ego development.

The Integration of Theology and Psychology

Four of the early dissertations reflect Dr. Wise's effort to integrate the domains of theology and psychology. Einar Nilsen (1952), Homer Jernigan (1959), Ronald R. Lee (1965), and Leila Foster (1966) each provided foundational work relating dynamics of faith and belief to particular psychological theory and insights about the human psyche. A recent study by Pierce (1987) supported left brain redemption oriented and right brain creation oriented belief patterns proposed by Ashbrook (1984) by identifying cognitive dimensions seminarians use in processing biblical material imagistically and analytically.

From this summary overview, one can sense the themes and emphases which have developed within the Pastoral Psychology and Counseling Department over the years. The generation of bibliographies and research reviews in so many areas related to pastoral care and counseling is in itself a major contribution. The research tradition which Dr. Wise initiated continues as the Doctor of Ministry research projects in pastoral counseling/psychotherapy are added to the collection and dissertations are completed in the Religion in Personality and Society focus of the new Ph.D. program.

Contributions to Research Methods and Analysis

Along with contributions made by individual research, these studies have foreshadowed developments in epistemology and research design that only had begun to germinate in the days of Carroll Wise. By researching topics that some said "couldn't be studied" empirically, his students were helping to move psychological science into a new era. It is now recognized that the logical positivist's dream of an entirely objective, quantified, observable, and replicable route to truth is quickly dying. In its stead is greater appreciation for the unity and

277

connectedness of experience and perception. Scientists now understand that they create what they discover by their methods of investigation. The process of observation itself always has an impact on both the observed and the observer. (Augros & Stanciu, 1984; VanLeeuwen, 1982)

Most of the studies reported here used experimental or quasi-experimental designs, as defined by Cook and Campbell. (Campbell & Stanley, 1966; 1979) Some were time-series designs; some pre-and-post-test designs. Either control and treatment groups were randomly assigned or groups were established as clearly differing on the basis of the trait being studied. Parametric statistics were used to verify that a change had occurred after treatment or that groups in fact were not of the same population in terms of their behavior (scores). Instruments were developed, using standard tests for validity and reliability. In some cases, correlational statistics and factor analysis were used to locate trends and show relationships within the data. State-of-the-art computer analysis was employed frequently. In spite of the advanced technology and rigorous design standards, one still does not lose the sense of the holy in the experience of persons. The sense of caring and commitment to healing for the persons being observed and measured are not overshadowed.

Evelyn Fox Keller, in describing a feminist approach to the practice of scientific research, uses the term "dynamic objectivity;"

> I define dynamic objectivity as the pursuit of a maximally reliable understanding of the world around one that actively draws on, rather than rejects, the sense of commonality between mind and nature as a resource for understanding. . . It permits the cognitive use of subjective identification with the object of study--possible, according to some scientists, even with chromosomes or electrons. In this, it is not unlike empathy--a form of knowledge of other persons that draws explicitly on the commonality of feelings and experience in order to enrich one's understanding of another in his or her own right. Dynamic objectivity is thus a pursuit of knowledge that makes use of subjective experience in the interests of a greater objectivity. (Keller, 1983)

Dr. Wise understood dynamic objectivity--empathy--whether it was practiced in the therapy room, the pastor's office, or the researcher's experiment. He would agree, I think, with Ken Wilbur who argues strongly for a new view of science which acknowledges multiple avenues to truth and multiple faculties of knowing:

> . . .when theologians talk empiric facts, they must be prepared to face scientists; when they talk mental principles, they must face philosophers or psychologists; only when they practice contemplation are they truly at home. And a comprehensive-transcendental paradigm should be able to embrace, charitably, all three. That makes it different from traditional religion, traditional

philosophy/psychology, and traditional science--because it includes and can potentially integrate all of them. . . .

We of today are in an extraordinarily favorable position: we can preserve the utterly unique position of possessing and championing a balanced and integrated approach to reality--a "new and higher" paradigm--one that can include the eye of flesh and the eye of reason and the eye of contemplation. And I think that the history of thought will eventually prove that to do more than that is impossible, to do less than that, disastrous. (Wilbur, 1983, pp.35,37)

I remember Carroll as a tough/objective and compassionate/empathic supervisor. I particularly treasure my experiences in a course he taught on creativity. Through the sharing of his photography, he communicated what he had learned over the years about the unconscious processes involved in genius and the ability to create works of art. Good research, as well as good art, begins with an intuitive hunch about how the world is--a preconscious knowing that breaks through into consciousness as a new insight, a new perspective, or a new way of asking an old question. Weaving the concepts and variables into a testable framework is itself an artform. The technical manipulation of the data is a hard-learned skill, as is the use of the tools and materials of art. However, the ability to apply the knowledge with a healing love for others is a gift of the Spirit. As Carroll wrote:

. . .the behavioral sciences are here to stay, and they will see great development in the years ahead. The love of truth which the Christian faith commands should teach us to appreciate the positive contribution of these sciences to the work of the Church and lead us to use their contribution for the benefit of persons. (Wise, 1966, p.127)

Aden, LeRoy. 1985. *Pastoral Care and the Gospel: A Theological Foundation for Hiltner's Pastoral Care, Journal of Psychology and Christianity*, Winter, Vol.4, No.4, pp.78-84.

Alpers, A. 1970. *The World of the Polynesians*. Melbourne: Oxford University.

American Psychiatric Association. 1987. *Diagnostic and Statistical Manual of Mental Disorders (Third Edition - Revised) DSM III - R*. Washington, D.C.: American Psychiatric Association.

Ashbrook, James. 1970. Testing for the Protestant Ministry. In William Bier, S.J., ed., *Psychological Testing for Ministerial Selection*. New York: Fordham University Press, pp.87-123.

Ashbrook, James. 1984. *The Human Mind and The Mind of God: theological promise in brain research*. Lanham, MD: University Press of America.

Ashbrook, James. 1985. Personal communications to the Ph.D. graduates of Pastoral Psychology, Garrett-Evangelical Theological Seminary.

Ashby, Homer. 1978. *An MMPI Scale for Narcissistic Personality Disorder*. Unpublished dissertation. Northwestern University.

Ashby, Homer U., J. Kristian Best, Michael F. Conroy, Gerald J. DeSobe, and J. Jeffrey Means. 1980. CPE and Academic Credit-Three Criteria of Eligibility, *Journal of Pastoral Care*, Vol. XXXV, No.2, pp.99-105.

Auden, W. 1945. *The Collected Poetry of W.H. Auden*. New York: Random House.

Augros, R.M. and G.N. Stanciv. 1984. *The New Story of Science: Mind and The Universe*. New York: Bantam Books.

Augsburger, David. 1986. *Pastoral Counseling Across Cultures*. Philadelphia: Westminster Press.

Berger, P.L. 1979. *The Heretical Imperative*. Garden City, N.Y.: Anchor Press.

Beesinger, Maria, Robert J. Nogosek, Patrick H. O'Leary. 1984. *The Enneagram: A Journey of Self-Discovery*. Denville, N.J.: Dimension Books.

Bettleheim, Bruno. 1979. *Surviving*. New York: Knopf.

Boisen, Anton. 1926. Personality Changes and Upheavals Arising Out of a Sense of Personal Failure, *American Journal of Psychiatry*, Vol.5, pp.531-551.

Boisen, Anton. 1928. The Sense of Isolation in Mental Disorder: Its Religious Significance, *American Journal of Sociology*, Vol.33, pp.555-567.

Boisen, Anton. 1960. *Out of the Depths*. New York: Harper and Brothers.

Bonhoeffer, D. 1953. *Letters and Papers from Prison*. New York: Macmillan.

Bova, B., and R. Phillips. 1982. *The Mentoring Relationship as an Educational Experience*. (Report No.CE 034 712). Albuquerque, NM: University of New Mexico. (ERIC Document Reproduction Service No. ED 224 944).

Bowers, M.K. 1963. *Conflicts of the Clergy: A Psychodynamic Study with Case Histories*. New York: Thomas Nelson & Sons.

Campbell, D.T. and J.C. Stanley. 1966. *Experimental and Quasi-Experimental Design for Research*. Chicago: Rand McNally.

Campbell, D.T. and T.D. Cook. 1979. *Quasi-Experimentation: Design and Analysis Issues For Field Settings*. Chicago: Rand McNally.

Campbell, Macfie. 1926. *Delusion and Belief*. Cambridge, MA: Harvard University Press.

Capps, Donald. 1984. The Bible's Role in Pastoral Care and Counseling: Four Basic Principles, *Journal of Psychology and Christianity*, Winter, Vol.3, No.4, pp.5-15.

Carr, John C. 1980. *The MMPI, Ministerial Personality and the Practice of Ministry*. Unpublished dissertation. Northwestern University.

Carr, John C., John E. Hinkle, Jr., and David M. Moss III. 1981. *The Organization & Administration of Pastoral Counseling Centers*. Nashville: Abingdon Press.

Carroll, Jackson W. 1985. The Professional Model of Ministry--Is It Worth Saving? *Theological Education*, pp.7-48

Chopp, Rebecca. 1986. *The Praxis of Suffering*. MaryKnoll: Orbis Books.

Christensen, Carl W., James McHolland, and Carroll A. Wise. 1968. Some Aspects of Training Pastoral Counselors, *The Journal of Pastoral Care*, Vol. XXII, No. 4, pp.212-222.

Christensen, Carl W. 1972. I Passed By The Church. In P.E. Johnson, ed. *Healers of the Mind*. Nashville: Abingdon Press.

Clinebell, Jr., Howard J. 1964. The Challenge of the Specialty of Pastoral Counseling, *Pastoral Psychology*, Vol. 15, No. 143, April, pp.17-28.

Clinebell, H. 1986. Forward by Howard Clinebell. In D. Augsburger, *Pastoral Counseling Across Cultures*. Philadelphia: Westminster Press.

Cobb, John B. 1982. *Beyond Dialogue: Toward a Mutual Transformation of Christianity and Buddhism*. Philadelphia: Fortress Press.

Crane, D. 1965. Scientists at Major and Minor Universities: A Study of Productivity and Recognition, *American Sociological Review*, 30, pp.699-714.

Crowne, D. and D. Marlowe. 1964. *The Approval Motive*. New York: Wiley.

Dahlstrom, W. Grant, George S. Welsh, and Leona E. Dahlstrom. 1972 & 1975. *An MMPI Handbook*, Vols. I & II, Minneapolis: University of Minnesota Press.

Division of Ordained Ministry. 1985. *Board of Ordained Ministry Handbook*. Nashville, Tenn: Abingdon Press.

Dolgin, L., D.S. Kemnitzer, and D.M. Schneider, eds. 1977. *Symbolic Anthropology*. New York: Columbia University.

Duff, F.L. 1965. Item Subtlety In Personality Inventory Scales, *Journal of Consulting Psychology*, Vol. 29, No.6, pp.565-570.

Dunne, J.S. 1972. *The Way of All the Earth*. New York: Macmillan.

Edlind, E., and P. Haensly. 1985. Gifts of Mentors. *Gifted Child Quarterly*, 29, pp.55-60.

Erikson, E. 1963. *Childhood and Society*. New York: W.W. Norton & Co.

Erikson, E. 1964. *Inner and Outer Space: Reflections on Womanhood.* *Daedulus,* 93, pp.582-606.

Feilding, Charles. 1966. *Education for Ministry,* Theological Education, III (Autumn).

Freud, S. (1914a) 1957. *Some Reflections on Schoolboy Psychology In* Standard Edition, 13:241-244. London: Hogarth Press.

Freud, S. (1914b) 1957. *On Narcissism, An Introduction. In* Standard Edition, 14:73-102.

Freud, Sigmund. (1917) 1957. *Mourning and Melancholia. In* Standard Edition , 14:237-258. London: Hogarth Press.

Fricke, B.G. 1957. *Subtle and Obvious Test Items and Response Set,* Journal Consulting Psychology, Vol. 21, No.3, pp.250-252.

Geertz, C. 1982. *From the Native's Point of View: On the Nature of Anthropological Understanding. In L. Dolgin, D.S. Kemnitzer, and D.M. Schneider, D.M., eds.* Symbolic Anthropology. New York: Columbia University.

Gerkin, Charles V. 1984. The Living Human Document: Revisioning Pastoral Counseling in a Hermeneutical Mode. *Nashville: Abingdon Press.*

Gilberstadt, Harold, and Janet Duker. 1965. A Handbook for Clinical and Acturial MMPI Interpretation, *Philadelphia: Wm. Saunders*

Gynther, M.O., B.R. Burkhardt, and C. Havanitz. 1979. *Do Face Valid Items Have More Predictive Validity Than Subtle Items? The Case Of The MMPI Pd Scale,* Journal Consulting and Clinical Psychology Vol. 47, No.2, pp.295-300.

Haight, Roger, S.J. 1985. An Alternative Vision: An Interpretation of Liberation Theology. *New York: Paulist Press.*

Hartmann, H. 1958. Ego Development and Adaptation. *New York: International Universities Press.*

Hiltner, S. 1962. *Conclusion: The Dialogue on Man's Nature. In S. Doninger, ed.* The Nature of Man in Theological and Psychological Perspective. *New York: Harper & Brothers.*

Hiltner, Seward. 1964a. *The American Association of Pastoral Counselors: A Critique,* Pastoral Psychology, Vol. 15, No. 143, April, pp.8-16.

Hiltner, Seward. 1964b. *Comment on A.A.P.C. Meeting Report,* Pastoral Psychology, Vol. 115, No. 146, September, pp.50-52.

Hiltner, Seward and Lowell Colston, 1961. The Context of Pastoral Counseling. *Nashville: Abingdon Press.*

Hinkle, Jr., John E. 1979. *Fitness for Ministry: An Address. Delivered at Garrett-Evangelical Theological Seminary on the occasion of the Consultation on Fitness, February 5th.*

Hinkle, Jr., John E. 1981. *Is the Ph.D. Necessary for Pastoral Counseling?* The Journal of Supervision and Training in Ministry, Vol. 4. *Published by the North Central Region of the Association for Clinical Pastoral Education and the Central Region of the American Association of Pastoral Counselors, P.O. Box 215, 950 E. 59th St., Chicago, IL.*

Hinkle, Jr., John E. 1982. *Utilizing Psychological Assessment in Ministerial Selection. Unpublished study.*

Hinkle, Jr., John E. 1985. *Psychological Testing of Candidates for Ministry*, *New Catholic World*, Vol. 229, No. 1371, June, pp. 117-122.

Holifield, E. Brooks. 1983. *A History of Pastoral Care in America: From Salvation to Self-realization*. Nashville: Abingdon Press.

Holliman, Pamela. 1985. *A Study of Psychological Assessment Procedures as Adjunctive to Personnel Selection Processes in a Religious Organization*. Unpublished dissertation, Northwestern University.

Holmes, Urban T. 1978. *The Priest in Community*. New York: Seabury Press.

Hordern, W. 1964. *Speaking of God: The Nature and Purpose of Theological Language*. New York: Macmillan.

Houck, J., and D. Moss. 1977. Pastoral Psychotherapy, the Fee-For-Service Model, & Professional Identity, *Journal of Religion & Health*, 16(3), pp.172-182.

Hsu, F.L.K. 1961. American Core Character. In F.L.K. Hsu, ed. *Psychological Anthropology*. Homewood, IL: The Dorsey Press.

Jaynes J. 1976. *The Origin of Consciousness in the Breakdown of The Bicameral Mind*. Boston: Houghton Mifflin.

Jones, Doris Moreland, ed. 1980. *Guidebook for Interviewing, Psychological Testing and Pastoral Evaluation*. Nashville, Tenn: Division of Ministry Press.

Justes, Emma. 1981. Basic degrees committee evaluation of assessment services program: A report. Unpublished Report.

Kassam, S. 1987. Coups and Earthquakes Only. *World Press Review*, 34(9).

Kegan, Robert. 1982. *The Evolving Self*. Cambridge: Harvard University Press.

Keller, E.F. 1983. Feminism as an Analytical Tool for the Study of Science, *Academe*, September-October.

Kernberg, O. 1970. A Psychoanalytic Classification of Character Pathology, *Journal of American TSA Association*. 800-822. Quoted by Samuel Bradshaw in "Ministers in Trouble. A Study of 140 Ministers Evaluated at the Menninger Foundation." Unpublished occasional paper.

Kiely, B. 1980. *Psychology and Moral Theology*. Rome: Georgian University Press.

Klein, Melanie. 1975. A Contribution to the Psychogenesis of Manic-Depressive States. *In Love, Guilt and Reparation, and Other Works*. London: Hogarth Press.

Kohut, Heinz. 1971. *The Analysis of the Self*. New York: International University Press.

Kohut, Heinz. 1977. *The Restoration of the Self*. New York: International University Press.

Kohut, Heinz. 1978. *The Search for the Self*. Vol. I & II. Ed. P. Ornstein. New York: International University Press.

Kohut, Heinz. 1984. *How Does Analysis Cure?* Ed. A. Goldberg. Chicago: Chicago University Press.

Kohut, Heinz. 1985. *Self Psychology and the Humanities: Reflections on a New Psychoanalytic Approach*. Ed. C. Strozier. New York: W.W.Norton & Co.

Kohut, Heinz. 1987. _The Kohut Seminars on Self Psychology and Psychotherapy With Adolescents and Young Adults._ Ed. M. Elson. New York: W.W.Norton & Co.

Koteskey, R.L. 1980. _Psychology From a Christian Perspective._ Nashville: Abingdon Press.

Kram, K. 1980. _Mentoring Processes at Work: Developing Relationships in Managerial Careers._ Unpublished doctoral dissertation, Yale University.

Kram, K. 1983. Phases of the Mentor Relationship, _Academy of Management Journal,_ 26, pp.608-625.

Kram, K. 1985. _Mentoring at Work: Developmental Relationships in Organizational Life._ Glenview, IL., Scott; Foresman & Co.

Kram, K., and L. Isabella. 1985. Mentoring Alternatives: The Role of Peer Relationships in Career Development, _Academy of Management Journal,_ 28, pp.110-132.

Kram, K. 1986. _Mentoring in the Workplace._ In Thomas Hall, et al, _Career Development in Organizations._ San Francisco: Jossey-Bass, pp.160-201.

Kuhn, T. 1970. _The Structure of Scientific Revolutions_ (Rev. ed.). Chicago: University of Chicago Press.

Leas, Speed. 1985. Clergy Move . . ., _The Circuit Rider,_ 1 August, 12.

Leiffer, Murray and Dorothy. 1987. _Enter the Old Portals, Reminiscences: Fifty Years on a Seminary Campus._ Garrett-Evangelical Theological Seminary, Evanston, IL: The Bureau of Social and Religious Research.

LeVine, R.A. 1973. _Culture, Behavior, and Personality._ Chicago: Aldine.

Long, Charles. 1986. _Significations._ Philadelphia: Fortress Press.

Macquarrie, J. 1966. _Principals of Christian Theology._ New York: Charles Scribner's Sons.

Malony, H.N. ed. 1983. _Wholeness and Holiness: Readings in the Psychology/Theology of Mental Health._ Grand Rapids, Michigan: Baker.

Marcella, A.J., G. Devos, and F.L.K. Hus, eds. 1985. _Culture and Self: Asian and Western Perspectives._ New York: Tavistock.

Martin, Colby. 1981. _Dimensions in the Grief Experience in Recently Bereaved Spouses._ Unpublished dissertation, Northwestern University.

Mason, R. 1980. The Psychology of the Self: Religion and Psychotherapy. In A. Goldberg, ed. _Advances in Self Psychology._ New York: International Universities Press, pp.407-425.

McNair, A.W. 1985. Remarks on the occasion of the C.A. Wise memorial dinner. Downington, PA, April 1985. Transcript of audio tape provided by Department of Pastoral Psychology and Counseling, Garrett-Evangelical Theological Seminary, Evanston, Illinois.

Meadow, M.J. and R.D. Kahoe. 1984. _Psychology of Religion: Religion in Individual Lives._ New York: Harper & Row.

Means, J. Jeffrey. 1980. _An Investigation of an Assessment Model for the Evaluation of the Capacity of Seminary Students to Utilize Clinical Pastoral Education as a Professional Learning Experience._ Unpublished dissertation, Northwestern University.

Meine, Franklin J. ed. 1954. _The Consolidated Webster Comprehensive_

Encyclopedic Dictionary. Chicago, IL: Consolidated Book Publisher.

Meissner, W.W. 1984. *Psychoanalysis and Religious Experience.* New Haven: Yale University Press.

Moore, B. and B. Find. 1968. *A Glossary of Psychoanalytic Terms and Concepts.* New York: American Psychoanalytic Association.

Moss, D. 1969. *Prolegomena Post Mortem Dei: A Critical Overview of the Nature and Structure of a Radical Theology.* Unpublished master thesis, Seabury-Western Theological Seminary, Evanston.

Moss, D. 1976a. Narcissism, Empathy and the Fragmentation of Self: An Interview with Heinz Kohut, *Pilgrimage: The Journal of Pastoral Psychotherapy,* Vol. 4, Number 1, pp.26-43.

Moss, D. 1976b. Pastoral Psychology in a Historical Perspective: An Interview with Carroll A. Wise, *Pilgrimage: The Journal of Pastoral Psychotherapy,* Vol. 4, Number 2, pp.14-26.

Moss, D., et.al. 1977a. Empathy, *Pilgrimage: The Journal of Pastoral Psychotherapy,* Vol. 5, Number 1.

Moss, D. 1977b. "Ein Gesprach mit Heinz Kohut." *Wege zum Menschen* (February/Marz) pp.49-68.

Moss, D. 1978. The Early Pastoral Psychology Movement: An Interview with Seward Hiltner, *Pilgrimage: The Journal of Pastoral Psychotherapy.* Vol. 6, Number 2, pp.83-101

Moss, D. 1979. Near-Fatal Experience, Crisis Intervention and the Anniversary Reaction, *Pastoral Psychology,* 28(2), pp.75-96.

Moss, D. 1984. Judicial Trauma-Juridical Traversty. In M.C. Nelson and M. Eigen, eds. *Self-in-Process Series: Vol. IV, Evil, Self and Culture.* New York: Human Sciences Press, pp.181-199.

Moss, D. 1986a. Epitaph: Carroll Alonzo Wise, Symbol of Pastoral Care, *Pastoral Psychology,* 34(3), pp.147-150.

Moss, D. 1986b. In Memoriam: Professor Carroll A. Wise, Th.D., *Journal of Religion and Health,* 25(2), pp.167-168.

Mowrer, O. Hobart. 1961. *The Crisis in Psychiatry and Religion.* Princeton, NJ: D. Van Nostrand Company, Inc.

Navran, L. 1954. A Rationally Derived MMPI Scale for Dependence, *Journal Consulting Psychology,* 18, p.192.

Norwood, Frederick A. 1978. *From Dawn to Midday at Garrett.* Evanston, IL: Garrett-Evangelical Theological School.

O'Neill, E. 1925. The Great God Brown. In *Nine Plays.* New York: The Modern Library, (1941 edition), pp.307-377.

Orthner, Dennis K. 1987. *Pastoral Counseling: Attitudes and Experiences of United Methodist Clergy.* Center of Work and Family Issues: University of Georgia, March.

Outler, A.C. 1954. *Psychotherapy and the Christian Message.* New York: Harper & Brothers.

Pasteur, Alfred B. and Ivory L. Toldson, *Roots of Soul: The Psychology of Black Expressiveness.* New York: Anchor.

Patton, John. 1981. Clinical Hermeneutics: Soft Focus in Pastoral Counseling and Theology, *Journal of Pastoral Care,* Vol.XXXV, No.3, September pp.161-162.

Patton, John. 1983. *Pastoral Counseling: A Ministry of the Church.* Nashville: Abingdon Press.

Peters, T.J., and Robert Waterman Jr. 1982. *In Search of Excellence*. New York: Harper & Row.

Pius XI. 1939. Divini Illius Magistri (1929). In *Five Great Encyclicals*. New York: Paulist Press.

Powell, Robert C. *Fifty Years of Learning Through Supervised Encounters with Living Human Documents*. New York, NY: Association for Clinical Pastoral Education, 1975.

Powell, Robert C. Anton T. Boisen: Breaking an Opening in the Wall Between Religion and Medicine, *AMHC Forum*, 1976, Vol.29, No.1.

Rahner, K. and H. Vorgrimer. 1965. *Theological Dictionary*. New York: Herder and Herder.

Ricoeur, Paul. 1980. Toward a Hermeneutic of the Idea of Revelation. In Lewis C. Mudge, ed., *Essays on Biblical Interpretation* Philadelphia: Fortress Press, pp.73-118.

Rizzuto, A. 1979. *The Birth of the Living God: A Psychoanalytic Study*. Chicago: The University of Chicago Press.

Roberts, J. Deotis. 1987. *Black Theology in Dialogue*. Philadlphia: Westminster Press.

Roche, G. 1979. Much Ado about Mentoring, *Harvard Business Review*, 57, pp.26-28.

Sacks, J.M. and D.D. Dirtley. 1972. Some Personality Characteristics Related to Response to Subtle and Obvious Items on the MMPI, *Journal Consulting Psychology*, Vol. 38, No.1, pp.66-69.

Schafer, R. 1968. *Aspects of Internalization*. New York: International Universities Press.

Scharfenberg, J. 1980. The Psychology of the Self and Religion. In A. Goldberg, ed., *Advances in Self Psychology*. New York: International Universities Press, pp.427-437.

Schillebeeckx, Edward. 1981. *Jesus: An Experiment in Christology*. New York: Vintage Books, 1979 (Eng. trans. from the 1974 Dutch).

Schreiter, Robert J. 1985. *Constructing Local Theologies*. Maryknoll: Orbis Press.

Schuller, David S., Merton P. Stromen, and Milo L. Brekke, eds. 1980. *Ministry in America*. San Francisco: Harper & Row.

Shackelford, James. 1986. In Memorium: Carroll A. Wise (1903-1985), *Chronical of Pastoral Care*, Fall, Vol. 6, Number 2.

Smith, Archie. 1982. *The Relational Self: Ethics and Therapy From a Black Church Perspective*. Nashville: Abingdon Press.

Smith, B. 1985. The Metaphorical Basis of Selfhood. In A.J. Marsella, G. Devos, and F.L.K. Hsu, eds., *Culture and Self: Asian and Western Perspectives*. New York: Tavistock.

Stone, I. 1971. *The Passions of the Mind*. New York: Doubleday & Company, Inc.

Stone, Leray A. 1964. Subtle and Obvious Response on the MMPI, *Psychology Reports*, 15, pp.721-722.

Stone, Leroy A. 1965. Subtle and Obvious Responses on the MMPI as a Function of Acquiescence Response Style, *Psychological Reports*, 16, pp.803-804.

Strunk, O., Jr. 1959. The Present Status of the Psychology of Religion. In O. Strunk, Jr., ed., *Readings in the Psychology of*

Religion. New York: Abingdon Press.

Sullivan, E.V. 1984. _A Critical Psychology_. New York: Plenum Press.

Tillich, Paul. 1952a. _The Courage To Be_. New Haven: Yale University Press.

Tillich, P. 1952b. _Autobiographical Reflections_. In C.W. Kegley and R. W. Bretall, eds., _The Theology of Paul Tillich_. New York: Macmillan.

Tillich, P. 1964. _A Theology of Culture_. New York: Oxford University.

Tolpin, Marion. 1971. On the Beginnings of a Cohesive Self, _Psychoanalytic Study of the Child_, Vol. 26, 316-352.

Tracy, David. 1975. _Blessed Rage for Order: The New Pluralism in Theology_. New York: Seabury Press.

Van Leeuwen, M.S. 1982. _The Sourcerer's Apprentice: A Christian Looks at the Changing Face of Psychology_. Downers Grove, IL: Intervarsity Press.

Van Leeuwen, M.S. 1985. _The Person in Psychology: A Contemporary Christian Appraisal_. Grand Rapids, Michigan: William B. Eerdmans.

Van Wagner, Charles A., II. 1986. _The AAPC: The Formative Years: A History of The American Association of Pastoral Counselors_ (1963-1970). Unpublished dissertation. Emory University.

Vayhinger, John M. and Carroll A. Wise. 1964. _A Psychological Study of Theological Students_. An unpublished study, two volumes. Evanston, IL: The United Library.

Vitz, P.C. 1977 _Psychology As Religion: The Cult of Self-Worship_. Grand Rapids, Michigan: William B. Eerdmans.

Vriezen, T.C. 1962. _An Outline of Old Testament Theology_. Oxford: Basil Blackwell.

Weidman, July. 1976. _Occasional Papers_, Vol. 1, No. 11, June.

Wiener, D.M. 1948. Subtle and Obvious Keys for the MMPI, _Journal Consulting Psychology_, 12, pp.164-170.

Wimberly, Edward. 1979. _Pastoral Care in The Black Church_. Nashville: Abingdon Press.

Winnicott, Donald. 1951. Transitional Objects and Transitional Phenomena, _International Journal of Psycho-Analysis_, Vol. XXIV, pp.229-242.

Wilbur, K. 1983. _Eye to Eye: The Quest for the New Paradigm_. Garden City, NY: Anchor.

Wong, Sam. 1971. _A Descriptive Study of Garrett Graduates_. Unpublished study. Garrett Theological Seminary.

Wright, C., and S. Wright. 1987. The Role of Mentors in the Career Development of Young Professionals, _Family Relations_, 36, pp.204-208.

Yeager, Richard. 1965. Continuing Education Needs, _The Interpreter_, September, 26.

CARROLL A. WISE BIBLIOGRAPHY

Prepared by John C. Carr

Books

Religion in Illness and Health. New York: Harper, 1942.

Pastoral Counseling, Its Theory and Practice. New York: Harper, 1951.

Psychiatry and the Bible. New York: Harper, 1956 (ChapelBook Edition under the title: *Mental Health and the Bible* in 1966).

The Meaning of Pastoral Care. New York: Harper, 1966.

Pastoral Psychotherapy: Theory and Practice. Northvale, NJ: Jason Aronson, Inc., 1983.

CONTRIBUTIONS TO BOOKS

"Religion As a Constructive Factor in Counseling." In *Religion in the State University: An Initial Exploration*, H.E. Allen, ed. Minneapolis: Burgess, 1950.

"Physical and Mental Health." In *Fruits of Faith*, R.J. Spann, ed. New York & Nashville: Abingdon, 1950.

"The Pastor-Parishioner Relationship." In *A Clinical Approach to the Problems of Pastoral Care*, J. Levy and R.K. McNickle, eds. Boulder, Colorado: Western Interstate Commission for Higher Education, 1964.

"Pastoral Problems of Sex." In *Sex and Religion Today*, S. Doniger, ed. New York: Association, 1953.

"Clinical Training in Preparation for Institutional Chaplaincy and Clinical Training Supervision." In *Clinical Pastoral Training*, S.Hiltner, ed. Federal Council of Churches of Christ in America, 1949.

"The Role of the Clergy in Relation to the Mentally Ill." In *Mental Health* (Publication of the American Association for the Advancement of Science, No.9) New York: Science House, 1939 (pp.438-444).

JOURNAL ARTICLES

The Garrett Tower

1948 (March), Vol. 23, No.2	*Announcement of the appointment of C.A. Wise as Profesor of Pastoral Psychology and Counseling at Garrett Theological Seminary*
1951 (June), Vol. 26, No. 3	*A Prayer*
1951 (Oct.), Vol. 26, No. 4,	*"Man's Desire for Peace"*
1954 (Mar.), Vol. 29, No. 2	*"The Ministry and the Communication of the Gospel"*
1964 (Sept.), Vol. 41, No.4	*Review of the The Meaning of Pastoral Care (edited verbatim of a discussion with Professors Wise, Thompson, and Lindgren)*

Journal of Clinical Pastoral Work

1947, Vol. 1, No. 1	*"The ministry to the physically ill" (pp.25 ff.)*
1948, Vol. 1, No. 3	*"Some practical problems in counseling in the parish" (pp.1 ff.)*
1949, Vol. 2, No. 2	*"When is counseling religious" (pp.83 ff.)*

Journal of Pastoral Care

1951, Vol. 5, No. 1	*"The place of Clinical Training in the department of Pastoral Theology" (pp.46-52)*
1953, Vol. 7, No. 3	*"Client-centered counseling and the pastor" (pp.127-136)*
1954, Vol. 8, No. 4	*"The relationship between Clinical Training and Field Work Supervision" (pp.189 ff.)*
1955, Vol. 9, No. 4	*Editorial: "Judgment and Acceptance in Counseling" (pp.232-234)*
1956, Vol.10, No. 4	*Editorial: "Recent developments" (p.239)*

1957, Vol. 11, No. 1	*Editorial: "Conversion" (pp.40-42)*
1957, Vol. 11, No. 4	*Editorial: "The Clergyman and Research" (pp.229-30)*
1962, Vol. 16, No. 2	*Editorial: "Human values in the Seminary" (pp.89-90)*
1966, Vol. 20, No. 2	*Communication: "A Project in the pastoral care of the ill" (pp.101-102)*
1967, Vol. 21, No. 4	*Editorial: "The question of religious faith in relation to suicide" (pp.235-236)*
1968, Vol. 22, No. 3	*Editorial: "Dealing with defenses in Clinical Pastoral Education" (pp.171-172)*
1968, Vol. 22, No. 4	*"Some aspects of training pastoral counselors" (pp.212 ff.) (With Carl W. Christensen and James D. McHolland)*
1970, Vol. 24, No. 1	*"The roots and resolution of conflict" (pp.8-13)*
1977, Vol. 31, No. 3	*"The Supervisory Alliance in Pastoral Psychotherapy" (pp.186-193)*
1979, Vol. 33, No. 4	*"Response to an Experience of Extreme Stress in the Light of the Ideas of Anton T. Boisen" (pp.220-229)*
1981, Vol. 35, No. 4	*"The Grandfather of CPE?" (pp.276-280)*

Ladies Home Journal

August 1959, Vol. 76   *"Sex and Religion" (pp.30 ff.)*

Lutheran Social Welfare Quarterly

Spring, 1967   *"Clinical Pastoral Education and Theological Education"*

Mental Hygiene

Jan. 1941, Vol. 25   *"The clergy and community education for mental hygiene" (pp.30-42) (see unpublished article on "Mental Hygiene and the Clergy")*

July 1945, Vol. 29   *"The relation of the Mental hospital to the community"* (pp.412-422) Commencement Address, Toledo State Hospital School of Nursing, June 11, 1943)

The New Christian Advocate

Date Uncertain   *"Guilt"* (Case comments in the column, *"Counselor at Work"*)

Nexus 22   (Alumni Magazine of the Boston University School of Theology)

Nov. 1964, Vol. VIII,   *"Pastoral Care for the Broken and*
No. 1   *Forgotten"* (Introductory Statement at Founder's Day seminary, March 12, 1964)

The Pastor

Feb. 1943, Vol. 6, No. 3   *"What do you say?"* (pp.8-13) (Counseling parents whose sons are in the Solomons or North Africa)

Pastoral Counselor

1967, Vol. 5, No. 2   Proceedings of the 1967 Annual Meeting of the AAPC *"Introduction"* (p.3)
"The Pastor as Counselor" (pp.4-11)

1968, Vol. 6, No. 2   *"Pastoral Counseling and human values"* (pp.1-8)

Pastoral Psychology

1950, Vol. 1, No. 8   Consultation Clinic: *"The Minister and the Psychiatrist"* (p.50)

1951, Vol. 2, No. 11   *"The Pastor as Counselor"* (pp.9-14) Carroll A. Wise: *"Man of the Month"* (pp.6 & 66)

1952, Vol. 2, No. 20   Consultation Clinic: *"Counseling with Neurotics"* (p.50)

1952, Vol. 3, No. 26   *"Pastoral problems of sex"* (pp.57-64)

1955, Vol. 6, No. 52   Readers' Forum: *"Theology Questions Counseling"* (pp.55-56) (Reply to R.R. Wright)

1955, Vol. 6, No. 57   Consultation Clinic: *"Counseling with neurotics"* (pp.50-52)

| 1956, Vol. 7, No. 62 | "Is psychotherapy a religious process?" (pp.40-41) |

1956, Vol. 7, No. 62   "Is psychotherapy a religious process?" (pp.40-41)

1958, Vol. 9, No. 89   "The Ministry as a Vocation" (pp.7-54) (Guest Editor)

1958, Vol. 9, No. 89   "Call to the Ministry" (pp.9-17) (Revision of 1953 paper in *Religion in Life*)

1959, Vol. 10, No. 99   "Education of the Pastor for marriage counseling" (pp.45-48)

1961, Vol. 11, No.111   "'Credentials' for Pastoral Counseling?" (pp.48-49) (Response to S. Hiltner)

1961, Vol. 12, No.112   Editorial: "The Ministry as a Vocation" (p.7)

1964, Vol. 15, No.146   "Meeting of the American Association of Pastoral Counselors in St. Louis: A Report" (pp.47-50) Comments by S. Hiltner

Pilgrimage: The Journal of Pastoral Psychotherapy

1976 (Winter)
Vol. 4, No.2   "Pastoral Psychology in a Historical Perspective" (pp.26-43) (An Interview with David Moss)

1979, Vol.7, No.2   "Sunrise" (p.82)

Religion in Life

1953, Vol.23, No.1   "The Call to the Christian Ministry" (pp.59-69)

Religious Education

1943 (May-June),
Vol.38, No.3   "The value of Clinical Training for Religious Education" (pp.160-168)

1947 (Sept.-Oct.),
Vol.42, No.5   "The role of emotions in the solution of personal problems: A Symposium on Emotions in Religious Education" (pp.257-261)

Zion's Herald

April 27/32   "The Church and Mental Disorder: Why should the Minister and Layman be interested in Mrs. Jones and the problems she represents?"

January 13/43   *"Personal Problems in War Time: To help the world, we must first work out our own troubles"*

Addresses and Sermons Referred to in the Text

August 10, 1947   *"The Lure of Superiority." Hennepin Avenue Methodist Church, Minneapolis.*

October 1950   *"The Place of Clinical Training in the Department of Pastoral Theology." The Silver Anniversary Conference of Clinical Pastoral Education, Chicago.*

N.d.   *"To Preach . . . To Heal." Chapel Garrett-Evangelical Theological Seminary.*

LIST OF CONTRIBUTORS

James B. Ashbrook, Ph.D., LL.D.

Professor, Pastoral Psychology and Counseling
Garrett-Evangelical Theological Seminary
2121 Sheridan Road
Evanston, IL 60201

Homer U. Ashby, Jr., Ph.D.

Professor, Pastoral Care and Counseling
McCormick Theological Seminary
5555 S. Woodlawn Avenue
Chicago, IL 60637

Richard E. Augspurger, Ph.D.

Executive Director, The Institute for Living
690 Oak Street
Winnetka, IL 60093

Richard B. Bruehl, Ph.D.

Private Practice of Pastoral Psychotherapy
2505 Hillsboro Rd. - Suite 204
Nashville, TN 37212

John C. Carr, Ph.D.

Executive Director, The Pastoral Institute of Edmonton
11112 - 109th Avenue
Edmonton, Alberta, Canada
T5H 1E1

Carl W. Christensen, M.D., FASCMS

Private Practice of Psychiatry (Retired)
702 Waukegan Road
Glenview, IL 60025

Leila M. Foster, J.D., Ph.D.

Private Practice of Clinical Psychology
500 Davis Street, Suite 600
Evanston, IL 60201

Allan R. Gilmore, Ph.D.

Executive Director, The Pastoral Counseling
and Consultation Centers of Greater Washington
P. O. Box 39
Oakton, VA 22124

Emily Demme Haight, Ph.D.

Assistant Professor, Pastoral Psychology and Counseling
Garrett-Evangelical Theological Seminary (1979-86)
Center for Religion and Psychotherapy of Chicago
192 South Kenilworth Street
Elmhurst, IL 60126

Paul Hessert, Ph.D.

Henry Pfeiffer Professor of Systematic Theology
Garrett-Evangelical Theological Seminary (1963-80)
Rural Route # 2, P. O. Box 58
Kingsley, PA 18826

John E. Hinkle, Jr., Ph.D.

Professor, Pastoral Psychology and Counseling
Garrett-Evangelical Theological Seminary
2121 Sheridan Road
Evanston, IL 60201

Donald C. Houts, Ph.D.

Area Director of Pastoral Care and Counseling
Illinois Area, United Methodist Church
1701 S. Prospect Street, Suite 19
Champaign, IL 61821

296

Ronald R. Lee, Ph.D.

Professor, Pastoral Psychology and Counseling
Garrett-Evangelical Theological Seminary (1970-79)
R. Redvers Lee and Associates, P. C.
Private Practice of Clinical Psychology
111 N. Wabash Avenue, Suite 1221
Chicago, IL 60602

J. Colby Martin, Ph.D.

Christian Brothers Counseling Center
1840 Mayfair
Westchester, IL 60153

J. Jeffrey Means, Ph.D.

Des Moines Pastoral Counseling Center
550 39th Street, Suite 100
Des Moines, IA 50312

David M. Moss, Ph.D., D.D.

Private Practice of Pastoral Psychotherapy
Director, The Coventry Association for Pastoral Psychology
2997 Piedmont Road, N. E.
Atlanta, GA 30305

Tyler Thompson, Ph.D.

Professor Emeritus, Philosophy of Religion
Garrett-Evangelical Theological Seminary
415 Oaklawn Avenue
South Pasadena, CA 91030

John M. Vayhinger, Ph.D.

Professor, Pastoral Psychology and Counseling
Garrett Evangelical Seminary (1958-64)
Professor Emeritus, Pastoral Care and Counseling
Anderson School of Theology
119 Illini Drive
Woodland Park, CO 80863

LINCOLN CHRISTIAN COLLEGE AND SEMINARY